THINKERTOYS

THINKERTOYS

A HANDBOOK OF BUSINESS CREATIVITY FOR THE '90s

MICHAEL MICHALKO

TEN SPEED PRESS
BERKELEY, CALIFORNIA

1🔟 TEN SPEED PRESS   Box 7123   Berkeley, CA 94707

Text design by Sarah Levin
Cover design by Fifth Street Design
Typeset by Wilsted & Taylor

Library of Congress Cataloging-in-Publication Data

Michalko, Michael, 1940–
    Thinkertoys / Michael Michalko.
       p.   cm.
    ISBN 0-89815-408-1
    1. Creative ability in business.   2. Creative thinking.
    I. Title.
HD53.M53   1991
650′.01′9—dc20   90-19336 CIP

First Printing, 1991
Printed in the United States of America

        8   9   10   —   97   96   95

Figure on page xi from *Can You Believe Your Eyes* copyright © 1989 by J. R. Block and H.E. Yuker. New York: Gardner Press, Inc. Used by permission of the publisher.

Figure on page 7 from *Drawing on the Artist Within* copyright © 1989 by Betty Edwards. New York: Simon & Schuster. Used by permission of the publisher.

Figure on page 10 from "Pattern recognition and modern computers" by O. G. Selfridge. Published in the proceedings of the Western Joint Computer Conference, New York. Copyright © 1955 by IRE (now IEEE). Used by permission.

Figure on page 12 from Ripley's Believe It or Not, property of Ripley's International, Inc., Toronto, Ontario. Used by permission.

Figure on page 25 from "Subjective Contours" by Gaetano Kanisza, illustration by Jerome Kuhl. Copyright © 1976 by *Scientific American*, New York. Used by permission of the publisher.

Figure on page 35 from *Can You Believe Your Eyes* copyright © 1989 by J. R. Block and H. E. Yuker. New York: Gardner Press, Inc. Used by permission of the publisher.

Figure on page 94 from *Can You Believe Your Eyes* copyright © 1989 by J. R. Block and H. E. Yuker. New York: Gardner Press, Inc. Used by permission of the publisher.

Figure on page 159 from "The Amateur Scientist" by Michael Goodman, illustration by Jearl Walker. Copyright © 1988 by *Scientific American*, New York. Used by permission of the publisher.

Figure on page 177 from "Figural aftereffects: an investigation of visual processes" by W. Kohler and H. Wallach. Published in the proceedings of the American Philosophical Society, 88, 269–357, copyright © 1944. Used by permission.

Figure on page 201 from *The Journal of General Psychology*, 7, 481–482 copyright © 1932. Published by Heldref Publications. Used by permission of the publisher.

Figure on page 230 from "The role of frequency in developing perceptual sets" by B. R. Bugleski and D. A. Alampay, published in the *Canadian Journal of Psychology*, 15, 205–211. Copyright © 1961 by the Canadian Psychological Association. Used by permission of the publisher.

Figure on page 290 from "Subjective Contours" by Gaetano Kanisza, illustration by Ilel Arbel. Copyright © 1976 by *Scientific American*, New York. Used by permission of the publisher.

DEDICATION

This book and my love are dedicated to Anne, my wife and partner, who has free rent in my heart, forever.

ACKNOWLEDGEMENTS

Writing a book of this nature is a slow and deliberate activity, like making flowered wallpaper for the White House ballroom by hand. To do the job right, I needed assistance. Accordingly, I gratefully acknowledge the help and support of Frances Michalko, Pat Lehmann, George and Maureen Michalko, Phil Pies, Sam Pies, Eric Zeller, David and Lynn Barclay, Gary Lehmann, Claude Blackcloud, Bill and Mary Stevenson, Clyde Kreckman, Susan Malone, Ed Homsey, Fred Regan, Alan Spiegel, Roger Heap, Gerry Gowing, Pete Adams, Richard Stratton, Paul Saeli, Sam Ajaeb, Bob Thomas, Jim Nye, Ron Taylor, Dow Drukker, Art Sotak, Kyle Wallace, and my faithful companion, B. J., who, I suspect, would probably prefer a bone.

A very special thanks are due Matthew McSain, artist; Mariah Bear, editor; George Young, Editorial Director; and, R. Wayne Oler, first-class friend and idea person. Their work runs like a perfectly detached composition by Mozart throughout all the lines of the book.

TABLE OF CONTENTS

WARNING:
THIS BOOK IS FOR MONKEYS

Your business attitude determines your potential for innovation, creativity, even genius, and success in your field. There are two basic business attitudes, which I call the "kitten" and the "monkey," because of how each animal deals with stress and change.

If a small kitten is confused or in danger, it will do nothing but mew until its mother comes and carries it to safety. By contrast, a baby monkey will run to its mother and jump on her back at the first sign of trouble. The baby monkey then rides to safety, hanging on for itself.

This book can do little for people with the "kitten" attitude—those who cry for help when faced with a challenge or problem. Thinkertoys is designed for the "monkeys," who are willing to work on themselves, work to develop their business creativity, and work on coming up with innovative ideas . . . and are ready to enjoy the very real benefits of that work.

If you have the "monkey" attitude and want a wealth of original ideas to improve your business or personal life, this book is for you. I invite you to take these Thinkertoys and use them to create the ideas you need to change your life. Thinkertoys are solid, creative techniques that show you how to get ideas. The rest is up to you.

(Hope for those with the "kitten" attitude: If you want to change, you will find the help you need in Chapter One, Original Spin, with exercises and encouragement for developing the "monkey" attitude.)

INTRODUCTION

Can you identify the figure below? If you have seen this puzzle before, you should have no trouble. If it is new to you, try to figure it out before reading further.

Observe *how* you scan the figure for meaning. You probably tend to focus on finding meaning in the irregular black shapes, which is useless—there is none. However, if you focus on the spaces *between* the shapes, the word "West" appears. Place a straightedge on the top or bottom border of the figure to make the word obvious. Once found, it seems so obvious that you wonder why you were, at first, blind to it.

By changing your perspective, you expand your possibilities until you see something that you were unable to see before. This is what you will experience when you use Thinkertoys: You will find yourself looking at the same information you had before in a new and different way. This "new and different way" will lead you to new ideas and unique insights.

No matter what business you're in, your future will be shaped, even determined by innovation occurring today. Where did all those health clubs come from? And those video stores? And who can remember when the only athletic footwear anybody owned was a pair of canvas-topped, flat-bottomed, solid-white sneakers? For that matter, when did you notice that there were Japanese cars and products everywhere? Can you recall the first Walkman you saw? Who thought these things up? Your future depends upon great ideas, and to come up with consistently great ideas, you can't rely on chance.

Thinkertoys train you how to get ideas. They are specific, hands-on techniques that enable you to come up with big or small ideas; ideas that make money, solve problems, beat the competition, and further your career; ideas for new products and new ways of doing things.

The techniques were selected for their practicality, and range from the classic to the most modern. They are divided into *linear* techniques, which allow you to manipulate information in ways that will generate new ideas, and *intuitive* techniques which show you how to find ideas by using your intuition and imagination.

A popular children's puzzle shows six fishermen whose lines are tangled together to form a sort of maze. One of the lines has caught a fish; the problem is to find which fisherman it belongs to. You are supposed to do this by following each line down through the maze, which may take up to six tries, depending on your luck. It is obviously easier to start at the other end and trace the line from the fish to the fisherman, as you have only one possible starting place, not six.

This is how I researched and developed Thinkertoys. Instead of presenting a catalog of all known creative techniques and abandoning you to puzzle out which ones actually work, I started with the *ideas* (fish) and worked backwards to each creator (fisherman). Then I identified the technique that caught the idea.

Some readers will feel that they profit more from the linear techniques and will discount the intuitive ones. Others will prefer the intuitive and discount the linear. You can produce ideas using both the linear and intuitive techniques, and should not limit yourself to one or the other—the more ideas you generate the better.

This book will change how you perceive your own creativity, while stripping creativity itself of its mystique. You will, perhaps for the first time, see endless possibilities stretching before you. You will learn how to:

- Generate ideas at will.
- Find new ways to make money.
- Create new business opportunities.
- Manipulate and modify ideas until you come up with the most innovative and powerful ideas possible.
- Create new products, services, and processes.
- Improve old products, services, and processes.
- Develop solutions to complex business problems.
- Revitalize markets.

- See problems as opportunities.
- Become more productive.
- Be the "idea person" in your organization.
- Know where to look for the "breakthrough idea."
- Become indispensable to your organization.

Thinkertoys do not *render* the creative experience, they *suggest* it. To illustrate, let us imagine me drawing a rabbit on a blackboard. You say "Yes, that's a rabbit," although in reality there is nothing on the blackboard but a simple chalk line. The rabbit appears because you have accepted my notion that the space within the line suggests a rabbit. The line limits the content by suggesting a *significant form*.

I must stress that it is not enough to read the book—to create your own ideas, you have to *use* the techniques. Try to explain the joy of skiing to a bushman who has never left the desert. You can show him some skis and a picture of a snowy mountain, and perhaps get some of the idea across. However, to fully realize the concept of skiing our bushman *must* put on the skis and head down a mountain. If you merely read these techniques, you will have no more than a suggestion of how to get ideas. You'll be like the bushman standing in the desert, staring at a pair of skis and a photo of the Matterhorn, with a small notion of what skiing might be.

Each Thinkertoy is a specific technique for getting ideas to solve your challenges. Each chapter contains a blueprint that gives precise instructions for using the technique and an explanation of why it works—including anecdotes, stories, and examples of how real heroes used each technique to produce ideas and breakthroughs. I call them heroes because they left behind a mark, a sign, an idea, an enterprise, a product, or a service that reminds us of their innovation.

I also use illustrations, puzzles, and charts, and hypothetical examples to demonstrate how various techniques work. Some of these hypothetical examples present usable ideas for new businesses, products, and services. These ideas are the gold beneath the river of words continually rushing past.

Each chapter begins with an inspirational quote from *The Art of War* by the legendary master, Sun Tzu. Sun Tzu wrote his extraordinary book in China more than 2,400 years ago, but his principles are as applicable to creativity in business as in warfare. Long a classic for Japanese businesspeople, his book is now required reading at many leading international business schools. From Tokyo to Wall Street, business leaders quote and apply the principles of Sun Tzu.

A friend of mine, Hank Zeller (an executive, entrepreneur, inventor, and poet), once described creativity this way: "When you realize that you just came up with an idea that betters anything that has been done, well, your hair stands up on end, you feel an incredible sense of awe; it's almost as if you heard a whisper from God."

INITIATION

The first chapter in this section, "Original Spin," will help you overcome your fears, doubts, and uncertainties about creativity. The second, "Mind Pumping," provides exercises to help you get started acting like an "idea person." To be creative, you have to believe and act as if you are creative.

Look at the illustration below. It appears to be two straight lines, but you can create a third line. To do this, tilt the book away from you so that it is perpendicular to your eyes. Position it so that the cross point is in front of you. Cross your eyes slightly to focus on the cross point. Do you see the third line? (It should look like a short pin sticking up out of the page.)

If you believe you are creative and act as if you are creative, you will begin to create ideas, like the third line, out of anything.

The worth of the ideas you create will depend in large part upon the way you define your problems. The third chapter, "Challenges," shows how to word problem statements so that the final statement has the feel of a well-hit golf ball.

CHAPTER ONE

ORIGINAL SPIN

"To secure ourselves against defeat
lies in our own hands."

SUN TZU

When you are depressed, your thoughts are quite different than when you are happy. When you feel rich and successful, your thoughts are quite different than when you feel poor and unsuccessful. Similarly, when you feel you are creative, your ideas are quite different than when you feel you are not.

Scientists have established that physiological responses can be consciously altered. You can condition yourself to trigger a particular chemical pattern in your brain that will affect your attitudes and your thinking in positive ways. This chapter contains some very simple exercises which will help you overcome your fears, doubts, and uncertainties, affirm your self-worth, and cultivate a creative attitude.

Nothing is more harmful to a positive creative attitude than fears, uncertainties, and doubts (FUDS); yet, most people let FUDS control their lives.

It is much more productive to learn to control your FUDS, to transform destructive negative attitudes into a new, positive reality. To do this, simply acknowledge the negative feelings and then focus your energies on what you want to substitute for them.

Suppose you are driving along and your oil pressure gauge comes on, warning you that your car is overheating. This is a negative indicator. However, you don't ignore it, nor do you become paralyzed with fear. You simply stop at a service station, have it corrected, and drive on.

Following this incident, you do not look at the oil pressure gauge continuously when you're driving, allowing the gauge to monopolize your thoughts. To do so would mean slow and erratic driving, if you had the courage to drive at all. So it is with your fears and doubts. You need to acknowledge them, and then replace them with positive thoughts.

Prescott Lecky, a pioneer of self-image psychology, developed a method that consisted of getting a subject to see that some negative concept of his was inconsistent with some other deeply held belief. Lecky believed that humans have an inherent need for consistency. If a thought is inconsistent with other, stronger ideas and concepts, the mind will reject it.

Lecky found that there were two powerful levers for changing beliefs and overcoming fears, convictions that are strongly felt by nearly everyone. These are:

1. The belief that one is capable of doing one's share, holding up one's end of the log, exerting a certain amount of independence.
2. The belief that there is something inside one that makes one equal in talent and ability to the rest of the world, and that one should not belittle oneself or allow oneself to suffer indignities.

One of his patients was a salesman who was afraid to call on top management clients. Lecky asked him, "Would you get down on all fours and crawl into the office, prostrating yourself before a superior personage?"

"I should say not!" the salesman replied.

"Then why do you mentally crawl and cringe? Can't you see that you are doing essentially the same thing, when you go in overly concerned with whether or not he will approve of you? Can't you see you are literally begging for his approval of you as a person?"

The important thing to remember is that you do not have to change your personality or your life, or somehow make yourself into a new and better person in order to understand and replace your negative thoughts.

General George Patton was once asked if he ever experienced fear or uncertainty before battle. He replied that he often experienced fear before, and even during, a battle, but the important thing was "I never take counsel of my fears."

TICK-TOCK

Tick-Tock is a very powerful exercise based on Lecky's work that is designed to help you overcome your fears, doubts, and uncertainties. In Tick-Tock you write out your fears, confront them head-on, and then substitute positive factors that will allow you to succeed.

1. *Zero in on and write down those negative thoughts that are preventing you from realizing your goal.* Write them under "Tick."

2. *Sit quietly and examine the negatives.* Learn how you are irrationally twisting things and blowing them out of proportion.

3. *Substitute an objective, positive thought for each subjective, negative one.* Write these under "Tock."

Following are two examples of Tick-Tock exercises with sample negative and positive thoughts. The first addresses the fear of presenting a new idea to management; the second, the fear of producing a new product.

TICK-TOCK #1

TICK	TOCK
Presenting this idea is pointless. Management is more experienced and skilled than I am and they probably thought of this before.	This is all or nothing thinking. The idea doesn't have to be a blockbuster—big endings come from small beginnings. Reverse roles; if I owned the company, wouldn't I want all the ideas I could get? I will write down all my self-doubting thoughts and refute them.
The idea is so nontraditional I'll be a laughingstock if I suggest it.	Even if the idea is rejected, people respect and admire those who are creative in their work and who are constantly trying to improve the current situation. No pain, no gain. The riskier the idea, the greater the potential for rewards.

I never had a new idea in my life. My best chance is not to take chances.

I assume my negative feelings necessarily reflect the way things are: I feel it, therefore it must be true. My real problem is a false image of myself: Would my company have hired me if they were as negative about me as I am?

My last idea failed miserably and Tom's didn't. I'm afraid to take another chance.

I exaggerate the importance of things (my failure, Tom's success). Thomas Edison once said that the only road to success was through failure. The only crime in life is never having tried. Instead of trying not to be wrong, try to be right.

TICK-TOCK #2

TICK

I'll never be able to do it.

TOCK

Just do a little bit at a time and get started. There's no reason why I have to do it all on a crash schedule.

I'll probably screw it up and then fail miserably.

It doesn't have to be perfect. I might learn something and imagine how I'll feel when it's finally finished. I have a good track record of doing things well. Concentrate on the project, and my attitude will improve.

I can't discipline myself. I have no self-control. I won't be able to manage my time on my own.

I must have self-control because I've done well in other things. Just work on it as best I can as long as I can. I have as much self-control as anyone I know. The project is so important and the benefits so tangible that time management will be more fun than a problem.

What's the point in doing all that work? I'll never find a company to market it.

I have no way of knowing that. Give it a try. Some company will be interested. Besides, you can learn things even if someone rejects it. Where there is a will there is a way. If I believe in it, others will as well. It's a question of finding the right company.

At first, the figures above look strange and meaningless. Because you are mentally conditioned to look at black shapes and figures, you ignore the white shapes in between the black ones. However, if you focus on the white shapes, you can see the words "FLY" and "WIN." The white shapes become dominant and the black ones recede in importance.

In Tick-Tock, your negative thoughts will recede like the black shapes as your positive thoughts become dominant. Once you have used Tick-Tock for some time, you will find yourself mentally replacing negative thoughts with positive ones "on cue," so to speak. When you experience doubts or fears, you will automatically use them as a signal to look for the "white" thoughts.

HOW TO SPIN THE ORIGINAL SPIN

Years back, a group of scientists visited a tribe in New Guinea that believed their world ended at a nearby river. After several months, one of the scientists had to leave, which involved crossing the river. Safely across the river, he turned around and waved. The tribesmen did not respond because, they said, they didn't see him. Their entrenched beliefs about the world had distorted their perception of reality.

Recently, the CEO of a major publishing house was concerned about the lack of creativity among his editorial and marketing staffs. He hired a group of high-priced psychologists to find out what differentiated the creative employees from the others.

After studying the staff for one year, the psychologists discovered that there was only one difference between the two groups: The creative people believed they were creative and the less creative people believed they were not. Like the New Guinea tribesmen, those who felt they were not creative had a distorted perception of reality. These employees had lost their original spin.

The psychologists recommended instituting a simple two-part program designed to change the belief systems of those who thought they were not creative. The CEO agreed, and within a year, the uncreative people became many more times creative than the original creative group. Once their attitudes changed, they began to pay attention to small and large challenges and to flex their creative muscles in extraordinary ways. The following year, many innovative programs and blockbuster books were generated by this group. These people regained their original spin and began to transform themselves and the world around them.

The first part of this extremely effective program addressed self-affirmation; the second part dealt with creative affirmation.

SELF-AFFIRMATION

To increase your self-affirmation, get in the habit of remembering your successes, your good qualities and characteristics, and forgetting your failures. It doesn't matter how many times you have failed in the past; what matters is the successful *attempt*, which should be remembered and reinforced. A successful salesperson, for example, must be willing to fail in closing an order several times before succeeding once.

Success breeds success. Small successes are stepping stones to greater ones. The first exercise is to write and maintain a self-affirmation list.

Record all the things you like about yourself—your positive qualities, characteristics, and traits. Include the successes you have had in every area of your life: work, home, school, and so on. Keep adding to this list as you think of more things and as you accomplish more. Acknowledging yourself, your abilities, and your own unique qualities will encourage you to get moving.

If you make a practice of remembering your successes and good personal qualities and paying less attention to your failures, you will begin to experience more success than you would have thought possible. Imagine a person learning to hit a baseball. At first, he will miss the ball many more times than he hits it. With practice, his misses will gradually diminish, and the hits will come more frequently. If mere repetition were the key to improved skill, his practice should make him more expert at missing the ball than hitting it. However, even though the misses outnumber the hits, he hits the ball more successfully because his mind remembers, reinforces, and dwells on the successful attempts rather than the misses.

CREATIVE AFFIRMATION

The second technique used by the psychologists is a deceptively simple yet incredibly powerful technique that uses written affirmations to cultivate and reinforce the belief that you are a creative person.

Human beings act, feel, and perform in accordance with what they *imagine* to be true about themselves and their environment. What you imagine to be true becomes, in fact, true. Hold a given picture of yourself long and steadily enough in your mind's eye and you will become that picture. Picture yourself vividly as defeated and that alone will make victory impossible. Picture yourself vividly as winning and that alone will contribute immeasurably to success.

To visualize yourself as creative, affirm that you believe it to be true. An affirmation is a positive statement that something is already so. It can be any positive statement, general ("I am creative") or specific ("I am always in the right place at the right time, engaged in the right activity in order to get ideas"). Take a few minutes and write down several different affirmations about your creativity.

Now, take one of these affirmations and write twenty variations of it, using the first, second, and third persons. For example, "I, Michael, am a creative person. Michael is a creative person. Michael, you are a creative person." "I'm truly creative. Michael is the most creative person in the group. You, Michael, are gifted with creativity," and so on.

As you write, take your time and really ponder each word *as you write it*. Keep changing the wording of the affirmations.

Whenever you feel negative thoughts, write them on the other side of the page, or on a separate piece of paper. For instance, you might write, "Michael has not had a new idea in two years. Others do not feel Mike is creative. Michael is too dull to think up a good idea. I'm too old to be creative. I'm not educated enough to come up with good ideas." Then, return to writing your positive affirmations.

When you're finished, look at the negatives. These are your obstacles to being creative. Nullify the negatives by writing additional, specific affirmations to address the negatives. For the negatives above, you might write, "Michael has new ideas every day. Others do not know Michael well enough to make a judgment. Michael is an exciting person, not a dull one. Most inventors and big idea people do not have much formal education," and so on.

Write your affirmations about being creative every day for five days. During this period, the negatives will almost certainly stop; at that point just continue writing the positive affirmations, until you no longer feel the need.

Read the following words.

TAE CAT

Anyone can see that these letters spell out "THE CAT," right? But look more closely. If you examine the "H" and the "A," you will see that they are identical. Your perception of the words was influenced by your expectations. You expected to see "THE" and not "TAE," and "CAT" and not "CHT." This expectation was so strong that you influenced your brain to see what you expected.

In the same way, when you expect to be creative you will influence your brain to be creative. Once you believe you are creative, you will begin to believe in the worth of your ideas, and you will have the persistence to implement them.

SUMMARY

Each one of us must affirm our own individual creativity. Although many facets of human creativity are similar, they are never identical. All pine trees are very much alike, yet none is exactly the same as another. Because of this range of similarity and difference, it is difficult to summarize the infinite variations of individual creativity. Each person has to do something different, something that is unique. The artist, after all, is not a special person; every person is a special kind of artist.

MIND PUMPING

"Anciently the skillfull warriors first made
themselves invincible and awaited the enemy's
moment of vulnerability."

SUN TZU

Tibetan monks say their prayers by whirling wheels on which their prayers are inscribed, spinning the prayers into divine space. Sometimes, a monk will keep a dozen or so prayer wheels rotating, like the juggling act in which whirling plates are balanced on top of long thin sticks.

The monk may be thinking about dinner, his religious future, or something else while he is spinning his prayer wheel. Similarly, there are priests who go through the motions of celebrating Mass without feeling a connection to the liturgy.

When the monk and priest assume the role of "religious person" and make it obvious to themselves and others by playing that role, their brains will soon follow. It is not enough for the monk or priest to have the *intention* of being religious: the monk must rotate the wheel; the priest must say the Mass. If one acts like a monk, one will become a monk. If one goes through the motions of being a priest, sooner or later, one will become emotionally involved in religion.

If you act like an idea person, you will become one. It is the intention and going through the motions of being creative that counts.

If you want to be an artist, and actually go through the motions of being one, you *will* become at least an adequate artist. You may not become another van Gogh, but you will be much more of an artist than someone who has neither had the intention nor gone through the motions. There is no way of knowing how far intention and action can take you. This world offers no guarantees, only opportunities and vicissitudes. When you reach for the stars you may not get one, but you won't come up with a handful of mud either.

This chapter contains eleven exercises that will encourage you to behave like an idea person.

IDEA QUOTA

Give your mind a workout every day. Set yourself an idea quota for a challenge you are working on, such as five new ideas every day for a week. You'll find the first five are the hardest, but these will quickly trigger other ideas. The more ideas you come up with, the greater your chances of coming up with a winner.

Set an Idea Quota

Get Tone

Don't Be a Duke of Habit

Feed Your Head

Do a Content Analysis

Make a Brain Bank

Be a Travel Junkie

Capture Your Thoughts

Think Right

Keep an Idea Log

Having a quota will force you to actively generate ideas and alternatives rather than waiting for them to occur to you. You will make an effort to fill the quota even if the ideas you come up with seem ridiculous or far-fetched. Having an idea quota does not stop you from generating more ideas than the quota, but it does ensure that you generate your minimum.

Thomas Edison held 1,093 patents. He was a great believer in exercising his mind and the minds of his workers and felt that without a quota he probably wouldn't have achieved very much. His personal invention quota was a minor invention every ten days and a major invention every six months. To Edison, an idea quota was the difference between eating beefsteak or a plateful of Black Beauty stew.

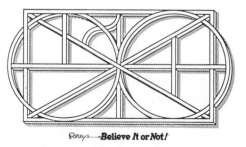

Ripley's——*Believe It or Not!*

The above puzzle is somewhat like your mind because every time you look at it you see something new. What are the entire contents?

Most probably you found some letters and numbers. If I told you your quota was to find all twenty-six letters of the alphabet and the numerals 0 through 9, chances are you would search the puzzle until you located them all. And you will find them all because they are all there. Similarly, you can stretch your mind to find ideas to fill idea quotas.

GETTING TONE

Fighter pilots say, "I've got tone" when their radar locks onto a target. That's the point at which the pilot and plane are totally focused on the target. "Getting tone" in everyday life means paying attention to what's happening around you.

How many f's are in the following paragraph:

The necessity of training farmhands for first class farms in the fatherly handling of farm livestock is foremost in the minds of farm owners. Since the forefathers of the farm owners trained the farmhands for first class farms in the fatherly handling of farm livestock, the farm owners feel they should carry on with the family tradition of training farmhands of first class farms in the fatherly handling of farm livestock because they believe it is the basis of good fundamental farm management.

Total number of f's _____

If you've got tone, you found thirty-six f's. If you found less, you probably ignored the f's in the word "of." In the latter case, you are probably thinking, "Of course, it was right in front of my eyes the whole time."

Ordinarily we do not make the fullest use of our ability to see. We move through life looking at a tremendous quantity of information, objects, and scenes, and yet we *look* but do not *see*.

Paying attention to the world around you will help you develop the extraordinary capacity to look at mundane things and see the miraculous. Really paying attention to what you see will enable you to develop a kind of binary vision, with which you perceive what others see, but notice something unexpected as well.

Did you see anything unexpected in the below illustration? If not, look again.

An idea can be found anywhere. Maybe it's up in the hills, under the leaves, or hiding in a ditch somewhere. Maybe it will never be found. But what you find by paying attention, whatever you find, will always lead to something.

TINY TRUTHS

This exercise is designed to help you pay pure attention to the world around you. It was developed by Minor White, who taught photography at MIT.

Select a photograph or picture that gives you pleasure, the more detailed the better. Get comfortable and relax. Set a timer or alarm for ten minutes. Look at the photograph or picture until the timer goes off, without moving a muscle. Stay focused on the image. Do not allow your mind to free-associate. Pay attention only to the image in front of you. After the timer goes off, turn away from the image and recall your experience. Review the experience visually rather than with words. Accept whatever the experience is for what it is. After your review and your experience becomes kind of a flavor, go about your everyday work, trying to recall the experience whenever you can. You'll begin to experience tiny truths that you can find only by paying pure attention. Recall the experience frequently and recall it visually. Some think these tiny truths are the voice of God.

DUKES OF HABIT

Dukes of Habit must always do things the same way, must have everything in its place, and are at a loss if something violates their routine. Because everything in their lives is precisely folded, labeled, and placed in neat little cubbyholes, Dukes of Habit are limited problem-solvers. Don't be a Duke of Habit.

Deliberately program changes into your daily life. Make a list of things you do by habit. Most of the items will probably be those little things that make life comfortable, but also make it unnecessary for you to think. Next, take the listed habits, one by one, and consciously try to change them for a day, a week, a month, or whatever.

- Take a different route to work.
- Change your sleeping hours.
- Change your working hours.
- Listen to a different radio station each day.
- Read a different newspaper.
- Make new friends.
- Try different recipes.
- If you normally vacation in the summer, vacation in the winter.
- Change your reading habits. If you normally read nonfiction, read fiction.
- Change your break habits. If you usually drink coffee, drink juice.
- Change the type of restaurants you go to.
- Change your recreation. Try boating instead of golf, and so on.
- Take a bath instead of a shower.
- Watch a different television news broadcaster.

FEEDING YOUR HEAD

Creative thinkers read to feed their minds new information and ideas. As Gore Vidal put it, "The brain that doesn't feed itself eats itself."

Here are some ideas to pump your mind when you read:

Select carefully. Before you read a book ask: "How good an exercise for my creative mind will this provide?" Make the most of your reading time by sampling broadly and reading selectively.

Take notes. In Albert Paine's biography of Mark Twain, Paine wrote: "On the table by him, and on his bed, and on the billiard-room shelves, he kept the books he read most. All, or nearly all, had annotations—spontaneously uttered marginal notes, title prefatories, or comments. They were the books he read again and again, and it was seldom that he had nothing to say with each fresh reading."

Outline. Outline a book before you read it, or read the first half, stop and write an outline of the latter half. Imagine what you will find before you read the table of contents or the book. This was George Bernard Shaw's favorite exercise; it will provide good, strenuous exercise for your imagination.

Read biographies. Biographies are treasure-houses of ideas.

Read how-to books on any subject. Exercise your mind by manipulating the ideas of others into new ideas. Read books on crafts, automobiles, carpentry, gardening, and so on. These books give you tools with which you can create unique ideas and products.

Read magazines on varied subjects. Walt Disney relied on the *Reader's Digest* for many of his ideas. He was quoted as saying: "Your imagination may be creaky or timid or dwarfed or frozen at points. The *Digest* can serve as a gymnasium for its training."

Read nonfiction. When reading nonfiction books, practice thinking up solutions to any problems presented in the book before the problem is solved. This was one of John F. Kennedy's favorite exercises.

Think. Think as you read. Search for new solutions to old problems, changes in business, trends in foreign countries, technological breakthroughs, connections, and parallels between what you read and your problems.

John Naisbitt, author of *Megatrends* and chairman of the Washington, D.C.-based Naisbitt Group, has been very successful in employing a method of trend spotting called "content analysis." He adapted this notion from methods used in a book he read about the Civil War. The historian who wrote the book, in turn, adapted content analysis from an article he had read about the CIA's intelligence-gathering methods. The CIA patterned it after methods used by the Allies in World War II. Allied forces discovered the strategic value of reading newspapers smuggled out of small German towns. These papers sometimes carried useful stories on fuel, food, and other items. Similarly, a small group of Swiss intelligence officers were able to figure out German troop movements by reading social pages to see where famous German officers were mentioned.

Content Analysis

Here's how to do your own content analysis:

- Scan your junk mail before you discard it. What trends in advertising, marketing, new products, and new values can you discern?
- Let your junk mail collect for a month or two before scanning it. Patterns and trends are more readily apparent, because you can see the repetitive nature of emerging trends.

- When you're on the road, read the local newspapers and shopping news giveaways. What inferences can you make about the local economy? Is it growing or declining? What new business opportunities do you see? What opportunities are transferable to your home town? What are the area's values, attitudes, and lifestyles?
- Actively observe popular culture. Watch network and cable TV, rent videos, read popular magazines and books, go to movies, and listen to popular songs. What are people interested in? What values and lifestyles are portrayed? Who are the popular heroes? Why are they heroes?
- Think about how your job has changed. What is in your in basket as compared with its contents this time last year? Has the corporate emphasis changed? Do you have more paperwork or less? More meetings or fewer? Where is the company heading? Talk to the people you work with for clues to the ways work attitudes, values, and commitments are changing.
- Attend as many business conferences, seminars, and lectures as you can.
- Listen to a different radio station every week to get a variety of perspectives. Who is the market for the station? What are they addressing? Who listens? Who advertises? Why?
- Make it a practice to scan the week's television schedule, and then tape the programs that interest you. When you're in the mood for television, watch the taped programs instead of whatever's on.

Your own content analysis will be infinitely more valuable to you than any of the available services, some of which charge clients $25,000 a year to provide them with this type of information. When you perceive trends and patterns of interest, begin to pump your mind for ideas, opportunities, and business possibilities. Look for connections and relationships between your content analysis and your business challenges.

BRAINBANKS

Collect and store ideas like a pack rat. Keep a container (coffee can, shoe box, desk drawer, or file folder) of ideas and idea starters. Begin collecting interesting advertisements, quotes, designs, ideas, questions, cartoons, pictures, doodles, and words that might trigger ideas by association.

When you are looking for new ideas, shake up the container and pull out two or more items at random to see if they can somehow trigger a thought that might lead to a new idea. If not, reshuffle and eventually you'll come up with some intriguing combinations of useful ideas.

The other day I shook up my Brainbank and pulled two clippings: One was about a man who invented a new coffin that is cheaper and more durable than the others on the market. The other was about a man who started a camcorder rental service. Free-associating with death, funerals, videos, rentals, and so on, I hit on what might be a viable enterprise: Video tributes to the deceased. Do short videos of scenes from the deceased's life that could be made by super-imposing photographs over peaceful landscapes.

TRAVEL JUNKIE

Be a travel junkie. Whenever you're feeling stale and bored, go to a store, trade show, exhibition, library, museum, flea market, craft show, old folks' home, toy shop, or high school. Pick up something at random and create connections and relationships in your mind with the object and your problem. Wander around with an open mind and wait for something to catch your attention. It will. Your mind is like vegetation. It flourishes in one soil or climate and droops in another.

George Smith made candy on a stick in the early 1900s. Competition was fierce. He tried hard to find a new marketing twist to differentiate his stick candy from others. One day, he decided to take a break and went to the race track. One of the finest racehorses of the day was racing, and he bet a substantial amount of money on it. The horse won. The name of the horse was Lolly Pop. Smith named his stick candy "lollipops" and made candy history.

CAPTURING IDEA BIRDS

Ralph Waldo Emerson once wrote: "Look sharply after your thoughts. They come unlooked for, like a new bird seen in your trees, and, if you turn to your usual task, disappear."

You have to record your own ideas, as, so far as I know, there is no store that sells Cliff Notes on your past thoughts. If you think it, write it. In the figure to the left, the "target" shape is the black figure above the design. Find the target shape in the design and stare at it for a few seconds. When you stare at it in the design, the target shape will blink out of your conscious perception.

Just as the target shape disappears right before your eyes, your thoughts will disappear unless you write them down.

Psychologists have demonstrated that we are able to keep only about five to nine pieces of information in our mind at a time. We have all had the experience of looking up a phone number, then being distracted before dialing and forgetting the number in a matter of seconds. What is happening is that new information is bumping out older information before your mind can ready the older information for long-term storage in your memory.

In general, short-term memory can hold items fairly well for the first few seconds. After about twelve seconds, however, recall is poor, and after twenty seconds the information will disappear entirely, unless you keep repeating it to yourself or write it down. Writing signals your brain that this piece of information is more crucial than others and should be stored in your long-term memory.

John Patterson, president of National Cash Register, was a fan of Napoleon. Patterson rode horseback with his executives every day at 5 A.M. He demanded that they maintain a "little red book" to record daily activities, thoughts, ideas and so on. He ruthlessly fired many an employee who failed to maintain a notebook. He died in the midst of his business travels while scribbling in his little book.

Interestingly, one sixth of the major U.S. companies were headed by ex-NCR employees between 1910 and 1930. Among the disenchanted former NCR employees was Tom Watson, founder of IBM.

THINK RIGHT

Consciously work to make your thinking more fluent and more flexible (fluency means the number of ideas, flexibility refers to creativity). Making lists is a powerful way to increase your thinking fluency, as it forces you to focus your energy in a very productive way. To illustrate this, take a few minutes to think about possible uses for the lubricant WD-40. You probably came up with some ideas, but you almost certainly had a little trouble focusing, you probably censored some thoughts, and came up with only the most obvious uses.

Actually *listing* possible uses for WD-40 will help you to feel more focused and interested, and to come up with a greater number of ideas. Giving yourself a time limit will make you even more productive. But fluency is not enough—you must also be flexible.

If your list included such uses as "quick lubrication, loosen rusted things, lubricate bicycle chains," and so on, you demonstrated fluency, but you listed the ordinary expected uses of the product. You are flexible if your list contained such unusual entries as:

- Loosen jammed garbage disposals.
- Spray on bird-house poles to keep animals away from the nest.
- Bait for mousetraps.
- Prevent deterioration of musical instrument strings.
- Fish bait.
- Restore used typewriter ribbons to make blacker impressions.
- A car safety product. Keep it in your glove compartment to unstick car doors in case of bad accidents.

Flexibility in thought means the ability to see beyond the ordinary and conventional roles. It means you are more improvisational and intuitive, can play with context and perspective, and focus on *process*es rather than *outcomes*.

Psychologist J. P. Guilford, a pioneer in the study of creativity, believed the following exercise helps exercise thinking fluency and flexibility, and enhances the ability to organize such complex projects as plots for novels, scientific theories, plans for new business organizations, or the building of any system which is interrelated and interconnected.

Play this game with friends. See who can get the most sentences in five minutes.

Write four-word sentences from the four letters of a given word:

| I | don't | enjoy | apricots |
| Irritated | dogs | eagerly | anger |

IDEA LOG

The idea log is one of the CIA's favorite techniques for recording information. There is a written log for each problem, which is used to record ideas, facts, thoughts, questions, and so on. This enables the agent to instantly focus on all the ideas, comparisons, interrelationships, and data relating to a given problem.

Maintain an idea log. Each section could be devoted to separate aspects of your business and personal life. Sections could include: marketing, product, selling, corporate, personal, services, special projects, and new business possibilities. There are many organizers and personal planners on the market these days, but it's much more fun, creative, and useful to design your own. Experiment with different methods of capturing ideas before you decide which is best for you.

Reviewing your recorded ideas periodically is a good way to titillate your imagination. Each time you review them, you will begin to search out connections between a recorded idea and your present situation or experience.

Suppose you are chewing gum to relieve stress and an idea occurs to you: Why not create a gum to measure stress? You record it in your idea log and review it from time to time. A few months later you read in a magazine that the body's pH can indicate health. While reviewing your idea log, an idea pops up: Develop a gum that uses the body's pH factor to measure health. The user would chew it for three minutes. If it turns dark pink, they're healthy. If it turns green, they should go home and go to bed.

SUMMARY

Effective ways to pump your mind for ideas are:

1. Set an idea quota.
2. Get tone.
3. Don't be a Duke of Habit.
4. Feed your head.
5. Do a content analysis.
6. Create a Brainbank.
7. Be a travel junkie.
8. Capture your thoughts.
9. Think right.
10. Keep an idea log.

Pumping your mind is like making a path through tall grass. Originally there is no path, yet as you walk the same way each time, one appears. In the same way, you may have no ideas at first, yet as you exercise your mind using these techniques, ideas appear.

CHAPTER THREE

CHALLENGES

"He who knows when he can fight and when
he cannot will be victorious."

SUN TZU

Imagine five brilliant entrepreneurs sitting down to consider new ideas. They can't get started until someone proposes something. But where does the proposal come from? How do they decide what problem to solve? Who decides the focus? How do they determine their goals?

If they try to come up with new ideas without having a specific goal, they could consume an infinite amount of time with no purpose. It would be like trying to climb these stairs—moving up and up and up forever, without purpose.

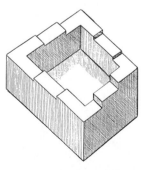

Before you start looking for ideas, you need to know what your goal is. This chapter will help you to identify worthwhile business problems and convert them into specific challenges to be solved using Thinkertoys.

A problem is nothing more than an opportunity in work clothes. A successful businessperson pays attention to problems, converting the problems into opportunities and deciding which opportunities are worth pursuing. These opportunities become productive challenges.

Anyone can learn how to pay attention. As a focusing exercise, select a color at random and spend an entire day looking for items that are that color or contain it. For instance, if you choose red you will discover an incredible number of red objects: cars, books, clothes, houses, fire trucks, chimneys, shoes, hats, paintings, and so on. Familiar objects will become new again, reds will become richer, and you will find that your perspective toward "red" has been dramatically changed. By tuning in "red" and tuning out other colors, you allowed yourself to understand the color red more deeply.

Consider the illustration in the margin.

This figure was drawn in 1900 by Joseph Jastrow, a psychologist. He drew the figure so that it can be viewed with equal validity as a duck or rabbit. When the face looks right it is a rabbit; when it looks left it is a duck. You tend to see the whole rabbit or the whole duck depending on which animal you select to focus on. It is difficult to concentrate and see both at the same time, rather than constantly shifting images.

Unless you set your business problems down in writing, your attention is constantly shifting and you become indecisive about what, if anything, you should focus on. Listing problems is a way for you to decide which ones are worth solving. It transforms a body of information into a set of components that can be restructured, checked, and searched.

Start keeping a journal of problems that you find to be personally interesting and that would be worthwhile to resolve. The following questions may help you get started:

- What would you like to have or to accomplish?
- What business idea would you like to work on?
- What do you wish would happen in your job?
- What business relationship would you like to improve?
- What would you like to do better?
- What do you wish you had more time to do?
- What more would you like to get out of your job?
- What are your unfulfilled goals?
- What excites you in your work?
- What angers you at your work?
- What misunderstandings do you have at work?
- What have you complained about?
- What changes for the worse do you see in the attitudes of others?
- What would you like to get others to do?

- What changes would you like to introduce?
- What takes too long?
- What is wasted?
- What is too complicated?
- Where are the bottlenecks?
- In what ways are you inefficient?
- What wears you out?
- What in your job turns you off?
- What would you like to organize better?
- In what ways could you make more money at work?

Following are typical business challenges:

- What creative suggestions can I make about new product ideas?
- How can I cut costs and increase production?
- How can we better differentiate our product from all others?
- What new product is needed? What extension of a current product's market?
- How can I sell 20 percent more than I am at present?
- What new selling techniques can I create? Can I reduce the cost of our current selling techniques?
- How can I become indispensable to my company?
- How can we better handle customer complaints?
- How can we improve the role service plays in the sale of our products?
- How can our advertising better communicate about our goods and services?
- Is it possible to encourage everyone in our organization to actively look for ways to better differentiate our products?
- What procedures could we institute that would reduce unnecessary paperwork?
- What awards would be more meaningful to employees?
- How can we become more customer-oriented?
- Is is possible to change our corporate image?
- In what ways might we outperform the competition?
- Which of our products can we make into silver bullets? (A silver bullet is the leading product or service in a particular industry.)

In the following illustration, there are two sets of parallel lines. The lines appear to form a contoured border between them. Either set of lines can be seen as covering the other. Yet, in reality, there is no border between the two sets. There is nothing there. This illusion is created because our minds try to make the gaps between the lines into something meaningful.

In the same way, the mere act of writing a challenge may trigger your mind to create something meaningful to fill in the gaps and solve it. A retired police detective who was looking for a business opportunity listed problems that were related to police work. One problem he listed was the difficulty in proving the identity of a stolen or kidnapped baby. Just writing the challenge provoked him to think of an idea for a new business venture: a DNA bank. He plans to store DNA samples for parents who worry about identifying their children in case of a kidnapping or a baby swap. It will cost $200 for collection and eighteen years of storage.

BUGS

Ideas sometimes grow out of irritation, like the pearls that grow when an oyster is irritated by grains of sand inside its shell. One creative soul was bugged by his inability to remember important dates such as anniversaries, birthdays, and so on. He was always a day late with presents. He made this bug into a challenge and created a novel product: vacuumed-packed canned roses to be stored and used for emergencies.

After you make your "bug list," select the challenges that you find most interesting. Remember that a worthwhile problem for one person may very well be boring to another. An accountant and salesperson will not likely be stimulated or challenged by the same problem; indeed two people in the same discipline may not be challenged by the same problem. Only you can identify the kind of challenges that will stimulate and drive you.

Take the challenge of sliced bread. Few people in the early 1900s were bugged by slicing their own bread, but one of them was Otto Frederick Rohwedder. He invested sixteen years of his life and all of his money in inventing

an automatic bread slicer, despite poor health, lack of enthusiasm from the industry, and financial ruin. In 1930, Continental adopted his slicer for Wonder Bread, and by 1933, about 80 percent of bread purchased was presliced. Rohwedder said he was not driven by money (he never became rich) but by the challenge of creating a workable bread slicer and an aversion to slicing his own bread.

BENEFITS

"Unhappy is the fate of one who tries to win his battles and succeed in his attacks without cultivating the spirit of enterprise, for the result is a waste of time and general stagnation."

SUN TZU

It's important to give yourself a compelling, personal reason for coming up with new ideas to solve them. Weigh each challenge for personal benefits before you commit yourself. The best ideas come from those hungry for success and those who cultivate the spirit of enterprise.

Thomas Edison learned the importance of realizing a personal benefit from his work early on. His first invention was an automatic vote recorder for Congress. When he presented the invention to a Congressman, he was told that efficiency in lawmaking was the last thing on Congress's agenda. From that point on, Edison would often state that the only reason he invented was to make a lot of money. He didn't have the time, energy, or interest to modify the world to fit his inventions.

Before you decide which challenge to resolve, make a list of the benefits that may be gained if you are successful in developing a creative solution. What are the direct benefits: money, pleasure, recognition, property, and so on? What are the indirect benefits: new skills, knowledge, attitudes, etc.? Do the benefits outweigh the costs in terms of your time and energy? Which challenges would be the most rewarding to resolve? What problems or situations do you want to accept personal responsibility for solving?

If you feel that it is not necessary to realize any personal benefits before you dedicate yourself to solving a challenge . . . just lean your head sideways and watch the sawdust pour out of your ear.

After you decide what challenges are most interesting and likely to yield solid benefits, it is important to *accept* the challenge. To accept a challenge means to accept responsibility for generating ideas as possible solutions to the problem. The more you accept responsibility and dedicate yourself to generating ideas, the higher your probability of reaching an innovative solution.

There are different levels of commitment to different problems. Some problems need total dedication, others may need little effort. Whenever I think of total dedication, I'm reminded of a story I once heard about a samurai who had the duty to avenge his overlord's murder. When he had cornered the murderer and was about to dispatch him with his sword, the man spat in the warrior's face. The warrior sheathed his sword and walked away.

Why? Because the spitting made him angry, and if he had killed that man in anger it would have been a personal act. He had accepted the responsibility to do another kind of act, an impersonal act of vengeance.

After you decide what challenges are interesting and will yield you solid benefits, it is time to state those challenges in the most useful way possible. This will allow you to most effectively use Thinkertoys to generate creative solutions.

Your Challenge Statement

"A victorious army wins its victories before
seeking battle."

Sun Tzu

The more time you devote to perfecting the wording of your challenge, the closer you will be to a solution. Conversely, the less time you take to define and center the challenge, the greater the chances for a not-so-great idea. You might end up with an idea that is as practical as a book about cattle ranching written by a cow.

One need only look at records from the U.S. Patent Office to find humorous examples of ideas generated by challenges that were not quite centered. These include: a golf ball that sends out smoke signals when it lands to help its owner find it, a diaper for parakeets, an alarm clock that squirts sleepers in the face, a fishing line for removing tapeworms from the stomach, and a machine that imprints dimples on the face.

Shape and center your challenge. Whenever I center a challenge, I think of sumo wrestling. Sumo wrestlers are those great big Japanese wrestlers. During the greater part of the wrestling contest, the two wrestlers are settled in a squat position, measuring each other. They assume a pose, hold it for awhile, then break, walk around, and assume their positions again. They repeat this act a number of times and then bang! They grab each other, one of the two hits the mat, and the bout is finished.

During all those rounds of squatting and posturing they are sizing each other up and searching for that center in themselves from which all action springs. The only protection for a sumo wrestler is to be in a perpetual state of centeredness, ever ready for the sudden attack and immediate response.

Similarly, when you have a problem, you can write a challenge statement, study it for awhile, then leave it, change it, stretch and squeeze it, and restate it until you feel that the challenge is centered. Then, like the sumo wrestler, you are ready.

You center your challenge with questions. Questions help you look at challenges from different perspectives. Sometimes a different perspective will stretch your eyes wide open. How many cubes can you count in the figure in the margin?

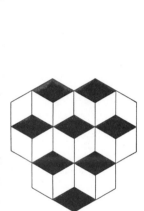

It is possible to count six or seven stacked cubes, depending on whether the black diamonds are viewed as the tops or bottoms of the cubes. What changes is not the picture you are looking at but your perception of it. Questions can help change your perception.

BLUEPRINT

To center a challenge:

1. *Write it as a definite question, beginning "In what ways might I . . . ?"*
2. *Vary the wording of the challenge by substituting synonyms for key words.*
3. *Stretch the challenge to see the broader perspective.*
4. *Squeeze the challenge to see the narrow perspective.*
    (a) Divide it into subproblems.
    (b) Solve the subproblems.
    (c) Keep asking "how else?" and "why else?"

To start with, it's helpful to coin problems in a particular way. Write the problem you want to solve as a definite question. Use the phrase "In what ways might I . . . ?" to start a problem statement. This is something known as the *invitational stem* and helps keep you from settling on a problem statement that may reflect only one perception of the problem.

Write several different problem statements using the invitational stem "In what ways might I . . . ?" Each different statement will encourage you to look at the problem from a new perspective, and will point your thinking toward new possibilities.

Imagine you are the person in the illustration below. Your challenge is to tie together the ends of the two strings suspended from the ceiling. The strings are located so you cannot reach one string with your outstretched hand while holding the second. The room is bare, and you have only the things with you that you have in your pocket today. How do you solve the problem?

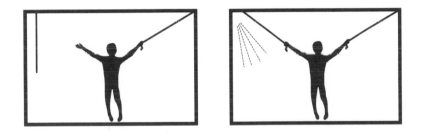

Initially, you might state the problem as: "How can I get to the second string?" However, you would then waste your energy trying to get to the second string, which is not possible. If, instead, you state the problem in a different way: "In what ways might the string and I get together?" you will likely come up with the solution—to tie a small object (such as a key, ring, watch, or belt) to the end of one string and set it in motion like a pendulum, then grab it while still holding the second string in your hand.

VARY THE WORDS

A simple technique to help you achieve different problem statements is to use synonyms or substitutes for key words in the challenge statement. The first step is to examine a particular challenge statement and identify the key words within it.

The product manager of OV' ACTION of Lievin, France, faced the following challenge: "In what ways might I develop a unique food product?"

He changed "unique" to "surprising" and "develop" to "transform" and restated the challenge to: "In what ways might I transform a product into a surprising food?"

He thought of things that might surprise him, and then about how food products could surprise consumers in similar ways. For instance, one thing that would surprise him would be to see a familiar object in an odd shape, such as an airplane shaped like a cow. Similarly, he would be surprised to see a familiar food product in a strange and different shape, such as a banana shaped like a loaf of bread, tomatoes in the shape of pyramids, or square potatoes. These thoughts led to his idea: a square egg.

He developed a precooked egg cube with a yolk in the middle which has a shelf life of twenty-one days and can be reheated in a microwave oven (unlike conventional eggs, which explode). Needless to say, OV'ACTION hopes Americans will scramble to buy their surprising new food product.

Making a few simple word changes may provide the stimuli for new ideas. It's like injecting a few raisins into the tasteless dough of a challenge.

STRETCHING THE CHALLENGE

The samurai warrior was trained to keep his senses open to all possibilities. With his attention focused as broadly as possible, a samurai was more likely to detect a surprise attack or sudden movement than when his attention was focused analytically on a single object or way.

To keep your mind open to all possibilities, stretch your challenge by asking "why?". Asking "why?" will help you identify your general objective and allow you to challenge your assumptions. This, in turn, enables you to redefine and shape your challenges.

Suppose your challenge is: "In what ways might I sell more IBM computers?"

Step one: Why do I want to sell more IBM computers? "Because our overall computer sales are down."

Step two: Why do I want to sell more computers? "In order to improve our overall sales volume."

Step three: Why do I want to increase our sales volume? "In order to improve our business."

Step four: Why do I want to improve our business? "To increase my personal wealth."

Step five: Why do I want to increase my wealth? "To lead a good life."

Now the challenge can be reshaped in a variety of ways including:

"In what ways might I sell more computers?"
"In what ways might I increase my overall sales volume?"
"In what ways might I improve my business?"
"In what ways might I increase my wealth?"
"In what ways might I lead a better life?"

The idea is to look for the appropriate level of abstraction, the best viewpoint from which to gather ideas. A phrase such as "increase my wealth" allows your thinking to embrace far more opportunities than "sell more computers." You could negotiate for higher commissions, go into another career, get a part-time job, make some investments, sell other products, and so on.

By coining your challenge as broadly as possible, you put yourself on the top of a mountain from which you can view all possible approaches to the top. If you don't look at all the possible approaches, you may preclude yourself from seeing the best route to the top.

The shipping industry provides a useful example of the consequences of not looking at all approaches to solving a problem.

In the 1950s, experts believed that the ocean-going freighter was dying. Costs were rising, and it took longer and longer to get merchandise delivered. This increased pilferage at the docks as goods piled up waiting to be loaded.

The shipping industry formulated their challenge as: "In what ways might we make ships more economical at sea and while in transit from one port to another?"

They built ships that were faster or required less fuel, and reduced crew size. Costs still kept going up, but the industry kept concentrating its efforts on reducing the specific costs related to ships while at sea and doing work.

They were doing things right, but they weren't doing the right thing. They were about as effective as an expert salesperson who spends all her energy, time, and talents trying to sell veal door-to-door.

A ship is capital equipment and the biggest cost for the capital equipment is the cost of *not working*, because interest has to be paid without income being generated to pay it. Finally, a consultant stretched the industry's challenge to: "In what ways might the shipping industry reduce costs?".

This allowed them to consider *all* aspects of shipping, including loading and stowing. The innovation that saved an industry was to separate loading from stowing, by doing the loading on land, before the ship is in port. It is much quicker to put on and take off preloaded freight. They decided to concentrate on the costs of *not working* rather than *working*, and reduce the amount of time a freighter does not work. The answer was the roll-on, roll-off ship and the container ship.

This simple solution was the direct result of reframing the challenge. The results have been startling. Freighter traffic has increased fivefold in the last thirty years, and costs are down by 60 percent. Port time has been reduced by three quarters, and with it, congestion and theft.

SQUEEZING THE CHALLENGE

Once you have a broad idea of what you are trying to find, narrow the objective from the general to the specific by squeezing it. This makes your challenge easier to solve by reducing the area within which problem solving takes place. Imagine trying to find an address, knowing only that it was somewhere in Montreal. If you knew that it was west of Old Montreal, it would be easier to find. If someone told you it was within walking distance of the Hotel Bonaventure, it would be still easier to find. So it is with challenges. You set your own limits within which to search for ideas.

To squeeze a challenge and ascertain its strengths, weaknesses, and boundaries, ask who, what, where, when, why, and how.

Who helps you identify individuals and groups who might be involved in the situation, have special strengths or resources or access to useful information, and who might gain from a resolution of the problem.

What helps identify all the things, objects, and items involved in the situation, the requirements, difficulties involved, rewards, and advantages and disadvantages of formulating a resolution.

Where considers the places, locations, and focal points of the problem.

When probes the schedules, dates, and timeliness of the situation.

Why helps you reach an understanding of your basic objective.

How helps you recognize how the situation developed, actions that may have been attempted or are now occurring, and steps that might be taken.

A design company framed their challenge as: "In what ways might we design a unique and convenient trash container?". To squeeze the challenge, they asked these questions:

"Who can help us design the container?"
"What material should we use?"
"Where can we get other materials?"
"When should we make it?"
"How can we make it more convenient?"
"What is a unique form?"
"Why will a new container be superior to existing ones?"

The subproblems became:

"In what ways might others help us design a better container?"
"In what ways might we make containers out of other materials?"
"In what ways might we obtain other materials?"
"In what ways might we schedule the project?"
"In what ways might we make containers more convenient?"
"In what ways might we design a unique container?"
"In what ways might we make our containers superior?"

These subproblems inspired the company to create an innovative product: the convertible trash can. This convertible can is made of recyclable plastic and is stored flat. Instructional graphics, locking tabs, and a quick-release system allow the user to turn flat sheets into cylindrical containers in seconds. The container is better-looking than other containers and devours less of the Earth's resources.

Squeezing the Challenge Further

Once you have asked these questions, go one step further—ask "how else?" and "what else?". You can almost always squeeze more out of your challenge.

O. M. Scott & Co., a leader in lawncare products, sells seeds, fertilizer, pesticides, and so on. At one time, they were a small seed retailer in competition with corporate giants such as Sears, Roebuck and Co. and Dow Chemical. Their products were good, but no better than the competition's.

Scott's general challenge was: "In what ways might we improve our market share?" They narrowed this to several specific challenges and then settled on one: "In what ways might we differentiate our products from the others?"

All the lawncare products were basically similar. All claimed to be "scientific," and described in meticulous detail how much of the stuff should be applied, given soil conditions and temperatures. All conveyed to the customer that growing a lawn is a precise, controlled scientific process. Customers did not seem to pay much attention to brand names.

Scott's salespeople asked their customers how the company could separate itself from the pack. The customers talked about their frustration in trying to plant their lawns in a precise and controlled way. Scott focused on this frustration and brainstormed ways to solve it. The challenge now became: "In what ways might we alleviate customer frustrations with planting?"

Asking "how else?" and "what else?", they came up with ideas ranging from more friendly directions to gardening classes for customers. Then they hit on the idea that made millions: a simple, mechanical gadget called the Scott Spreader. This small, lightweight wheelbarrow has holes that can be set to allow the proper quantities of Scott's products to pass through in an even flow. Before the Scott Spreader, no lawncare supplier had given the customers a tool to *control* the process. Scott designed its product line around the Spreader and, overnight, the small seed retailer became the market leader in lawncare.

Here's a challenge that seems to have no solution—certainly no obvious one. In the illustration below, remove three matches to leave four.

How can six minus three equal four? Just because the answer isn't obvious doesn't mean it's not there. By asking: "How else can I make a four?" and "What else is a four?" you can solve the challenge. Remove the matches at the top, bottom, and right, and now the answer is obvious.

THINKERTOYS

In order to get original ideas, you need to be able to look at the same information everyone else does, and organize it into a new and different pattern. This is *active thinking*.

Here is an equation of Roman numerals, made with ten matches. It is incorrect. Can you correct the equation without touching the matches, adding new matches, or taking away any matches?

To solve this problem, you have to break away from the obvious way of looking at things. If you look at a situation from only one perspective, it's like drawing a boundary around the way you think and working only within that boundary. You can solve this problem by looking at it in a new way. To make the equation correct, turn the book upside down.

How would you describe the figure in the margin?

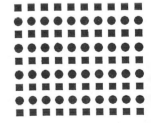

Most people describe it as a square of smaller squares and circles or as alternate rows of squares and circles. Few people will spontaneously see it as columns of alternate squares and circles. This is because we tend to passively organize similar items together in our minds. Once it's pointed out that it can also be viewed as columns of alternate squares and circles, we, of course, see it.

To go beyond the boundaries in your mind, you need to become an active thinker, to organize information into new patterns. It is the formation and the use of new patterns of information that gives rise to new ideas.

Take two accomplished waffle-makers whose waffles are equal in quality and price. One is a passive thinker, the other active. For some reason, people stop buying waffles. The passive thinker does nothing and goes out of business; the active thinker fashions the waffle into a cone and creates a whole new product: the ice cream cone. A passive thinker is unable to move beyond the given information to new ideas, while an active thinker is constantly organizing information into new ideas.

Thinkertoys provide concrete techniques to help you become an active thinker. Thinkertoys reflect linear *and* intuitive thinking, both of which are necessary for optimum creativity. The basic difference between the two is that the linear Thinkertoys structure existing information, while the intuitive toys generate new information using insight, imagination, and intuition.

We have two eyes, two ears, two hands, and two minds. Our left brain thinks in terms of words and symbols while our right brain thinks in terms of images. Linear Thinkertoys are for the left brain, intuitive Thinkertoys for the right brain.

The following chart summarizes some of the major differences between left-brain and right-brain functions:

LEFT BRAIN	RIGHT BRAIN
dealing with one thing at a time	integrating many inputs at once
processing information in a linear fashion	holistic perception or thinking
operating sequentially	seat of dreams
writing	awareness without definition
analyzing	seeing whole solutions at once
idea-linking	seeing similarities
abstracting	intuition
categorizing	insight
logic	gut feeling
reasoning	synthesizing
judgment	visualizing
mathematical	visual memory
verbal memory	recognizing patterns
using symbols	relating things to the present

The left side is the side used more by writers, mathematicians, and scientists; the right side by artists, craftspeople, and musicians. Remembering a person's name is a function of the left-brain memory while remembering their face is a function of the right brain. Reading books on how to play golf is a job for the left brain, while getting a "gut feel" for the golf swing is a job for the right brain.

Imagine a long passenger train traveling down a railroad track. One person is staring straight ahead at the train as it passes him. He sees that part of the train that is passing in front of him, from car to car. First, the engine, then the first car, the second car, and so on. If he has good peripheral vision, he might glimpse parts of those cars that have already passed him by, and parts of those cars which have yet to pass.

Another person views the same train from an airplane high above. She sees the whole train all at once, from beginning to end. This is the difference between the two sides of our brain. The left brain processes pieces of information sequentially, one by one, bit by bit. The right brain processes information all at once, holistically, intuitionally.

GUIDELINES

I do not recommend working through this book from start to finish, reading one Thinkertoy at a time, as though it were a textbook. You can best profit by *playing* with these toys, in your own unique style, to stimulate ideas from your imagination. Invent your own singular method for using them. You might be tempted to just use the one or two Thinkertoys you like best, but playing with a variety will be more productive.

If you pick just one, you might choose a perfectly adequate technique for getting ideas, but that does not mean there cannot be a better way. In school, when you add a column of numbers, you get a sum. If you have the right answer, you move on to the next problem.

Many people carry that idiom over into creative thinking. As soon as they have an answer, they stop thinking. They are satisfied with the first answer that comes along. Reality, though, is different from arithmetic. Some answers are better than others: They cost less, afford more status, are made better, easier to use, more aesthetic, are easier to install, or whatever. There is no reason for supposing that the first answer is the best one.

One day I set out for my favorite restaurant. Some friends set out from the same place at the same time, and got there long before I did. I asked them what route they had taken. They explained that they had taken the obvious route: They had turned down an alley that led them directly to the restaurant.

My own route had always seemed the best way to go, so I had never looked for another one. I was not even aware of the *possibility* of a better route. I had driven by that alley several times but never explored it. After all, I knew the best way to go. Because I never explored the alley, I never found out how useful it was. At the entrance to an unlikely approach, there is usually nothing to indicate that it is worth exploring, and yet it may lead to something useful. So it is with creative techniques. Unless you investigate them, you will never discover their usefulness.

The second reason for using a variety of different techniques is to cultivate a creative attitude. A good actor plays many different parts, and plays each to the fullest, depending on which mask he is wearing. A good actor will take pride in being versatile, in being able to play many different types, in comedies and tragedies. The more parts he plays, the more accomplished he becomes. The varied experiences give depth to the actor's performance.

In the same way, you need to take pride in your skill as a creative thinker. The ability to use *all* the techniques and to carry through the thinking that goes along with them will give depth to your creativity. Once you have experienced all the Thinkertoys, you can call up any one of them to help you with a particular problem. Some of these toys are like the reverse gear on a car. It's there, but you rarely use it—you seldom see people driving their cars down the road in reverse. On the other hand, one needs to have it and know how to use it for maneuverability whenever you're stuck and can't move forward.

The key is to *use* the Thinkertoys. Merely reading and not using them is like dropping a rose petal down the Grand Canyon and waiting for the echo.

Following are some ways to use Thinkertoys:

Work with one particular Thinkertoy at a time. Use it over and over again until you are thoroughly familiar with the technique. Spend several hours or even several days.

Select one linear and one intuitive Thinkertoy to take advantage of both sides of your brain. The left side handles logic and language while the right side excels at nonverbal tasks. Research into the thought processes of highly creative people reveals that they utilize both sides of their brains.

Select a Thinkertoy at random. Write the Thinkertoy titles on slips of paper and put them in a container. When you have a challenge, shake the box and randomly retrieve the name of the toy to use.

Thinkertoys produce an enormous quantity of ideas, and quantity is a key to creativity. Alex Osborn, a pioneer of creativity research, said: "Quantity! Quantity! and more Quantity! is the order of the day." And he added, "The more sights you take, the more likely you are to hit port." The writer Stendahl said, "I require three or four cubic feet of ideas per day, as a steamboat requires coal."

Thinkertoys generate so many good ideas that you will feel like you're in a candy store where you want to eat it all. Of course, if you tried, you would get sick to your stomach. You can't try all your ideas either, so you'll need guidelines to help sort through and judge them.

1. Inventory all the ideas in the sequence in which they occurred.

2. Browse through the list. As you do, you will find that you are subconsciously prioritizing the ideas. If you have difficulty prioritizing, try the technique described in *Worrywillie's Guide to Prioritizing.*

3. Develop criteria for judging the ideas. They should be ideal criteria, regardless of how impossible they might seem to fulfill. These criteria, of course, depend upon the specific challenge and will vary according to your objectives. The criteria to judge a new sales promotion will differ from those used to judge a shoe design. A bonus program will not be evaluated the same way as a negotiations program. And so on.

Some key questions to ask when developing criteria are:

- What standards might be applied to these ideas?
- How might we determine the strengths and weaknesses of the ideas?
- Which criteria are essential? Desirable? Optional?
- How might we best compare or analyze the ideas?
- Which criteria will best help us to refine and develop ideas?

4. Use judgment and intuition to choose the best ideas. Using your criteria, you should be able to funnel the huge quantity of ideas into a select few. Do not allow yourself to be wholly analytical. Your intuition may tell you when an idea that does not meet your criteria is, nevertheless, so powerful that it is the one to adopt.

Use a simple classification scheme to label ideas:

> excellent
> likely — needs refinement
> possible chance — needs improvement
> 50/50 — could go either way
> long shot — remote

You may never choose to back a long shot or a 50/50 idea; however, if you list and classify them, you have the choice of rejecting or improving them. If you do not list them, you have no choice in the matter at all.

5. Take your best ideas and get feedback. Use the techniques described in *Murder Board.*

PART ONE

——

LINEAR
THINKERTOYS

Group A

This group reorganizes known information in different ways by listing, dividing, combining, or manipulating it to give you new entry points for solving problems. Proceeding from these entry points, you can jump from one idea to another until you find the one you need. Just as we use stepping stones to move across a river, we can use ideas to move across a challenge.

FALSE FACES

Technique: Reversal.
Profile: How to find ideas by reversing conventional assumptions.

SLICE AND DICE

Technique: Attribute listing.
Profile: How to get new ideas from a challenge's attributes.

CHERRY SPLIT

Technique: Fractionation.
Profile: How to get ideas by dividing a challenge into two or more components and then reassembling them in new and different ways.

THINK BUBBLES

Technique: Mind mapping.
Profile: How to map your thoughts so as to spark new ideas.

SCAMPER

Technique: Questions.
Profile: How to manipulate what exists into something different.

FALSE FACES

"All warfare is based on deception."

SUN TZU

Which line is longer, AB or CD?

If you assumed that AB is longer, you are incorrect. The lines are equal in length, but you are not likely to discover this without challenging what you see and measuring the lines.

Suppose you built a house using a "yard" stick that was actually an inch short. If you assumed that it was a full yard and used it to measure everything you built, then everything would be wrong, and your ceilings, doors, and windows would be too low. If you had started by questioning the measuring stick, there would have been no problem. It is the same with all problems: If you start with incorrect assumptions, your solutions will be poorly constructed.

Sometimes assumptions seem so basic, so fundamental, that we never think to challenge them. Consider the illustration on the next page. We assume that far-away figure which looks as large as a nearby one must, in fact, be larger, because things are supposed to grow smaller as they move away from us. Yet this assumption doesn't hold up. Measure the figures with a ruler and you'll find that they are all the same size.

Assumptions are maintained by the hug of history. Yet, history does not guarantee their validity, nor does it ever reassess their validity. At times, an

assumption presents a false face that we mistake for something immutable; a truth that cannot be challenged.

Try to link the nine dots below with no more than three straight lines which will cross through all nine dots, without lifting your pencil.

A surprising number of people will make two assumptions: (1) you must not extend beyond the outside dots, and (2) the lines must pass through the center of each dot. Neither of these "rules" was mentioned above, and once you challenge those assumptions, the problem is easily solved (see p. 46).

Whenever Thomas Edison was about to hire a new employee, he would invite the applicant over for a bowl of soup. If the person salted his soup before tasting it, Edison would not offer him the job. He did not hire people who had too many assumptions built into their everyday life. Edison wanted people who consistently challenged assumptions.

Problems are often salted with assumptions that hinder creativity. Suppose you tell an architect that you want a certain kind of knob on the door between the dining room and kitchen so that it can be easily opened and shut. This illustrates the assumption that the answer to traffic between the two rooms *is* a door, rather than a redefinition of the space, or of the design, or of how we prepare and eat food. The assumption that a knob is the solution precludes numerous other possibilities.

I put so much emphasis on challenging assumptions to show that any assumption *can* be challenged. Obviously, many things must be taken for granted, and nobody has the time or need to challenge every assumption. However, it is important to realize that nothing is sacrosanct. Once you truly realize this, you are open to all sorts of wonderful discoveries. Imagine diving into a lake that everyone assumes is freezing—and discovering balmy, warm water. Until you jump, you will never know for sure.

BLUEPRINT

1. *State your challenge.*

2. *List your assumptions.*

3. *Challenge your fundamental assumptions.*

4. *Reverse each assumption.* Write down the opposite of each one.

5. *Record differing viewpoints that might prove useful to you.*

6. *Ask yourself how to accomplish each reversal.* List as many useful viewpoints and ideas as you can.

For years, bankers assumed that their customers preferred human tellers. In the early 1980s, Citibank concluded that installing automatic tellers would help them cut costs. However, the Citibank executives did not imagine that customers would prefer dealing with machines, so they reserved human tellers for people with more than $5,000 in their accounts and relegated modest despositors to the machines. The machines were unpopular, and Citibank stopped using them in 1983. Bank executives took this as proof of their assumption about people and machines.

Months later, another banker challenged this assumption and looked at the situation from the customer's perspective. He discovered that small depositors refused to use the machines because they resented being treated as second-class customers. He reinstituted the automatic tellers with no "class distinctions," and they were an instant success. Today, even Citibank reports that 70 percent of their transactions are handled by machine.

The banker challenged the dominant assumption by looking at it from the customer's perspective. A good way to challenge *any* assumption is by looking at it from someone else's perspective. Try writing a paragraph about your challenge as you see it. Next, change your perspective. If you're male, write it from a female standpoint; if you are a salesperson, write it from a customer's perspective; if you are a subordinate, write it from a superior's point of view, and so on.

REVERSE ASSUMPTIONS

Reversing your assumptions broadens your thinking. You may often find yourself looking at the same thing as everybody else, yet seeing something different. Many creative thinkers get their most original ideas when they challenge and reverse the obvious.

Consider Henry Ford. Instead of answering the usual question, "How can we get the workers to the material?", Ford asked, "How can we get the work to the people?" With this reversal of a basic assumption, the assembly line was born.

Alfred Sloan took over General Motors when it was on the verge of bankruptcy and turned it around. His genius was to take an assumption and reverse it into a "breakthrough idea." For instance, it had always been assumed that you had to buy a car before you drove it. Sloan reversed this to mean you could buy it while driving it, pioneering the concept of installment buying for car dealers.

He also changed the American corporate structure by challenging the conventional assumptions about how organizations were run. He quickly realized that GM's haphazard growth was stifling its potential. So he reversed the basic assumption that major companies are run by an all-powerful individual, creating a new theory that allowed for entrepreneurial decision-making, while still maintaining ultimate control. Under Sloan, GM grew into one of the world's biggest companies, and his reversal became the blueprint for the modern American corporation.

Reverse some of your basic assumptions about business. For instance, you might start with the idea that "A salesperson organizes the sales territory," then reverse it to "The sales territory organizes (controls) the salesperson."

This reversal would lead you to consider the demand for new salespeople as territories become more complex. A salesperson with a large territory may be too well "controlled" by it to react to new accounts and sales possibilities.

Another reversal might be: "A salesperson *dis*organizes the sales territory." This would lead to a consideration of how to make salespeople more efficient. You could add telemarketing support personnel, in-office follow-up systems, and so on, to organize the territories for salespeople.

Harry Seifert, CEO of Winter Gardens Salads, used reversal to cook up a winning recipe for productivity. Instead of giving employees a bonus *after* the busy times of the year, he gives them their bonus *before* the busiest time of the year.

Just before Memorial Day, when they have the largest demand for coleslaw and potato salad, Siefert dishes out $50 to each of his 140 employees to arouse their enthusiasm for filling all of the holiday orders as efficiently as possible. "Because employees are trying to achieve a goal," he observes, "they don't feel like they are being taken advantage of during the intense periods." Production has risen 50 percent during the bonus period.

How To?

After you reverse your assumptions about a challenge, ask yourself how to accomplish the reversals. You are not necessarily looking for one right answer, but for a different way of viewing existing information.

Consider the challenge of motivating city dwellers to recycle their paper products (newspapers, magazines, and cardboard). The basic assumption is that people give paper products to a pickup person for recycling.

Reverse it to giving paper products to people. How could doing this promote recycling?

The idea: The pickup person hands out a certain number of rolls of toilet paper or boxes of tissue, according to the weight of the material he collects. By giving as well as receiving, you motivate people to recycle their used paper products.

When a woman gives birth, she loses the shape of her pregnant belly. A California entrepreneur wondered how to reverse this fact. What if a woman *kept* the shape of her pregnant belly? He thought about it and hit on a novel idea.

The idea: He sells kits for women who want to keep a plaster of paris model of their pregnant belly. The $19.95 kit contains wire, gauze, plaster of paris, blue and pink ribbons, and instructions.

Once an assumption is reversed and a breakthrough idea achieved, you may be startled by how obvious the idea seems. The reversal need not be a 180-degree turn—just a different angle on a problem. Years ago, shopkeepers assumed they had to serve customers. Someone changed that to shoppers serving themselves and the supermarket was born.

Suppose my challenge is: "In what ways might I create a new business for airports and train stations?"

My basic assumptions are:

- Airports and train stations are for people who are traveling from one point to another.
- Planes and trains are constantly arriving and departing.
- People depart rapidly.

I reverse these assumptions to:

- Airports and train stations are for people who are *not* traveling.
- Planes and trains are *not* arriving and departing.
- People are *not* departing rapidly.

I now have a new perspective on the challenge. Perhaps I could create a business to serve people caught by bad weather, strikes, missed trains or planes, or those who have long delays or layovers and want to rest—people who, for some reason, are not able to travel. They would need lodging, but would not want or be able to leave the terminal.

The idea: A capsule hotel that would provide basic amenities in modular, prefab, Pullman-style sleeping compartments that could be stacked two or three high. Each capsule would come with a TV, radio, alarm clock, and reading light. A community shower would be available to all guests. The front desk would be staffed twenty-four hours a day and would carry razors, soap, toothpaste, toothbrushes, and so on. The price for a twenty-four-hour stay would be 50 percent cheaper than airport hotels and would also have low hourly rates, perhaps $10 an hour. Such hotels are already in use in Japan, and are quite popular.

The capsules would be easy to clean and maintain. Because they are modular, they could be easily moved between locations. They could also be leased to cities as temporary lodging for the homeless or for people who are forced out of their homes by fires and floods.

The figure below is known as Schroeder's staircase. It will appear right side up even when turned upside down.

Assumptions can also appear right side up when turned upside down, and this may lead to a new idea. Consider the assumption that banks loan money to people to buy land. Reverse this to people loaning land to banks. How might this work? What ideas can you think of?

One idea: People who have unused land could enter into an agreement whereby they loan the land to the bank to develop. The bank would figure out the finances, hire the builder, and rent and manage the property; the owner would get a biannual dividend from the bank for the use of the property. At the end of an agreed-upon period, the property would revert to the owner. By reversing a basic assumption, you could realize a mutual profit with a bank by "lending" them your land.

Summary

Assumption reversal enables you to:

1. Escape from looking at a challenge in the traditional way.
2. Free up information so that it can come together in new ways.
3. Think provocatively. You can take a novel position and then work out its implications.
4. Look for a breakthrough.

Assumption reversal helps your imagination escape daily circumstance, as a bough that has been held down suddenly straightens itself out.

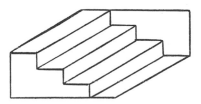

CHAPTER SIX

SLICE AND DICE

"When he is united, divide him."

SUN TZU

Imagine renovating a house with many rooms. Each of the rooms is part of the function of a house, and we tend to think of one "house" instead of a building composed of many different rooms.

Each room, however, is separate from the others, and we may think of them, accordingly, as separate entities: bedrooms, bathrooms, garage, living room, den, kitchen, and so on. Regarded this way, they are separate attributes that together constitute a house.

To change the nature of the house, you do not blow it up and start building a new and different one. It is much more productive to shift your focus from the one "house" to the many separate "rooms" and improve or change one room at a time. By changing a few rooms, you can convert a large house made up of many rooms into a mansion.

Every problem is a house with many rooms. To stimulate new ideas, identify and list the various attributes of a problem and work on one attribute at a time.

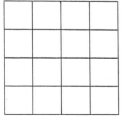

Imagine that the box in the margin represents your challenge, with each square representing an attribute. Divide the box into as many squares as you can. What is your final total?

Some people will see sixteen, or perhaps seventeen (if they counted the square which contains the smaller ones) squares; others will see more, and a few will see all thirty. The more you slice and dice your challenge, the more attributes you will be able to improve or change. Try to be as comprehensive as possible—if you omit something, you won't be able to bring it back later. Quantity is more important than quality at this point.

People define attributes differently. When listing the attributes of a problem, think of them simply as its components, and make a general list without worrying about how correct it is. Trusting yourself will make your solutions unique, and may produce an idea that will shake you down to your kneecaps.

Some common ways to describe attributes are descriptive, process, function, social, price, and ecological.

Common *descriptive* attributes are: substance, structure, color, shape, texture, sound, taste, odor, space, and density.

Common *process* attributes are: marketing, manufacturing, selling, function, and time.

Common *social* attributes are: responsibilities, politics, and taboos.

Common *price* attributes are: cost to manufacturer, wholesaler, retailer, and consumer.

Common *ecological* attributes are: positive or negative impact on the environment.

The attributes of a pencil might be listed as: used for writing, yellow, lead, eraser, sharp, hexagonal, has printing on it, and is cylindrical.

The attributes of a challenge to pay for a corporate acquisition might be: amount of payment, time of payment, type of payment, security, source of financing, management responsibilities, corporate politics, press relations, time to close the deal, and employee relations.

ATTRIBUTES OF A SCREWDRIVER

Consider the attributes of a common screwdriver.

1. Round.
2. Steel shank.
3. Wooden handle.
4. Wedge-shaped end.
5. Manually operated. Power is provided by a twisting motion.
6. Used for tightening and loosening screws.

To invent a better screwdriver, focus on each specific attribute and try to improve it. Look at each attribute or component and ask "How else can this be accomplished?" or "Why does this have to be this way?"

AB Bacho Tools of Sweden studied the screwdriver handle. They discovered that most craftspeople use both hands to turn a screwdriver even though the handle isn't designed for it. So, they developed a screwdriver handle with space for both hands, called the Bacho Ergo screwdriver, and what they call the "ergo" concept soon extended to their entire tool line. Since then, Ergo tools have gone on to win design prizes and have even been shown in museums. Bacho claims that redesigning the lowly screwdriver handle allowed them to maintain a strong position in the tool market.

We usually describe an object by listing its functions. The way we use something is not inherent in the object itself—it grows out of experience and observation. A screwdriver's primary function is to tighten or loosen screws. To discover new applications and ideas, you need flexibility of thought.

In the illustration to the left, the lone dot attracts your attention because it seems different somehow. We tend to assume that items that happen to be close together will have more in common than those which are distant. By separating the attribute "steel shank" from the screwdriver's other attributes, you are able to get some distance from the other attributes and focus on it without being influenced by them. The more you are able to focus on a specific attribute, the more likely you are to think flexibly and discover alternative ideas.

By examining "steel shank" as a separate attribute, we can move away from our stereotypic label of a screwdriver and come up with new applications. Possible other uses could include: weapon, probe, pointer, plug, pipe bowl cleaner, head and back scratcher, shoe horn, paint-can opener, measuring tool, tool to remove paper jams from copiers, scraper, prying device, telephone dialer, tapping tool, mini-dowel, and so on. Can you think of more uses? How might economic considerations affect possible uses? How about aesthetic considerations?

BLUEPRINT

1. *State your challenge.*

2. *Analyze the challenge and list as many attributes as you can.*

3. *Take each attribute, one at a time, and try thinking of ways to change or improve it. Ask "How else can this be accomplished?" and "Why does this have to be this way?"*

4. *Strive to make your thinking both fluent and flexible.*

Many years ago, bicycle manufacturers improved the design of the bicycle by examining the following attributes:

1. Frame.
2. Handlebars.
3. Pedals.
4. Brakes.
5. Tires.
6. Chain.
7. Drive sprocket.

They improved each attribute of the bicycle, including the following:

1. Lightweight frames made out of new materials.
2. Racing handlebars replacing traditional handlebars.
3. Pedals with straps and grips.
4. Hand brakes replacing axle brakes.
5. Lightweight, solid tires replacing inflatable ones.
6. Chains with clamps to make changing them easier.
7. Sprockets that provided ten gears.

If you tried to improve the bicycle by thinking of a bike as a whole entity, you may have left something out of consideration. What if they had improved everything but the tires? Of course, mountain bike manufacturers have improved on most of these items, as well as some new ones such as twenty-six gears, reinforced frames, and oval (instead of circular) chain rings. What have *they* left out?

Read the following:

Since the words "I love Paris in the springtime" are very familiar to most people, they fail to notice that the word "the" appears twice. However, if you concentrate on reading one word at a time, you automatically see the second "the." In the same way, Slice and Dice forces you to methodically rotate your attention to each attribute, one at a time.

Even trivial attributes sometimes provide the clue to a solution. Everything has meaning, no matter how small or seemingly insignificant. Even tiny pine needles have a clean fresh smell. Tiny improvements in a thousand places can lead to an innovation in almost any product or service. When you pay attention to attributes and improve them one by one you build a wave of ideas, drop by drop.

U.S. Precision Lens Co. developed a sophisticated new plastic projection TV lens. Happy with the item's sales, they went on to other things. Tethered to their original idea for the lens, they depleted the idea's capital by not trying to refine or improve it.

In Japan, Matsushita Electric "sliced and diced" the lens into its various attributes. Discovering that the original plastic was ill-suited for laser-based products such as videodiscs and CD ROM, they focused on improving that one simple attribute.

Lenses in general were the bottleneck in cost and performance for many laser-based products, so Matsushita worked quietly and methodically to make one small improvement in the U.S. Precision lens. In 1986, they unveiled it: an aspheric lens made of glass. Smaller and more precise than the original lens, it slashed manufacturing costs by 90 percent—another classic triumph brought about by improving one component of an already successful product. It was also another case of a U.S. company overlooking its own creative capital.

When you are invited to a banquet, you take what is set before you. If you demanded that your host serve a special fish or perhaps a certain type of bread, you would be deemed rude and absurd. Take your challenge as it is served to you, and slice and dice it into separate pieces or attributes with the sharp knife of your mind.

The Boatmen's National Bank of St. Louis was looking for better ways to advertise their cash-management services. They divided all their services into attributes, and discovered that one of those attributes—their early reporting of checks clearing a company's account—was unique. So they made this the focus of a major ad campaign.

Rather than sending out another brochure, they mailed boxes containing English muffins, jars of jelly, a knife, and a napkin to 1,400 prospective customers. The accompanying message read, "While you're having breakfast, Boatmen's already has available to you the information you'll need about your checks at the opening of the business day." This innovative campaign produced leads that were as warm as toast.

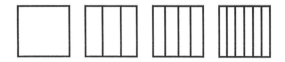

Which figure is the widest of the above?

They are the same size. However, as the number of subdivisions increases, the squares appear to become progressively wider. (This is known as the Opel-Kundt illusion and was first demonstrated in 1895.)

In the same way, when you subdivide a challenge into many separate parts, the nature of the challenge does not change. However, your perception of it does. It is this expansion of consciousness that leads to new ideas.

A frozen-fish processor was concerned that his product tasted bland. He tried everything to keep the fish fresh-tasting, including keeping them in fish tanks right up to processing. Nothing worked; the fish remained listless. To find a solution, he listed the attributes of a fish, including:

> Lives underwater
> Has gills and fins
> Constantly moves to escape from predators
> Cold-blooded
> Changes color out of water

He looked at each attribute separately, trying to find ideas to solve his problem. Finally, he hit upon the solution: He put a small shark in the tank with the fish. The fish kept moving to escape being eaten and retained their vitality and thus their fresh flavor.

His challenge did not change, but by subdividing it into attributes he expanded his consciousness to include predators, which proved to be the key to his solution.

Sometimes listing and then *clustering* related attributes will inspire an idea. The owner of a fast-food franchise had trouble with employee turnover. The majority of his employees were teenage students.

He sliced and diced the attributes of students into:

They go to school	Young
Like instant gratification	Parental supervision
Pride in grades	Like money
Competitive	Seek parental approval
Developing a work ethic	Seek teacher approval
Worried about future	Thinking about college
Seek recognition	Working to buy things

He focused his attention on the following cluster:

Pride in grades	Competitive
Work ethic	Recognition
Money	Parental approval
Teacher approval	College

The idea blared out at him from behind the cluster of attributes, honking like a saxophone for his attention.

The idea: A bonus plan based on grade-point averages. Any student who works for a whole semester and earns a 2.5 to 3.0 GPA is awarded a fifteen-cent-per-hour bonus for all hours worked that semester. The ante would be upped to 25 cents per hour for students earning better than 3.0.

The cost is marginal, probably less than 5 percent of his payroll costs for the time period. The advantages are many:

- Students are encouraged to work for the entire semester.
- The bonus attracted better students, who tend to be better workers.
- Guidance counselors and teachers do his recruiting for him, recommending his restaurant to students looking for work.
- Parents encourage their children to work at his place.
- Great PR for the restaurant. He gets free newspaper and television coverage.

SUMMARY

Sometimes ideas are just new information grafted onto an attribute and spliced with another thought. Two Manhattan psychotherapists contemplated some of the common attributes of their patients (shy, busy, housebound, and so on). These patient attributes sparked a new idea—counseling by mail. They launched a new enterprise designed to provide mail-order therapy for shy, busy, or housebound people.

A first-class idea person can slice and dice challenges into separate, simple attributes and then combine them into new, more complex structures, just as stars do.

CHAPTER SEVEN

—

CHERRY SPLIT

*"Who can determine where one ends
and the other begins?"*

SUN TZU

Sometimes the solution to a problem lies within the problem itself. Cherry Split allows you to take a challenge apart and then reassemble the parts into new ideas. It's titled "Cherry Split" after the first example of its use diagrammed in this chapter.

Giving a child a complete model fort is giving him a place where his ideas go to die—he has little choice but to use it as is. However, if you give him a set of building blocks, he can create any number of new and unique structures.

Cherry Split divides a challenge into separate blocks which you can reassemble in different ways to create any number of alternative ideas.

Do you see a square in the following illustration?

There is no actual, printed square. Yet, by splitting a target into halves, we can perceive a square where none exists (the curved sections end abruptly at what we perceive as the edges of a square). In the same way, by splitting attributes, we can shape and reshape components of a problem into ideas where none existed before.

1. *State the essence of your challenge in two words.* For instance, if your challenge is "In what ways might I improve my sales of Canon copiers?" the two-word phrase that captures the essence of your challenge is: "Selling copiers." In the example that follows, the challenge is "In what ways might we improve the methodology of picking cherries?"; the two-word phrase is "Cherry picking."

2. *Split the challenge into two separate units.* In the diagram note how "cherry" and "picking" are handled.

3. *Split each attribute into two* more *attributes.* For instance, "cherry" is split into "delicate" and "separate," "picking" is split into "remove" and "transport."

   Do not worry about the correctness of the split; no two people will split attributes in the same way. One person will look down a street and see an indescribable beauty in the shadows, the light, the brick walls, the dark porches, and the grayed snowbanks. Another person will see only rubble. You have to define attributes for yourself, taking your clues where you find them.

4. *Continue splitting the attributes until you feel that you have enough to work with.* In the cherry example, I split "delicate" into "damaged" and "blemished," "separate" into "selecting" and "closeness to each other," "remove" into "touch and hold" and "picking," and "transport" into "ground" and "boxes."

5. *Examine each attribute for ideas.* The wonder of this method is that big ideas can dwell in the most insignificant attribute just as the flavor of an entire ocean is contained in one drop.

6. *Try reassembling the attributes.* New combinations can induce new perspectives and new ideas. Splitting a challenge into several attributes is like removing a dividing panel from between chambers of very hot and very cold air: New forces rush together, creating new ideas.

CHERRY PICKING PROBLEM

Challenge: "In what ways might we improve the methodology of picking cherries?"

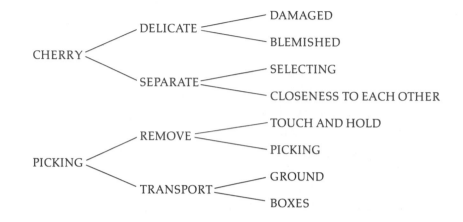

As our illustration shows, we split our challenge into the following attributes:

delicate	selecting
separate	closeness to each other
remove	touch and hold
transport	picking
damaged	ground
blemished	boxes

You could focus on just one attribute, such as "delicate," and decide to create a new type of cherry with stronger skin, to better withstand human handling.

You might reassemble attributes, such as "remove," "selecting," and "picking," and then look for a new way to accomplish these three attributes. One idea might be to shake the trees by hand and catch the fruit in large nets to minimize bruising.

Or, you might put "touching and holding," "selecting," "picking," and "transporting to the ground" together. Free-associating from this combination of attributes, one could come up with the idea of a hydraulic lift which would raise the cherry pickers up to the cherries. Picking by lift would help to minimize the number of times fruit is handled, thus reducing damage.

The separated attributes encourage rearranging of information, provoking you to search out new ways of doing things. It does not matter how many of the attributes you use, or how you link them when you generate ideas. It's just a way to add a few more ball bearings to your imagination.

CUSTOMER SERVICE PROBLEM

Imagine a company has a problem with customer service. We might separate out the attributes of customer service in the following manner:

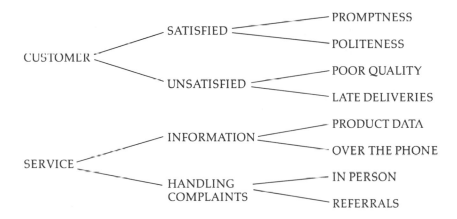

You could focus on one attribute, "politeness," and think of ways to incorporate more politeness into your customer service program. One idea might be to have everyone in the company perform one five-minute act of exceptional courtesy per day.

You might connect "information," "over the phone," and "unsatisfied customers," and suggest that customer service reps call unsatisfied customers, collect information about their dissatisfaction, write a report containing detailed suggestions for improvement, and distribute it to the people involved in the problem.

Or, you might connect "unsatisfied customers," "late deliveries," "information," and "over the phone," and suggest that customer service reps call to inform customers about possible late deliveries, and give them daily updates. The idea here would be to alert the customers to problems before they themselves became aware of them.

Cherry Splitting allows you to replace the inhibiting unity of a fixed problem with the more creative situation of working with several attributes in a variety of ways, generating so many combinations that you'll have to brush them away from your face.

Let's try one more example. A sports magazine publisher's challenge was "In what ways might I extend the market for my sports magazine?"
He cherry split the challenge:

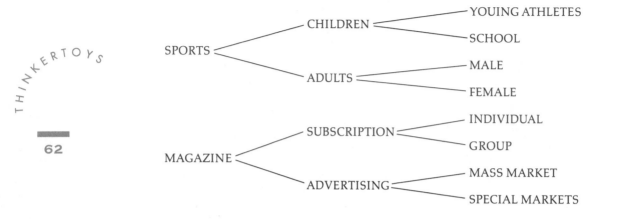

By putting "sports," "magazine," "children," "school," and "young athletes" together, he came up with the idea of modifying his adult sports magazine to appeal to kids. He plans to add a few special features to the basic magazine, such as a monthly profile of outstanding young athletes. The company intends to sell subscriptions through schools, and to provide free subscriptions to underprivileged kids as part of the Kids Literacy Program, which distributes magazines to schools and provides teaching guidelines. The children's version will attract an ever-larger crop of readers who will be likely to subscribe to the adult version in a few years.

GROUP EXERCISE

To use Cherry Split as a group exercise, present a challenge to a group and ask them to split it into as many attributes as possible. List the attributes as they are suggested, and keep going as long as anyone has ideas for further splitting. It doesn't matter if some of the suggestions overlap, but do ask anyone who volunteers a seemingly similar attribute to explain how it's different. If they believe it offers something new, go ahead and list it.

Ask each member of the group to reassemble the attributes into a new way of looking at the challenge. Start with one person's idea, and ask the rest of the group to build on it, until you've exhausted all possibilities. Then, go on to the next person and repeat the process again and again, until you're satisfied that you have drawn out as many creative ideas as possible.

A few years ago, a beer company was looking for new products to sell. In a group exercise, they split the challenge into clusters of attributes. Here is one of the clusters:

distribution network   flavored
rural   six-packs
liquid   spring water

This particular cluster led to an idea for a new product: a line of bottled water. At present, bottled water is distributed to urban areas nationally, but is less available in rural communities. The beer company, with its established distribution network, found that they could penetrate the rural market.

The water comes from the same mountain springs as water used in its beer. They intend to sell the water plain and with lemon-lime and cherry flavors and will package it in six-packs.

The obviousness of this particular beer company selling bottled water became apparent only when executives studied the challenge and fractionated it into the particular attributes of selling beer.

Summary

Cherry Split enables you to break apart a challenge into separate pieces. When you do this, you begin to see new material that had once been part of something else. When you first try to fit the pieces back together, you will be like a child fitting together his first model fort—awkward and slow, but when a piece slips into a proper slot, ideas begin to jump and take shape like coveys of startled birds into the air.

—

CHAPTER EIGHT

THINK BUBBLES

"Order or disorder depends upon
organization."

SUN TZU

When you look at the ceiling in an auditorium, you might say that the *lights* are on, or you might say that the *light* is on. In the first case, you are placing emphasis on the individual bulbs, in the second you are emphasizing their output. The important thing is not the *emphasis* but the *process,* the light.

When you map a challenge, you can emphasize either individual thoughts or the challenge as a whole. In making a mind map, emphasis is not important—the *process* is. It provides a way to communicate with your mind.

Think Bubbles is a graphic technique for organizing your thoughts. It creates an actual, physical picture of the way your mind blueprints a challenge. Think Bubbles allows you to record, store, and manipulate information about a challenge in a variety of ways, as well as letting you see relationships between different parts of the problem.

How would you describe the figure below?

● ● ● ●   ● ● ● ●   ● ● ● ●

They are twelve separate and unrelated dots. However, because of the way they are organized, we perceive them as three separate *groups* of dots. In fact, it is almost impossible to see them any other way. By organizing the dots into groups, one can give them a new identity.

This is what happens when you take your separate thoughts and organize them on paper by mapping them—the thoughts are immediately given a new identity. This new identity can be evaluated, developed, and resolved if resolution proves possible: altered or discarded if it does not. Once you project your blurred mental images onto paper, the process of idea evolution can really begin.

Because the map is designed to help you communicate with yourself, it's okay if the relationships between items are confusing to everyone but you. Similarly, your map can be as messy as you like, so long as you can read it. Some maps look like they were slapped down on paper by the testy tail of a barnyard animal. With practice, you will form and refine a method of mind mapping that is uniquely your own. What matters is that it makes sense to you, the creator.

BLUEPRINT

The mapping process usually goes like this: When you are caught with a challenge that defies solution, map out your impressions and thoughts about it. Study the map. If no ideas come after prolonged study, you will probably feel uneasy. In that case, put the map away for a few days. When you return to it, you will find that your mind is more focused on the challenge, and you will usually experience a moment of insight. This should be followed by a period of concentrated thought, during which the insight unfolds into a complete idea. Although maps can and should be highly individualized, all mind maps share five basic characteristics:

1. *Organization.* Mapping presents information organized in the way you think it. It displays the way your mind works, complete with patterns and interrelationships, and has an amazing capacity to convey precise information, no matter how crudely drawn.

   You can make your map of think bubbles as simple or as complex as you want. You can use large paper, a blackboard, or anything you like. You can group related ideas of equal importance horizontally and use connecting arrows to denote special relationships or color code different types of relationships. The visual, flexible nature of mapping makes it extremely useful as a device to help us see, express, and think about complex problems.

   You can readily add to the map later—and should be prepared to, as your first map will rarely produce an idea that meets all of your criteria.

2. *Key words.* Ignore all irrelevant words and phrases and concentrate only on expressing the essentials, and what associations these "essences" excite in your mind.

3. *Association.* Make connections, links, and relationships between seemingly isolated and unconnected pieces of information. These connections open the door to more possibilities. You can feel free to make any association you wish, without worrying whether or not others will understand you.

An entrepreneur looking for new products mapped out various ideas. The map reminded him of analysis, which reminded him of psychotherapy, which reminded him of Sigmund Freud. He wrote "Sigmund Freud" and drew a bubble around it. The bubble reminded him of a pillow, and that association inspired his idea.

The idea: He's manufacturing a pillow with Freud's picture on it, and marketing it as a tool for do-it-yourself analysis.

4. *Clustering.* The map's organization comes close to the way your mind clusters concepts, making the mapped information more accessible to the brain. Once your ideas are clustered, try to adopt the viewpoint of a critic seeing the ideas for the first time. This allows you to test your associations, spot missing information, and pinpoint areas where you need more and better ideas. Mind mapping is an idea generator. It does *not* supply raw material, so your map may show areas where you need to collect more information.

5. *Conscious involvement.* Making the map requires you to concentrate on your challenge, which helps get information about it transfered from short-term to long-term memory. In addition, continuous conscious involvement allows you to group and regroup concepts, encouraging comparisons. Moving think bubbles around into new juxtapositions often provokes new ideas.

Suppose my challenge is: "In what ways might I better market my consulting services?"

I write the essence of the challenge, "marketing consulting services," in the center of the page and draw a bubble around it. Then I free-associate another thought about the challenge. I write it. I draw a bubble around it and draw a line connecting it to the original. I continue to write whatever comes to mind, drawing bubbles and connecting related think bubbles with lines. The resulting map appears on the following pages.

The clusters of bubbles stimulate the following ideas to help me market my consulting services:

1. *Marketing through referrals by former clients and nonclients*, such as bankers and trade association executives.
2. *Personal marketing:* Personal cold-call selling, writing personal letters, and joining professional organizations.
3. *Nonpersonal marketing:* Direct mail, public relations, publishing, and advertising.
4. *Targets of influence.* This would include other professionals who serve the same clients, decision makers in client organizations, managers and directors of trade and professional associations, and leaders of industry.
5. *Targets of opportunity.* This includes former clients with new needs, potential new clients, and targeted market niches.

The marketing plan I get from the map is to market my services through referrals and both personal and nonpersonal marketing. In addition, the map shows me where more and better information is needed, specifically on targets of opportunity.

The vice president of a light-bulb company wanted to increase sales. He wrote "light bulbs" in the middle of a page and connected it with a *process*, "lighting," and a *system*, "4,000 distributors." He wrote down what came to mind, drew bubbles, and made connections.

His initial map appears on page 69.

The key concepts featured on his initial map were:

1. Attributes of light bulbs: lifespan, lighting, colors, and decoration.
2. Markets: industrial, institutional, and retail.
3. 4,000 distributors to reach his present markets.
4. Energy management to conserve costs.
5. "Decoration management," to enhance lighting quality.

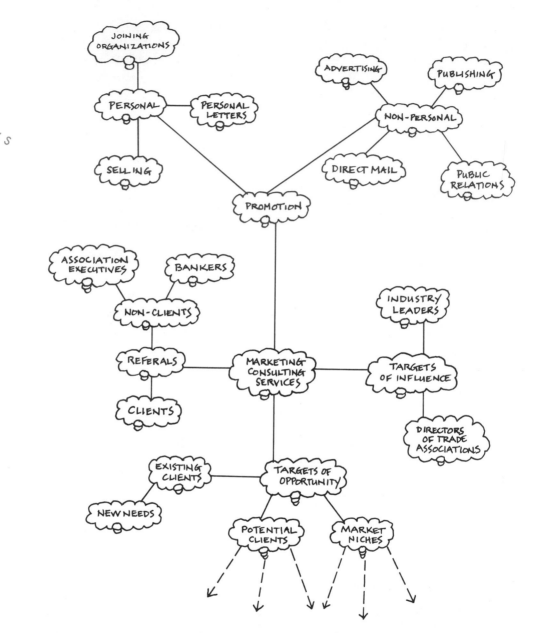

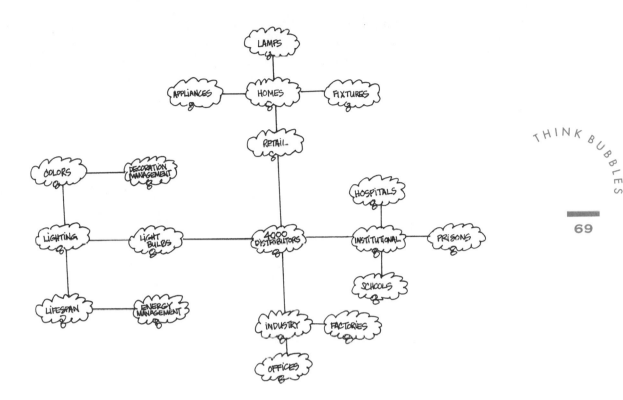

The map became increasingly complex as he worked on it over time, and prompted him to think about his business in various new ways. The bubble that produced the final idea was the one containing "energy management."

The idea: He created an energy management division, which bypassed the distributors and focused on industrial and institutional markets, allowing clients to cut energy costs. As a consequence, the company closed massive orders for light bulbs. He put it this way: "The map led to a cascade of ideas that motivated us to act and create a whole new division."

SUMMARY

Mapping a challenge or an idea allows you access to a certain mental spark: It flares up in the mind, is conducted to the hand, flows to the paper, and bursts into a tiny fire that, when seen, closes the circle by traveling back into the eye and farther into the subconscious.

Sometimes these tiny fires become the very ideas that you need to resolve your challenge; sometimes they need to be tended and fueled with more information before they flare into ideas. And, sometimes, these tiny fires smolder for days, weeks, or months before they blaze. However, if you take no action when that spark flares up in your mind, its spark burns out, turns cold, and is forgotten.

SCAMPER

"He who can modify his tactics in relation to his
opponent, and thereby succeed in winning,
may be called a heaven-borne captain."

SUN TZU

Manipulation is the brother of creativity. When your imagination is as blank as a waiter's stare, take an existing item and manipulate it into a new idea. Remember that everything new is just an addition or modification to something that already existed.

You will note that SCAMPER is much longer than any other chapter in this book. This is because it is actually a collection of nine techniques for transforming any object, service, or process into something new. Much of this Thinkertoy is devoted to specific examples, which may be skimmed or skipped. You should, however, pay close attention to the nine techniques; as you read about them, try asking yourself how a TV, suitcase, hamburger, home mortgage, or any other object or process can be improved. Ideas will appear almost involuntarily.

Can you transform the rabbit on the next page into a duck?

If you have trouble doing this, manipulate the page by turning it a quarter-turn to the left—suddenly, the duck takes form. You can also manipulate existing ideas and products into new things.

The new thing can then be changed into still other new things. To limit yourself to your first idea is a disaster for your imagination. The best way to get a good idea is to get as many ideas as you can. Any particular way of looking at things is just one of many other possible ways.

If you had a bag filled with thousands of white marbles and just one ruby one, the odds of anyone picking out that ruby marble would be very low. If you kept adding ruby marbles, the chances of picking one would keep increasing. Generating alternative ideas is as solid and positive a procedure as putting more ruby marbles into the bag. You still may not get a ruby marble, but it never hurts to increase your odds. There is nothing to lose when you generate alternatives, and everything to gain.

Several things happen when you search out alternative ideas:

1. One of the alternative ideas may solve your problem.
2. An alternative idea may help you rearrange the components of your problem, thereby solving it indirectly.
3. The alternative might prove to be a better starting point.
4. One alternative might be a breakthrough idea that has nothing to do with the problem at hand. When that happens, when you get this kind of breakthrough, your hair stands on end, your mouth goes dry, and you want to stand up and holler. Alexander Graham Bell found *his* breakthrough while he was trying to invent a hearing aid; he invented the telephone instead. Ray Kroc was trying to develop a market for his Multimixers when he discovered "fast food"—a concept that would change America's eating habits.
5. You may generate a number of alternatives and then return to your original idea. Compiling numerous alternative ideas in no way prevents you from using the most obvious approach, but it makes the decision to use it much more meaningful. Instead of being chosen because it seems the only option, it is chosen after it becomes apparent that it is the *best* one.

How many different answers can you think of to the question: "What is half of thirteen?" Of course, the obvious answer is six and a half. However, see how many other possible answers you can come up with before you read further.

There are six alternatives: Halving the *numeral* 13 gives you 1 and 3 (⅓).

Halving the *word* "thirteen" gives you 4 . . . letters on each side. Converting 13 into Roman numerals and halving it one way gives you 11 and 2 (XI/II). Halving it a different way gives you 8 (~~XIII~~).

Alternatives are provocative; they force you to overcome your clichéd patterns of thinking. After reading this chapter, you will find yourself walking down the most unlikely pathways, because you know that they often lead to surprising insights and ideas—ideas as startling as finding a trout swimming in your morning cereal.

BLUEPRINT

SCAMPER is a checklist of idea-spurring questions. Some of the questions were first suggested by Alex Osborn, a pioneer teacher of creativity. They were later arranged by Bob Eberle into this mnemonic.

> S = Substitute?
> C = Combine?
> A = Adapt?
> M = Modify? = Magnify?
> P = Put to other uses?
> E = Eliminate or minify?
> R = Reverse? – Rearrange?

To use SCAMPER:

1. *Isolate the challenge or subject you want to think about.*

2. *Ask SCAMPER questions about each step of the challenge or subject and see what new ideas emerge. Asking the questions is like tapping all over the challenge with a hammer to see where the hollow spots are.*

Consider the challenge: "In what ways might I improve my selling techniques?" First, identify all the stages in the selling process (i.e., prospecting, presenting, overcoming objections, closing, follow-up, paperwork, time management, and so on.) Then, ask SCAMPER questions to generate a wide variety of ideas about reshaping and manipulating each stage of the selling process.

For instance, let's say you have decided to isolate "prospecting." Now apply SCAMPER to that one step. Ask yourself:

- What procedure can I *substitute* for my current one?
- How can I *combine* prospecting with some other procedure?
- What can I *adapt* or copy from someone else's prospecting methods?
- How can I *modify* or alter the way I prospect?
- What can I *magnify* or add to the way I prospect?
- How can I *put* my prospecting *to other uses*?
- What can I *eliminate* from the way I prospect?
- What is the *reverse* of prospecting?
- What *rearrangement* of prospecting procedures might be better?

Prod your imagination with SCAMPER questions, and then continue asking "How can . . . ?" "What else . . . ?" "How else . . . ?" If you do this for each stage of the selling process, you will generate the maximum number of ideas for improving your selling techniques.

Suppose a paper clip manufacturer wants to improve his product. He would start looking for ideas by asking:

- What can be *substituted* in the clip?
- What can I *combine* the clip with to make something else?
- What can I *adapt* to the clip?
- How can I *modify* the clip?
- What can I *magnify* or add to the clip?
- What *other uses* can I find for the clip?
- What can be *eliminated* from the clip?
- What is the *reverse* of clipping?
- What *rearrangement* of the clip might be better?

One manufacturer *substituted* plastic for metal, *added* color, and produced plastic clips in various colors so that clipped papers could be color-coded, thereby creating *another use* for clips.

SCAMPERING BURGERS

Ray Kroc was a middle-class high-school dropout, a former piano player and real estate salesman who sold paper cups for seventeen years. In his fifties, Ray Kroc left the paper cup business and hit the road selling Multimixers, a little machine that could make six milkshakes at a time.

One day in 1954, a little hamburger stand ordered eight Multimixers.

Curious, Kroc drove his dusty little car out to investigate. He was stunned by the volume of business that Dick and Maurice McDonald were doing. They had unwittingly hit on the concept of fast food—homogenized, predictable items that are quick and easy to prepare. The McDonalds had simplified, economized, and minimized the hamburger stand.

Kroc and the McDonalds formed a partnership that allowed Kroc to find new sites, and open and run them. What followed was *not* instant success, but obstacles and challenges. Ray Kroc became a billionaire because he identified the right challenges and manipulated existing information into new ideas to solve them.

Following are some of the challenges he faced and how the SCAMPER principles shaped his ideas:

S = SUBSTITUTE?

Problem: The McDonalds proved to be lethargic business partners. Kroc was worried that they might sell out to someone who didn't want him around.

SCAMPER Solution: Substitute a different partner. Kroc was cash poor, but he was determined to buy out the McDonalds. Kroc raised the $2.7 million asking price from John Bristol, a venture capitalist whose clients (college endowment funds) realized a $14 million return on their investment. The next substitution was to go public, which he did in 1963, making many investors rich.

C = COMBINE?

Problem: Ray Kroc's first hamburger stand was planned for Des Plaines, Illinois, but he couldn't afford to finance construction.

SCAMPER Solution: Combine purposes with someone else. He sold the construction company half-ownership in return for constructing his first building.

A = ADAPT?

Problem: Ray Kroc was interested in developing a new twist on the food business but he lacked ideas.

SCAMPER Solution: Adapt someone else's idea. Kroc was amazed at the volume of business the McDonalds were doing by selling a hamburger in a paper bag here, or a helping of french fries there. Kroc's big idea was adapting the McDonalds' simple merchandising methods to create a brand new concept—fast food.

M = MODIFY?

Problem: The french fries made in Kroc's first stand in Illinois didn't taste like the originals; they were tasteless and mushy. He tried the McDonalds' recipe again and again, to no avail. A friend finally solved the mystery—Kroc stored his potatoes in the basement, while the McDonalds' kept theirs outside in chicken-wire bins, exposed to desert winds that cured the potatoes.

SCAMPER Solution: Modify the storage area. Kroc cured the potatoes by installing large electric fans in the basement.

M = MAGNIFY?

Problem: A number of franchise owners wanted to expand the basic menu.

SCAMPER Solution: Exaggerate the burger and add new items to the menu. He created the popular "Big Mac" by way of a $10 million dollar "Build a Big Mac" contest. Later additions included the Egg McMuffin, Filet-o-Fish, and Chicken McNuggets.

P = PUT TO OTHER USES?

Problem: Kroc needed to develop other sources of income.

SCAMPER Solution: Get McDonald's into the real estate business. Kroc's company would lease and develop a site, then re-lease it to the franchisee, who would have to pay rent as well as franchise fees. Today, 10 percent of the company's revenue comes from rentals. In the 1960s, Kroc also bought back as many of the original sites as he could. While this policy initially accrued huge debts, it gave McDonald's the upper hand against competitors, who periodically face massive rent hikes.

E = ELIMINATE OR MINIFY?

Problem: Hamburger patty distributors packed their burgers in a way that was efficient for them, but meant that McDonald's employees had to restack them to keep the bottom patties from getting crushed.

SCAMPER Solution: Eliminate the problem. Kroc refused to do business with packagers unless they shipped fewer burgers in each stack. Employees no longer had to restack burgers, saving McDonald's time and money. He also eliminated the middle man by buying entire crops of Idaho Russet Burbank potatoes.

R = REARRANGE?

Problem: Kroc wanted to differentiate his establishments from the competition.

SCAMPER Solution: Rearrange the architecture. Kroc kept changing the original red-and-white, box-shaped prototype, adding seating in the 1960s and drive-through in the 1970s.

Even the hot dog, as we know it, is the result of asking the right SCAMPER question at the right time. In 1904, Antoine Feutchwanger was selling sausages at the Louisiana Exposition. First he tried offering them on individual plates, but this proved too expensive. He then offered his customers white cotton gloves to keep the franks from burning their fingers. The gloves were expensive, too, and customers tended to walk off with them. Antoine and his brother-in-law, a baker, sat down to figure out what inexpensive item could be *added* (magnify?) to the frankfurter to prevent people from burning their fingers. His brother-in-law said something like "What if I baked a long bun and slit it to hold the frank? Then you can sell the franks, and I can sell you the buns. Who knows, it might catch on."

When the lines at the left are combined to form the figure on the right, we can no longer perceive the original two patterns without great effort. Instead, we see a continuous wavy line running through a series of bars.

By manipulating the lines, we have created something new out of already-existing items. With SCAMPER, you also take something that already exists and do something to it. Then you do something else to it. You keep doing something to it until you invent an original idea that can exist on its own. In group problem-solving sessions, SCAMPER questions can get ideas flowing and direct the group's imagination.

Following are more than one hundred SCAMPER questions and a collection of examples that show how SCAMPER has fostered innovation. The examples range from ancient to modern, from individuals to corporations, and from gimmicks to breakthrough ideas. The questions blink in and out like fireflies throughout the history of innovation, from the creation of flying doggie snacks to the restructuring of corporate America with junk bonds.

SUBSTITUTE?

You can substitute things, places, procedures, people, ideas, and even emotions. Substitution is a trial-and-error method of replacing one thing with another until you find the right idea. Scientist Paul Ehrlich tried well over five hundred colors before he found the right one to dye the veins of laboratory mice, making many new experiments possible.

To find ideas using substitution, ask:
- What can be substituted? Who else? What else?
- Can the rules be changed?
- Other ingredient? Other material?
- Other process or procedure?
- Other power?
- Other place?
- Other approach?
- What else instead? What other part instead of this?

WHAT CAN BE SUBSTITUTED?

One substitution that changed the history of marketing is the shopping cart. In 1937 Sylvan Goldman, a supermarket owner, asked himself, "What can I substitute for the shopping baskets people carry, so I can sell more goods?" After a number of trial-and-error experiments, he designed the simple shopping cart. While other supermarkets were concentrating on providing bigger boxes and bags, Goldman addressed the real challenge: "In what ways might I increase the number of things people buy in my store?" Today, there are more shopping carts in America than automobiles.

One Batavia, New York, department store owner gave each of his employees a thermal mug, reducing disposable-cup trash by 85 percent. This simple substitution generated an incredible amount of free publicity.

WHO ELSE?

A Japanese company came up with a unique service by asking "Who else could be used to fulfill this need?" A Japanese wedding reception is considered a failure if no executives and bureaucrats attend. So, a company was created to provide plausible stand-ins. For instance, at one wedding, an actor played the part of an executive from a bride's company; he gave a five-minute speech, full of praise for the excellent job she was doing at the office. The groom knew it was a sham, but neither his parents nor his new in-laws figured it out. At another wedding, the company provided seventy-five of the groom's eighty guests.

WHAT OTHER PROCEDURE MIGHT WORK BETTER?

Information companies, such as TRW and Knight-Ridder, are successfully offering new services that let customers with personal computers hook directly into the company's database to extract certain information. These self-service procedures eliminate the time and expense of having employees package the data, yet the savings are not passed on to the customer (in fact, companies are considering charging more for the convenience). The benefit to the customer is speed, efficiency, and not having to deal with a human being. Personal computers are allowing creative information companies to substitute one procedure for another, do less work, and turn a higher profit.

A Rochester lawyer was sued. Lacking the money to defend himself, he came up with a new procedure to finance a countersuit. He is going to sell shares of common stock for five dollars a share. If he gets a settlement, the investors get back their investment and a percentage of the remaining profits.

OTHER INGREDIENT?

Substituting one ingredient for another created an American delight. The ice cream soda was invented in 1874 by Robert Green, a Philadelphia soda fountain maker. Clergymen inveighed against the act of "sucking soda" on Sundays, and many communities passed laws against sucking Sunday sodas. Green got around the ban by serving ice cream on Sundays with the sweet syrups but no soda water—hence, the sundae.

OTHER MATERIAL?

New York designers Constantin Boym and Laurene Leon substituted biscotti and a "clay-like substance" for wood and graphite to create edible pencils. They won first prize in a writing instrument design contest.

OTHER COLOR?

What would happen if you changed the color? When vodka arrived in the U.S. in the 1930s, Americans ignored it—clear alcohol just wasn't popular. The Russian emigré who tried and failed to market vodka finally gave up and sold the rights for a pint-sized $14,000 in 1939 to Heublein. John Martin, the Heublein president who bought the brand, immediately went to work looking for other ingredients to color the drink and popularize it; hence, the Moscow Mule, Screwdriver, and Bloody Mary. Vodka sales rose from 6,000 cases a year to 38 million in 1988.

OTHER APPROACH?

If music can soothe the savage beast, might it also charm out a holed-up gunman? The Houston police department's hostage-negotiating team counts music—everything from soothing gospel tunes to rousing martial airs—among their "secret weapons."

Not long ago, they had to deal with an eighteen-year-old boy who ended an all-night drinking binge by threatening to commit suicide. He held his mother hostage and randomly shot at the police. The team waited six hours. Then they figured that he was not only tired but was probably also suffering from a tremendous hangover. They figured right. When they played "Stars and Stripes Forever" at a deafening level over their loudspeakers, the teen promptly surrendered—unarmed and wincing.

CHANGE FORMAT?

World War I created a demand for national and international news which the *New York Times* and other city newspapers and magazines tried to meet without success. Henry Luce asked: "What other format would be successful?", and identified the key points that had to be changed: the magazine had to be national, or there would not be enough readers or advertisers; it could not be a daily, as there was not enough news to fill one, and the format had to be unique. When his magazine, *Time*, came out, it was the world's first weekly news magazine, and one of the biggest successes in publishing history.

COMBINE?

Much creative thinking involves synthesis, the process of combining previously unrelated ideas, goods, or services to create something new. The printing press was created when Gutenberg combined the coin punch with the wine press. Gregor Mendel combined mathematics and biology to create the new science of genetics.

Look at the illustration below. Hold the book level and place a pencil about halfway between yourself and the figure, and focus on the pencil's point. Your eyes will gradually cross, and the two figures will eventually combine to form a three-dimensional pyramid. You can also see this effect when you focus on a point between the two figures and slowly bring the book toward the tip of your nose.

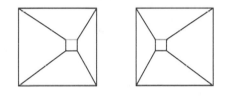

A three-dimensional pyramid came into being when two individual objects merged. In the same way, an idea can become something else by annexing its neighbor.

To combine, ask:
- What ideas can be combined?
- Can we combine purposes?
- How about an assortment?
- How about a blend, an alloy, an ensemble?
- Combine units?
- What other article could be merged with this?
- How could we package a combination?
- What can be combined to multiply possible uses?
- What materials could we combine?
- Combine appeals?

What Materials Can I Combine?

A barber in St. Louis combines hair clippings with peat and other substances to form an unusually rich potting soil, which experts believe may help restore drought-ravaged soil in Asia and Africa. Another "combination" idea that may one day benefit underdeveloped nations was invented by chemist John Albert. After trying many combinations, he created an economical heating fuel made from elephant dung and whole wheat flour.

What Units Can Be Combined?

ARCO customers enjoy a whole menu of combined units because someone asked this question. After you pump your gas, you can walk over to the adjacent AM/PM convenience store and serve yourself a ready-to-eat hamburger before you pick up a quart of milk to take home. Only then do you pay for everything you've bought. Gas pumped, dinner eaten, and shopping done in minutes, because some bright innovator combined units.

What Ideas Can be Combined?

Many creative individuals have made their fortunes by combining the ideas of others. In 1909 Henry Ford had this to say about the Model T: "I invented nothing new. I simply combined the inventions of others into a car. Had I worked fifty or ten or even five years before, I would have failed."

Examine any idea you come up with to see whether it could be combined with other ideas to create even *better* ideas. In the mid-1880s, new technology enabled George Eastman to develop a cellulose film that weighed almost nothing and was impervious to the rough handling, which threatened heavy glass photographic plates. This idea by itself was a great one . . . and then Eastman designed a lightweight camera to use with the new film. This combination made Eastman Kodak the world leader in photography within ten years.

Combine Purposes?

Suppose you combined a household toilet with devices that measure blood pressure, pulse, urine, temperature, and body weight? A Japanese company has done just that. It's called the "smart toilet," and can display the user's results on a built-in monitor.

What would happen if you combined the power of persuasion with food or music? One marketing study showed that subjects who were given a snack of peanuts and Pepsi-Cola were more likely to be persuaded by a written message than subjects who went snackless. In another study, subjects were more influenced by messages that were accompanied by folk music than by ones that were unaccompanied. It's no accident that the people in charge of "selling" presidential candidates tend to include pleasant background music in every television commercial.

A sake brewer in Fukushima, Japan, has combined the playing of classical music with his product's fermentation. He claims that the sake's flavor has improved since he began playing music and is now marketing Mozart Sake.

COMBINE TALENTS?

Samuel Goldwyn was something of an industry joke in the early 1920s; an ignorant, striving guy who had experienced some luck that no one had expected or wanted to last. Goldwyn realized the incredible importance of image in the motion picture industry, and assiduously set out to create himself a new one. In a brilliant move, he hired James Roosevelt as his vice president, combining Goldwyn's street sense with Roosevelt's style and connections to the elite. Within a year, Goldwyn was considered a serious artist and a dean of American producers. (Goldwyn got rid of Roosevelt once he had served his purpose.)

WHAT OTHER ARTICLE COULD BE MERGED WITH THIS?

A Japanese hosiery company is embedding millions of microcapsules of vitamin C and mineral-rich seaweed extract in every pair of pantyhose. The capsules supposedly burst when the pantyhose are worn and the nutrients are absorbed into one's skin.

HOW ABOUT AN ASSORTMENT?

Until Miller Lite, the average beer brewer's attitude was that if God had wanted us to brew a different beer, he would have mentioned it to Granddaddy. Since Miller Lite shook up the market, all the major brewers have come out with various assortments of beer. There is dry beer, draft beer, light beer, red beer, seasonal beer, super beer, and super premium beer. It seems just a question of time before barbecue-flavored, dry, light beer appears on the shelves.

ADAPT?

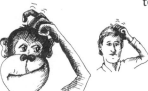
One of the paradoxes of creativity is that in order to think originally, one must first be familiar with the ideas of others. A classic case in point is the development of the steam engine. Popular legend has it that James Watt got the idea of the steam engine as he watched steam rising from the spout of a tea kettle, but the truth is that his engine was an adaptation of the Newcomen steam engines that were already operating in England. Thomas Newcomen is not the inventor of the steam engine either. He built on the work done before him by a French scientist, Denis Papin, who had developed a steam-operated piston-and-cylinder apparatus. Papin, in turn, probably adapted the idea from someone else before him. All new ideas or inventions are borrowed to some degree.

Thomas Edison put it this way: "Make it a habit to keep on the lookout for novel and interesting ideas that others have used successfully. Your idea needs to be original only in its adaptation to the problem you are working on."

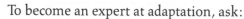

To become an expert at adaptation, ask:
- What else is like this?
- What other idea does this suggest?
- Does the past offer a parallel?
- What could I copy?
- Whom could I emulate?
- What idea could I incorporate?
- What other process could be adapted?
- What else could be adapted?
- What different contexts can I put my concept in?
- What ideas outside my field can I incorporate?

WHAT IDEA CAN I INCORPORATE?

William Durant, the founder of General Motors, had great ideas and dreams but could not run the company profitably. Finally, he was replaced as CEO by

Alfred Sloan, who was able to take many of Durant's ideas and turn them into orderly reality. Durant bitterly said to a friend: "If a clever man can figure out how to hold up a cow by its ears, even a moron can milk it."

Think of all the "of-the-month" clubs that were spawned by the Book-of-the-Month Club. One of the newest is the Panty-of-the-Month Club, which delivers designer silk panties once a month, gift wrapped and perfumed.

WHAT OTHER PROCESS CAN BE ADAPTED?

Breakfast cereals came into the marketplace as the result of a series of adaptations by different people. In 1893, a Denver man whose name has long been forgotten developed a process for compressing dried wheat fibers into biscuits. John and Will Kellogg of Battle Creek, Michigan, adapted it to produce a cereal called Granose that was an instant success.

In addition to the cereal, the Kelloggs ran Battle Creek Sanitarium where people with a variety of ailments could find physical and spiritual comfort. Among the patients was Charles W. Post, who emulated the Kelloggs' process of making cereal and invented Postum and Grape Nuts, the latter called Elijah's Manna until marketing problems provoked a change in name. By the turn of the century, more than forty companies had copied and adapted the process from Kellogg and were marketing such breakfast favorites as Food of Eden, Tryabita, and Cero-Fruito.

WHOM COULD I EMULATE?

Frank Winfield Woolworth was a struggling twenty-one-year-old store clerk in Watertown, N.Y. One day his boss decided to get rid of unwanted inventory by displaying it on a "five-cent counter." Woolworth liked the idea so much that he thought it could support a store of its own. So he took the idea and left.

He started the "Great Five-Cent Store" in Utica and failed. His second store opened in Lancaster, Pennsylvania, on June 21, 1879, timed to coincide with the circus coming to town. The crowds that came to see the circus bought a third of his inventory, and he was off and running.

Woolworth was always on the lookout for ideas he could adapt and use. He liked the bright red storefronts of the growing A & P grocery store chain so much that he adopted it as his trademark.

What Different Contexts Can I Put the Concept In?

In the figure below, the inner circles are the same size. However, the one on the left appears larger because the *context* in which it appears influences what you see. When you place any subject in a different context, your imagination can stimulate new ideas.

In 1956, a couple of brothers named Jacuzzi, who sold water pumps for farm use, designed a special whirlpool bath as a treatment for their cousin's arthritis. They did little with this new product until 1968, when Roy Jacuzzi put the concept into a different context—the luxury bath market—and bathrooms were never the same again. The Jacuzzi sold like crazy across the country, from California to the White House.

What Can I Copy?

The hub-and-spoke transportation system that makes Federal Express work was a feature of at least three air freight services as early as the 1930s. What was new in Fred Smith's elegant and successful concept was its enormous scale.

What Ideas Outside My Field Can Be Adapted?

Clarence Birdseye ground out a living as a fur trader in Labrador in the years before World War I. He noted that Eskimos preserved fish by quick-freezing it, and that the fish, when thawed, was tender, flaky, and moist. The same was true for the frozen caribou, geese, and heads of cabbage that he stored outside his cabin during the long Canadian winter. Birdseye emulated what the Eskimos were doing and made quick-frozen foods available to the general public. The quick-freeze process quickly replaced the old slow-freeze one, which left cooked food dry and tasteless. This adaptation of a process from another culture led to the creation of General Foods.

In 1930, Charles Merrill left Wall Street to build the Safeway grocery store chain. He returned to Wall Street in 1940, and promoted a new approach to buying stocks and bonds that was adapted from supermarket retailing techniques. His firm courted the small investor, advertised widely, offered free services, put salespeople on salary instead of commission, encouraged the public to come into the office to watch the ticker, and had the firm's partners publicly disclose the contents of their own portfolios.

WHAT ELSE CAN BE ADAPTED?

In New Mexico, a research project is underway to adapt jimsonweed, poisonous to humans, to help clean up heavy metal pollution in the environment.

MAGNIFY?

Americans tend to believe that bigger is better. People often perceive objects they value highly as being larger than objects they value less. Bruner and Goldman, in 1947, did a study that demonstrated that poor children perceived coins as being much larger than rich children did.

Which tree above attracts your attention?

Notice how your attention is automatically attracted to the large tree. This is why magnification is often used in advertising and equipment design.

Search for ways to magnify, add to, or multiply your idea, product, or service.

- What can be magnified, made larger, or extended?
- What can be exaggerated? Overstated?
- What can be added? More time? Stronger? Higher? Longer?
- How about greater frequency? Extra features?

- What can add extra value?
- What can be duplicated?
- How could I carry it to a dramatic extreme?

WHAT CAN BE MADE LARGER?

In the 1920s, George Cullen was a branch manager for Kroger Grocery & Baking Co. One day he wondered what would happen if he expanded the store to heroic proportions. He prepared a proposal that reads like a complete blueprint of the future, including self service, a full line of food and produce, and much, much bigger stores. Kroger thought the idea was crazy, so Cullen quit and started his own store. In 1930 he opened the first American supermarket in Jamaica, Queens, called King Kullen.

From that single store came the entire U.S. supermarket industry, which in 1988 sold $240.4 billion worth of food through 30,400 outlets, according to *Progressive Grocer*—and this may be just the beginning. Major food chains are watching the development of the "hypermarket," based on an idea that originated in France. Hypermarkets measure at least 150,000 square feet, with 25 percent of the space devoted to food.

WHAT CAN BE EXAGGERATED?

Will Kellogg, CEO of Kellogg's, was a marketing whiz who understood how to use exaggeration and overstatement. During the Great Depression, most cereal companies reduced their advertising and cut costs. Kellogg's response was to double his ad budget, increase the size of the cereal's package, and erect the world's largest billboard in Times Square. He not only survived the Depression but thrived.

WHAT IF YOU MADE IT ENORMOUS?

To promote the cheese industry, the state of Wisconsin created the world's largest cheese, a 40,060-pound cheddar they rolled from city to city on tour.

WHAT CAN BE ADDED?

Vic Mills, of Proctor & Gamble, invented Ivory soap when he ran some soap through an ice cream machine to add air. This increased its sudsing ability and allowed the bar to float.

The little toys that were added to Cracker Jacks elevated a snack food to an American tradition. Cracker Jacks had been around since the 1870s, but sales soared to a phenomenal 240,000,000 in 1948 because inventor Frederick Rueckheim asked the question: "What can be added to Cracker Jacks that will make it a unique product?"

A Japanese added a microchip to the base of the condom and created the "singing" condom. It plays "Love Me Do" by The Beatles.

WHAT CAN BE EXTENDED?

One of the reasons for the Heinz company's success in the early 1900s was Henry Heinz's insistence on extending his line of food products; hence, the famous slogan "Heinz 57 Good Things for the Table." Eventually, Heinz had many more than a thousand different food products for the market.

LONGER?

Japanese engineer Yuma Shiraishi developed a whole new entertainment concept—the home VCR—by suggesting that videotapes needed to be long enough for a feature-length movie. This simple idea helped lead to the VCR revolution.

HIGHER?

Random House had trouble making their children's books stand out until they tried magnification. They published a book by Richard Scary, titled *Biggest Word Book*, which is two feet high, almost taller than many of its intended users (ages three to five). The size of the book sets it apart from all competition and justifies a higher price.

OVERSTATED?

Carter-Wallace, Inc. is now marketing condoms that are 20 percent larger than the standard "one size fits all." The brawny Magnum Condom may just be the best marketing ploy ever. After all, what man in his right mind would ask for one of the smaller brands?

EXTRA FEATURES?

The experts said that no child would buy a doll that needed a wardrobe. Then, in 1959, a well-groomed platinum blonde standing less than a foot tall arrived with an accompanying line of fashions. Last year, Barbie and her playmates produced more than $450 million for Mattel, Inc. of California. In thirty years, children have bought and dressed more than 500 million of them.

Barbie was created by Ruth Handler and named after her oldest daughter. She also produced Barbie's friend Ken, named for her son, a gallery of companions and pets, and cars (the latest, a Ferrari). The extra wardrobes for Barbie have included: ballerina, nurse, flight attendant, astronaut, candy striper, newscaster, and rock star.

WHAT IF IT WERE MORE FREQUENT?

What one thing did Tom Monaghan add to Domino's pizza business that obliterated his competition? Home delivery with a guaranteed delivery time of thirty minutes or less.

WHAT CAN ADD EXTRA VALUE?

Lucy's Canvas, a Boston company, took the lowly shoelace and added extra value by printing rainbows, stars, hearts, and other designs on them. The firm has sold more than 7 million pairs at $1.50 to $2 each. By adding something of value to the shoelace, Lucy's Canvas invented a new accessory.

MODIFY?

At one time, the Ford Motor Company controlled 60 percent of the automobile market. Then General Motors asked some questions about modification and came out with a philosophy that stated, "A car with every shape and color for every purse and purpose." Henry Ford responded with "Any customer can have a car painted any color so long as it is black." Ford's sales slumped, and by the 1940s they had just 20 percent of the new car market. GM, by modifying their products to the market, had taken the lead.

What can be modified? Just about any aspect of anything. Even a perfect square can be modified by a circular background to appear bent when it is not.

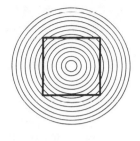

To modify your ideas, ask:
- How can this be altered for the better?
- What can be modified?
- Is there a new twist?
- Change meaning, color, motion, sound, odor, form, shape?
- Change name?
- Other changes?
- What changes can be made in the plans? In the process? In marketing?
- What other form could this take? What other package?
- Can the package be combined with the form?

WHAT OTHER FORM?

The ordinary ice cream cone is the result of modification. Ernest Hamwi was trying to sell paper-thin Persian waffles at the 1905 World's Fair. For days he watched people walk by his little stand to a nearby ice cream stand. When the ice cream stand ran out of dishes, Hamwi brought some hot waffles over. He fashioned the waffles into cones, let them cool, and served ice cream on top of them. By modifying the waffles to the ice cream he invented a new food product.

HOW CAN THIS BE ALTERED FOR THE BETTER?

The franchise business has become so competitive that many companies are having trouble finding qualified franchisees. Heavenly Hot Dogs, Inc. has modified the design of their hot dog stands so that they can be operated by franchisees in wheelchairs. The company is also designing mobile units that can be driven and operated by handicapped people. The response was overwhelming, and the CEO expects that handicapped people will account for 50 percent of the company's total franchisees. Also, the company discovered that it can take a tax write-off of $35,000 of the $60,000 cost of adaptations for handicapped people. Handicapped entrepreneurs are eligible for low-interest loans and priority locations at military sites and government buildings.

CHANGE MEANING?

The Copeland Corporation asked: "How can we change the nature of the grocery business?" and then modified the grocery business into a "convenience business" with 7-Eleven stores, which had a whole new sort of inventory, marketing strategy, and profit margin.

WHAT OTHER SHAPE?

Quaker Oats is marketing dog treats shaped like Frisbees in two flavors, bacon and beef. The dogs catch and eat them.

NEW TWIST?

In the years following World War II, Philip Morris was not a major player in the cigarette industry. They introduced a new filter cigarette, Marlboro, targeted at the female market, but sales were slow. Desperate, the chairman and marketing vice-president of Philip Morris asked Leo Burnett, the founder of the advertising agency that bears his name, for help. After some deliberation, he returned. "Here's your ad," he said, throwing it on the table. "Says it all right here. New from Philip Morris. The cowboy is a symbol of masculine virility. Filter. Flavor. Flip-top box." Phillip Morris ran the ad with the new twist in various newspapers, and thirty days later Marlboro was America's best-selling cigarette.

WHAT CHANGES CAN BE MADE IN THE PLANS?

Famous Supply Co., a building products distributor in Akron, Ohio, changed the standard benefits plan when they created "wellness dividends." They increased the deductible from $100 to $150 and required workers to pay a monthly premium for medical coverage: $25 for individuals and $50 for familics. Each year, workers who haven't submitted any claims receive back two thirds of their premiums. The system has made employees more conscious about their medical bills and their health. That, in turn, has enabled Famous Supply to keep their healthcare costs below the national average.

Modify Attitude?

Can you persuade people to try new things by changing your approach? A marketing group, attempting to create a demand for grasshoppers as a gourmet food, conducted some test marketing by attempting to persuade Americans to eat grasshoppers. Their first persuader was a relaxed and friendly person who presented his arguments in a pleasant manner. Few people tried the grasshoppers and those who did disliked them. Next, they tried a persuader who was cold, distant, and hostile. Remarkably, more people tried and liked the grasshoppers.

Modify Marketing?

3M's famous Post-it pads almost bit the dust because the marketing people relied on advertisements and brochures to introduce the new product, which did not generate much interest. Then general sales manager Joe Ramey noticed that people who started playing with the pads couldn't stop. Ramey immediately convinced the company to modify its marketing approach, and give free samples away to as many people as possible. The result was that the Post-it became one of 3M's all-time champion products.

Put to Other Uses?

These questions will help you find an idea, product, or service and then imagine what else can be done with it. George Washington Carver, botanist and chemist, discovered more than 300 uses for the lowly peanut because he never stopped looking.

In the following illustration, the middle figure can be seen either as "13," if you read it top to bottom, or as "B," if you read from left to right. Every subject takes its meaning from the way it is used.

12

A 13 C

14

Creative people can take just about anything and make something useful out of it. In 1857, Joseph Gayetty took ordinary unbleached pure manila hemp paper and had his name watermarked on each sheet. He marketed it as "Gayetty's Medicated Paper—a perfectly pure article for the toilet and for the prevention of piles." In this new context, manila hemp paper became the first toilet paper.

History is full of inventions, innovations, and products that developed from something else. Post-it pads, Silly Putty, and vulcanized rubber were all developed by people attempting to make something else. Bright entrepreneurs would willingly stand at street corners, hat in hand, begging passersby to drop their unused ideas into it.

To find other uses, ask:
- What else can this be used for?
- Are there new ways to use as is?
- Other uses if modified?
- What else could be made from this?
- Other extensions? Other markets?

WHAT ELSE?

In the early 1900s, Westinghouse engineer Frank Conrad built a radio receiver to catch the Naval Observatory time signals from Alexandria, Va., so he could check the accuracy of his $12 watch. He then built a transmitter and began to read baseball scores and play records for fellow ham radio enthusiasts. A friend of his who owned a record store asked: "What else can ham radio be used for?" and gave him free records in exchange for free ads. A local department store manager heard those commercials and ran a newspaper ad boasting that they had radio receivers for sale. A Westinghouse vice president, H. P. Davis, read the department store's ad and saw a vast new market. On November 2, 1920, Westinghouse station KDKA went on the air with federal license No. 1 and a marathon broadcast of Warren Harding's election.

In 1920, the U.S. had 5,000 radio receivers; by 1924, there were 2.5 million; by 1934 they outnumbered telephones. In 1989, manufacturers shipped 80 million radios. H. P. Davis went on to become president of NBC. This milestone in American business occurred because an enterprising record store owner wondered: "What else?"

WHAT ELSE CAN BE DONE WITH WASTE?

The above question has led to several imaginative solutions. Consider the following: rubber bands are made from surgical tubing; garbage is compressed into construction blocks or processed into polyactic acid to make garbage bags; sawdust is sold as compressed firelogs; slag is used as a soil conditioner; petrochemical waste is sold as Silly Putty, and the byproducts of coke ovens provide hundreds of products in the chemical and drug fields.

The Goodyear Tire Company has a pollution-free heating plant in Jackson, Michigan, that uses discarded tires as its only fuel. Similarly, Firestone has shown that a ton of tires can yield 150 gallons of oil and 1,500 cubic feet of heating gas. This process could eliminate the ecologist's nightmare of billions of tires littering the landscape. (Only 9 percent of tires are recycled at present.) It's illegal to burn tires, and landfills are getting scarcer and scarcer.

OTHER USES AS IS?

A toilet tissue manufacturer discovered a carload of paper that was too thick and heavy to be made into tissue. He was unable to return it, so he asked himself, "What else could be done with this paper?", and paper towels were born.

Whatever you think of Michael Milken, consider what he did by finding another use for junk bonds. Not since J. P. Morgan has anyone had so much influence on American business. He didn't invent junk bonds, but he did discover a novel use for them. Milken turned junk bonds into a potent force for thousands of companies that, because of weak balance sheets or poor track records, were unable to raise money by traditional means.

In the 1980s, he began using the bonds to finance hostile takeovers that helped restructure large sectors of corporate America, including Gulf Oil, Crown Zellerbach, and Beatrice. Many giant companies were merged out of existence or taken private in deals based on Milken's ideas about financing.

In the end, he became the target of the biggest securities investigation in history.

OTHER USES IF MODIFIED?

Medical waste has become a major problem for America. Currently, about 13,000 tons of medical waste is generated by the nation's 6,800 hospitals each day. Most of it is incinerated, a process that involves high handling costs and raises the risk of airborne pollutants. The high cost of transporting and disposing of medical waste has led some hospitals to dump it illegally. Some has washed up on beaches.

Combustion Engineering of Stamford, Connecticut, has developed a way of disinfecting medical waste using modified microwaves that can be moved from site to site. The disinfected waste can then be compressed and deposited safely in landfills or burned without danger of airborne pollutants. The process takes only twenty minutes.

OTHER EXTENSIONS?

Clarence Birdseye extended his process of fast-freezing foods to the citrus industry and created a brand new product—frozen orange juice.

OTHER MARKETS?

Fortunes have also been made by people taking existing products into new markets. 3M began as a supplier of abrasives and adhesives to industry; they never thought about the consumer market. When no industrial user seemed to want one of their new tapes, the product was abandoned. An engineer who had worked on the project took some discarded samples home and, to his surprise, his teenage daughters found that the samples were perfect for setting their hair overnight. 3M had stumbled upon a consumer market for the product, eventually known as Scotch Tape.

Another very successful 3M product, the Post-it pad, was made possible by a glue that was initially developed to be used on fixed surfaces, like bulletin boards. Arthur Fry, a 3M chemist, kept wondering about other uses for the adhesive. One day in 1974, while he was singing in the choir of the North Presbyterian Church in St. Paul, he had a creative insight: The adhesive would be just the ticket to keep a bookmark in place. He realized that the primary market was paper to paper, *not* paper to bulletin boards.

Other Fields?

A conservative think tank took the concept of private ownership and applied it to a serious environmental problem. Their idea: Increase private ownership of elephants to help fend off poachers.

Eliminate or Minify?

The original American doughnut did not have a hole. According to one legend, a small boy who was watching his mother make doughnuts noticed that the centers weren't thoroughly cooked. He took a fork and poked out the centers, creating the doughnut hole and the doughnut as we know it.

Ideas sometimes come from minifying a subject. Through repeated trimming of ideas, objects, and processes, you can gradually narrow your challenge down to that part or function that is really necessary—or, perhaps, is appropriate for another use. For instance, if you omit the war-making functions from a tank and keep only the weight and caterpillar track, you create a tractor.

A	B	C	D	E
F	G	H	I	J
K	M	N	O	P
Q	R	S	T	U
V	W	X	Y	Z

Can you figure out what single-word Christmas greeting the design above conveys?

The Christmas message is "Noel" (no L).

Find things to reduce, eliminate, streamline, omit, and miniaturize by asking the following questions:

- What if this were smaller?
- What should I omit?
- Should I divide it? Split it up? Separate it into different parts?
- Understate?
- Streamline? Make miniature? Condense? Compact?
- Subtract? Delete?
- Can the rules be eliminated?
- What's not necessary?

WHAT CAN BE STREAMLINED?

Who streamlined the potato? One day in 1853, George Crum, head chef at a posh Saratoga Springs resort, prepared fried potatoes as part of the evening's menu. A finicky customer kept returning his potatoes to the kitchen, complaining that they were too thick. Finally, an enraged Crum picked up his sharpest knife, sliced some potatoes wafer thin, and deep-fried them in boiling fat. Rather than being annoyed, the troublesome customer loved them. Soon other guests wanted to order the "Saratoga chip." The rest is potato chip history.

The Japanese auto industry learned about streamlining from an unexpected source. Kiichiro Toyoda, the founder of Toyota, was intrigued by American supermarkets. He noticed that they require great quantities of food—much of it perishable—which can't be stored on site, because of spoilage and space considerations. When supplies run low, the staff alerts the appropriate supplier and the items arrive "just in time." Toyota adapted this concept and streamlined their operations, eliminating waste and warehouses, and reducing costs dramatically. Toyota's "just-in-time" concept gave the company a significant competitive edge over every other automobile manufacturer in the world.

What Can Be Omitted?

To minify, think not only about what you can eliminate, but about what you can avoid altogether. Samuel Goldwyn once worked as a salesman for Elite Fitwell Gloves. The company's slogan and philosophy was "Making fewer, better." Goldwyn transferred this philosophy to the motion picture industry, and worked with only the best talent, making only films that he could personally supervise. This philosophy helped his company become one of the giants of entertainment.

Make It Smaller?

William Shockley, Walter Brittaïn, and John Bardeen aren't household names. But the midget device they invented in 1947, the transistor, has made products from pocket radios to personal computers practical and affordable. Thousands of new products have resulted from this revolutionary idea, and thousands more have benefitted from miniaturization.

A rancher in Mexico is breeding cows that weigh 25 percent less than average, yet produce the same quantity of milk as a normal cow.

Tomatoes with truncated roots can be grown in three-inch pots, producing three times as much fruit per volume of soil than plants with normal roots.

Could We Divide? Split Up?

Most brides want a set of good china. However, a whole set is too expensive for one person, and guests rarely know what the bride already has or what pattern she wants.

Lenox China asked: "How can we divide a set so people can purchase just a few pieces?" They adapted an old idea, the bridal register, so that the bride registers only Lenox china. The prospective bride picks one merchant with whom she registers her pattern of Lenox china, and to whom she refers wedding guests. This simple idea—dividing a major purchase—has made Lenox the favorite "good china" manufacturer and one of the fastest-growing medium-sized American manufacturing companies.

What's Not Necessary?

The postal service as we know it was invented in 1836 by an Englishman named Rowland Hill. He contributed absolutely nothing new; he simply

asked: "What's not necessary?" Before Hill, mail had always been paid for by the addressee, with the fee computed according to distance and weight. This made correspondence expensive and slow, as every letter had to be brought to the post office and weighed. For instance, it would take a merchant three hours to get a bill accepted by the postal clerk, and then the addressee would sometimes have to pay more to get the letter than the actual bill itself.

Hill proposed that postage be uniform regardless of distance, and that the fee be prepaid by buying and affixing a stamp. Overnight, mail became easy, convenient, and absurdly cheap. By eliminating what was not necessary, he created an explosion in mail: Stores could now send bills, and people could now communicate over great distances. Volume doubled in the first four years and quadrupled again in the next ten.

UNDERSTATE?

In the illustration below, the inner squares are the same size. However, the one on the right seems larger. This is the result of understating the squares surrounding the figure on the right.

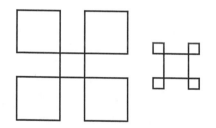

By understating the surrounding squares of the figure on the right, the inner square is made to seem larger than the one on the left.

Think of a product as an object surrounded by a cluster of advertising, marketing, and sales promotions and programs, like the squares that surround the figures in the illustration. Sometimes when these promotions and programs are understated, the quality of the product (the inner square) they surround is perceived to be greater than it is in reality.

For instance, compare the understated promotions of Rolls Royces with the overstated promotions of GM's cars. In reality, the actual value of a Rolls is not even close to what the average person perceives it to be. The average (modern) Rolls will last about as long as the average GM car (100,000 miles), and will have as many maintenance problems. But the ads work.

REARRANGE?

Consider the alphabet: ABCDEFGHIJKLMNOPQRSTUVWXYZ. These 26 marks have been rearranged in ways that can make you laugh, cry, worry, wonder, question, love, hate, and ponder. They've been arranged to form Hamlet, Tom Sawyer, the Bible, and the General Theory of Relativity.

Creativity, it could be said, consists largely of rearranging what we know in order to find out what we do not know. Rearrangement usually offers countless alternatives for ideas, goods, and services. A baseball manager, for example, can shuffle his lineup 362,880 times.

This puzzle, which probably originated in Japan, can be solved quickly if you make the right rearrangement. Arrange eight toothpicks, as shown below, in the shape of a fish swimming to the left. Add a dime to represent the fish's eye.

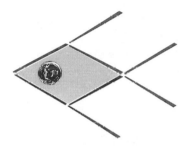

The challenge: Can you move just three toothpicks, and the dime, to make the fish swim in the opposite direction? (The solution is found at the end of this section.)

Just as we can move the fish in different directions by rearranging the toothpicks, so can we create new ideas by rearranging existing information.

Ask:

- What other arrangement might be better?
- Interchange components?
- Other pattern? Other layout?
- Other sequence? Change the order?
- Transpose cause and effect?

- Change pace?
- Change schedule?

What Other Corporate Arrangement Might Be Better?

In the 1970s and early 1980s, Exxon diversified into many different areas including office equipment and automobile engines. In the mid-1980s, new president Lee Raymond realized that Exxon management knew little about manufacturing or marketing, and even less about pricing. The first challenge he threw out to them was: "What rearrangement of corporate resources would be better than our current situation?" Acting on this challenge, management decided to sell the numerous outside businesses and reorganize Exxon into three separate businesses: basic commodities, polymers, and specialty chemicals. By rearranging its resources, Exxon has become a textbook case of excellent corporate performance in a tough business environment. These days, a price collapse in one of Exxon's three areas almost automatically sets off a boom in another one.

What Other Payment Plan Might Be Better?

The key to Xerox's success was a better pricing arrangement. Their first copier sold for $4,000. Few companies would pay such a sum for a copying machine when carbon paper cost practically nothing; few managers were willing to make such a capital appropriations request, as it meant going to the board of directors and showing the return on investment for this gadget.

Xerox understood this. They decided not to sell the *machine*, but what it produced: copies. At five or ten cents a copy, managers and secretaries could pay for them out of petty cash, without going to the board. The copy revolution was really one of a better pricing arrangement.

Other Pattern?

What would happen if you changed the pattern of communication between a company and its truck drivers? Sony and Geostar have developed a satellite communications system that uses automatic location maps to keep track of trucks continuously. This saves time, as drivers no longer have to make frequent stops to report their location. Soon, this system will allow the home base to talk to drivers through the dashboard, and to monitor the truck's performance and operating capabilities.

CHANGE PACE?

What happens when salespeople change the pace of their presentation? Fast-talking salespeople are sometimes regarded with suspicion, but rapid speech may actually increase one's persuasiveness. Norman Miller and his coworkers approached Los Angeles residents in parks and shopping malls and asked them to listen to a tape-recorded speech arguing that caffeine should be regarded as a dangerous drug. All subjects heard the same message, but half heard it at the slow rate of 102 words per minute and half at the fast rate of 195 words per minute. The fast-talking communicator was viewed as being the more knowledgeable and objective, and was more effective at changing the subject's attitudes. Within limits, the faster you talk, the more likely people are to assume that you know what you're talking about.

INTERCHANGE COMPONENTS?

"Can we interchange the components of a product to solve a new problem?" That question helped a young Japanese businessman make one of the fastest fortunes in Japanese history. As late as 1965, Japan had almost no paved roads outside of big cities. The country was shifting rapidly to the automobile and most Japanese could and did travel at high speeds, but the roads had hardly changed since the tenth century. They were scarcely wide enough for two cars to pass, with blind corners, hidden entrances, and junctions every few kilometers at which half a dozen roads met at every conceivable angle. Accidents mounted at an alarming rate, especially at night. The press clamored for the government to do something, but paving the roads would take twenty years, and a "Drive Safely" campaign had virtually no effect.

Then Tamon Iwasa looked at the traditional highway reflector and simply rearranged the little glass beads that serve as mirrors so that they could be adjusted to reflect oncoming headlights *from* any direction *to* any direction. The government installed the Iwasa reflector by the hundreds of thousands and the accident rate plummeted.

CHANGE LAYOUT?

John Hartford, president of A & P, was the first food retailer to recognize the value of store layout. He insisted on uniformity; all his stores were laid out and stocked the same way. Hartford used to brag, "I can walk into any one of my stores blindfolded and lay my hands right on the pork and beans."

FISH SOLUTION

Solution to the fish puzzle: Move the dime and three toothpicks as shown below.

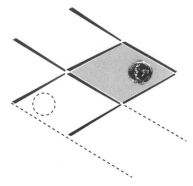

REVERSE?

Reversing your perspective on your ideas, goods or services opens up your thinking. Look at opposites and you'll see things you normally miss.

This figure was designed by Edgar Rubin in 1915 and can be seen as either a vase or a pair of faces. In the reversal method, one takes things as they are and reverses them to get more ideas.

Dr. Albert Rothenberg, a noted researcher on the creative process, has identified a process he terms "janusian thinking," named for the Roman god Janus, who had two faces that looked in opposite directions. In janusian thinking, two or more opposites or antitheses are conceived simultaneously, either as existing side by side, or as equally operative, valid, or true. Dr. Rothenberg has identified traces of janusian thinking in the works of Einstein, Mozart, Picasso, and Conrad. The way to use janusian thinking is to ask "What is the opposite of this?" and then try to imagine both opposites existing at the same time.

Questions to ask when using the reversal principle are:

- Can I transpose positive and negative?
- What are the opposites?

- What are the negatives?
- Should I turn it around? Up instead of down? Down instead of up?
- Consider it backwards?
- Reverse roles?
- Do the unexpected?

WHAT ARE THE NEGATIVES?

Henry Kravis turned corporate debt, a negative, into one of the most controversial tools in modern business: the leveraged buyout. The leveraged buyout transformed corporate philosophy by using debt to buy control from stockholders.

Kravis's biggest victory to date has been the $25 billion deal for Nabisco. Whatever the judgment of history, the deals that he made by capitalizing on the negative have changed the face of business in America.

REVERSE IT?

After Clarence Birdseye sold his company for millions, he examined the quick-freezing process that made him rich, and figured out how to reverse it. Working in his kitchen with a fan, heat from an electric coffee maker, and a batch of bread cubes, he developed the first process for dehydrating foods.

CONSIDER IT BACKWARDS?

Amana's George Foerstner knew how to use reversal in selling. He pioneered the market for home freezers, eventually wiping out the cold storage locker industry. He did this not by selling freezers—which were big, ugly and expensive—but by selling wholesale food door to door. Once people bought huge quantities of cheap food, they needed something to store it in. And there stood George, with a smile and an order pad.

DOWN INSTEAD OF UP?

Marketing experts Al Ries and Jack Trout took the concept of "top down marketing," in which strategy dictates tactics, and reversed it to create a hot new marketing concept: bottoms up marketing, in which the marketing tactics dictate marketing strategy.

Traditional theory says that top management should first set the strategy for a marketing campaign. Then the strategy should be turned over to middle managers who select the tactics to use to execute the strategy. Ries and Trout's concept says just the opposite.

DO THE OPPOSITE?

For years, engineers have replaced wooden bridges with steel ones. Now, the Pennsylvania Transportation Department is doing the opposite, with the theory that because it doesn't rust, wood may be more cost-effective than steel.

REVERSE ROLES?

Tires Nationwide has reversed roles with their customers. Instead of customers coming to them for tires, they come to where the customers are, with a truck stocked with tires and changing and balancing equipment. You pay for the brand name tires but not the delivery.

TURN IT AROUND?

The following story is an example of an enterprising storekeeper turning a slogan around. There were two furniture stores on Main Street in Elmira, N.Y. One day one of the stores put up a sign reading "The Cheapest Furniture on This Street." The other responded with "The Cheapest Furniture in This Town."

"...in this County."

"...in this State."

"...in America."

"...in the Free World."

"...in the World."

"...in the Universe."

After a pause of a few days, the first store owner quietly replaced his original sign: "The Cheapest Furniture on This Street." He realized that all he had to do was claim to be cheaper than his competitor on that street.

DO THE UNEXPECTED?

The American intelligence community spent billions on electronic intelligence (ELINT) to replace human sources. After ELINT was in place, President

Jimmy Carter recalled our human agents from the Middle East. Since then the United States has not apprehended one major terrorist because the terrorists have reversed their method of communications and reverted back to ancient techniques of using human couriers and messengers. They no longer communicate by telephone or radio, thus nullifying the effectiveness of ELINT.

Reverse your perspective. Look at the following illustration. Is the airplane coming toward you or moving away from you?

Study it again; can you make it switch direction? If you can't see the plane coming toward you, imagine yourself looking down on it from above. If you can't see it flying away, imagine yourself under it watching it fly off to your left. Chances are that when you first looked at it, you saw it moving in one direction only. It took a few moments, but after some concentration, you experienced a new perception, a new way of looking at the plane. It is the same with ideas. If you take a few moments and concentrate, you can experience a new perception.

SUMMARY

The Walkman evolved from a failure into today's best-selling electronic device because a number of people in management, engineering, and marketing asked the right SCAMPER questions at the right time, and created a product miracle.

In 1978, Sony engineers tried to design a small, portable stereo tape recorder. They failed. They ended up with a small stereo tape player that couldn't record. They gave up, and used the useless machine to play music while they worked on other projects.

One day Masaru Ibuka, honorary chairman of Sony, wandered into the workshop and noted the engineers listening to this "failed machine." He also remembered an entirely unrelated project going on elsewhere in the building, in which an engineer was working to develop lightweight portable headphones. "What if you combined them?" he asked (combine). "Could you leave out the recorder altogether and make a successful product that just plays music?" *(minify)*.

Ibuka was mixing up functions. The idea that tape players also record was so well established that no one had considered reversing it *(reverse)*. Even after Ibuka made his creative association, no one wanted to hear about it. They couldn't imagine that anyone would want a playback machine with no speaker and no recorder. Ibuka was not discouraged. "Young people who want to listen to stereo sound while playing tennis or golf and on the beach without disturbing others are the market," he said. "Think of it as not a tape recorder, but as a new concept in entertainment" *(put to other uses)*. Ibuka's idea meant that teenagers could carry music anywhere—even to the library or church.

"Add headphones," he said, "and you will dramatically magnify the quality of the music played" *(magnify)*. Sony finally agreed to produce a limited quantity, on the understanding that no more would be done if the first batch died on the market.

The marketing group received only $100,000 for advertising, nothing for promotion. Most of their budget consisted of Walkman samples. They decided to risk substituting an unconventional market introduction for what might be expected *(substitute)*. They targeted the youth market; their free samples all went to celebrities in music and show business. The Walkman's press announcement came out on cassette rather than on paper. And the day of the product release, Sony bused the press (each of them with a brand-new Walkman) to Yoyogi Park in Tokyo, where a throng of teenagers, all listening to free Walkmans and shimmying to the beat, roller-skated circles around the reporters. The press was delighted and gave the Walkman extraordinary coverage the next day and throughout the following months.

Guess what? The teenage market did not respond to the Walkman, but sales exploded anyway, because yuppies bought them. This affluent and active group made recorded music a pervasive influence in their lives. They already owned prerecorded cassettes and enjoyed being conspicuous consumers, and now they could drive, jog, play golf, and commute while listening to perfect sound. Sony recognized this market and quickly modified their pricing, advertising, and marketing campaigns *(modify)*.

By asking SCAMPER questions, Ibuka had taken the odd notion of a tape player with headphones but no recorder and made a product that introduced the whole world to the "headphone culture."

There is free dance in which the dancers improvise from moment to moment in order to express the overall theme. Then there is the formal ballet in which each step is precisely determined by the choreography. These linear techniques precisely choreograph information in such a manner that you move in determined steps toward a new idea.

Group B

TUG-OF-WAR

Technique: Force field analysis.
Profile: How to graph a challenge's positive and negative forces and then maximize the positives and minimize the negatives.

IDEA BOX

Technique: Morphological analysis.
Profile: How to identify and box the parameters of a challenge to quickly produce thousands of new ideas.

IDEA GRID

Technique: FCB grid
Profile: How to find new ideas and creative strategies using a grid to organize complex masses of information.

TOOTHACHE TREE

Technique: Diagramming.
Profile: How to diagram obstacles and then use them to reach your goal.

PHOENIX

Technique: Questions.
Profile: How to use a checklist of problem-solving questions—originated by the CIA—to guide your thinking.

THE GREAT TRANSPACIFIC AIRLINE AND STORM DOOR COMPANY

Technique: Matrix.
Profile: How to create a key-word index and mix and match the key words in a matrix to produce new ideas.

FUTURE FRUIT

Technique: Future scenarios.
Profile: How to project a future scenario in order to take advantage of unexpected opportunities.

CHAPTER TEN

TUG-OF-WAR

"One defends when his strength is inadequate;
he attacks when it is abundant."

SUN TZU

A good football coach does not say, "There is one way all great football teams win games, and we must do it the same way." Rather, he tries to determine which positions on his team are strong and which are weak by testing and observing each individual football player. Then, he replaces the weaker players, or teaches them to overcome or disguise their weaknesses. For example, if a defensive end is an ineffective pass rusher, the coach might teach him ways to trick the blocker. Only in this way can the coach bring his team's unique talents into play.

A football team has one goal: To win. To win, the coach will develop a strategy to maximize the team's strengths and minimize its weaknesses. For instance, if a team has a weak defense, his strategy might be to control the ball and keep his defense off the field; if the offense is weak, he might teach his team to keep the other team deep in their own territory. By being aware of the positive and negative aspects of his team, the coach most efficiently uses football knowledge to win games.

It is the same with challenges. You must be aware of the positive and negative forces operating in a challenge before you develop a strategy for solving it. Your strategy should allow you to take advantage of the positive factors while eliminating or diminishing the negative ones.

This Thinkertoy is modeled after *force field analysis,* a technique first developed by social psychologist Kurt Lewin. It allows you to see how positive and negative forces push and pull you toward a best case or worst case scenario.

Positive and negative forces won't sit still for a portrait. They are constantly vibrating, pushing and pulling. Tug-of-War is a frame on which you can fasten down these forces and study them. It can help you to:

1. Better define your challenge.
2. Identify strengths you can maximize.
3. Identify weaknesses you can minimize.

BLUEPRINT

1. *Write the challenge you are trying to solve.*
2. *Describe the best-case scenario and the worst-case scenario;* the best that can happen and the worst.
3. *List the conditions of the situation.* Conditions are anything that modifies or restricts the nature or existence of your subject. They are whatever requirements you perceive to be essential to solving a particular challenge.
4. *Note the "tug-of-war."* As you list the conditions, you will find the forces pushing you to the best case and those pulling you toward catastrophe. Pit each condition against its opposite on the continuum by specifying its push and pull powers.

In the example below, the situation being analyzed is an individual's job security. The conditions listed for job security are: track record, customer relations, working with peers, energy level, creativity, leadership ability, and job dedication. Beside each condition are best-case and worst-case scenarios.

In the next illustration, assume the center represents the current situation, while the best- and worst-case scenarios are playing tug-of-war with the conditions of job security. The best case is promotion, the worst case is getting fired. Most of the conditions are being pushed toward the best case. However, two conditions, customer relations and creativity, are being pulled toward the worst case.

There are three ways to move a condition toward the best-case scenario:

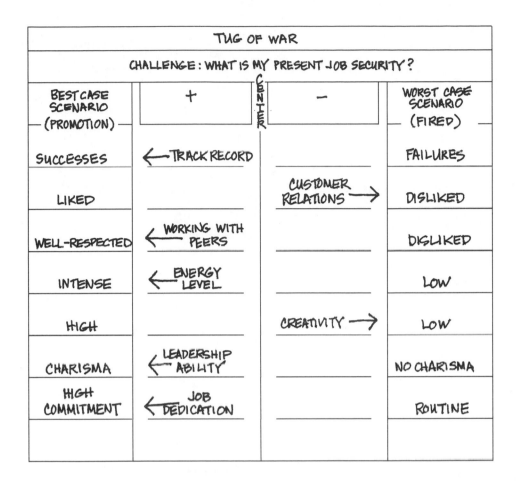

TUG OF WAR			
CHALLENGE: WHAT IS MY PRESENT JOB SECURITY?			
BEST CASE SCENARIO (PROMOTION)	+	CENTER —	WORST CASE SCENARIO (FIRED)
SUCCESSES	←—TRACK RECORD		FAILURES
LIKED		CUSTOMER RELATIONS →	DISLIKED
WELL-RESPECTED	← WORKING WITH PEERS		DISLIKED
INTENSE	← ENERGY LEVEL		LOW
HIGH		CREATIVITY →	LOW
CHARISMA	← LEADERSHIP ABILITY		NO CHARISMA
HIGH COMMITMENT	← JOB DEDICATION		ROUTINE

1. Maximize your strengths.
2. Minimize your weaknesses.
3. Add more positive forces.

You might choose to further strengthen the positive forces: track record, working with peers, energy level, leadership ability, and job dedication.

To minimize weaknesses, reframe them as challenges:

"In what ways might I improve my customer relations?"

"In what ways might I improve my creativity?"

Finally, you could create new positive forces to further outweigh the negative ones; for instance, you might work on a new positive condition of report writing and add that force to your analysis.

The key is to work on the conditions. A clay pot sitting in the sun will always remain a clay pot. It has to go through the white heat of a furnace to

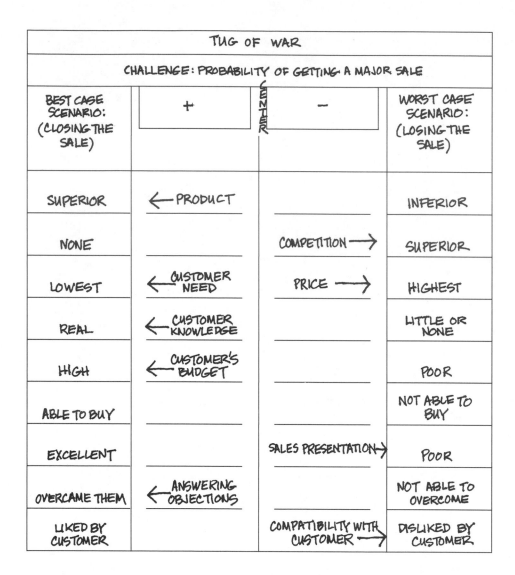

TUG OF WAR			
CHALLENGE: PROBABILITY OF GETTING A MAJOR SALE			
BEST CASE SCENARIO: (CLOSING THE SALE)	+	− (CENTER)	WORST CASE SCENARIO: (LOSING THE SALE)
SUPERIOR	← PRODUCT		INFERIOR
NONE		COMPETITION →	SUPERIOR
LOWEST	← CUSTOMER NEED	PRICE →	HIGHEST
REAL	← CUSTOMER KNOWLEDGE		LITTLE OR NONE
HIGH	← CUSTOMER'S BUDGET		POOR
ABLE TO BUY			NOT ABLE TO BUY
EXCELLENT		SALES PRESENTATION →	POOR
OVERCAME THEM	← ANSWERING OBJECTIONS		NOT ABLE TO OVERCOME
LIKED BY CUSTOMER		COMPATIBILITY WITH CUSTOMER →	DISLIKED BY CUSTOMER

become porcelain. This technique can give you insight into the "clay" of your challenge. However, you have to do something to it to make the "best case" happen.

Now let's consider the probability of a certain company getting a major sale. The best-case scenario would be closing the sale, the worst case would be losing the sale entirely.

Our negative forces are:

- Our competitors' products are perceived as superior.
- Our price is higher than alternative products.
- We gave a poor presentation.
- Our relationship with the customer could be better.

Our positive forces are:

- Our product is better than other comparable products.
- The customer has a real need for the product.
- Our customer is able and ready to buy.
- We answered and overcame all raised objections.

Our options are:

1. We can further strengthen our positive forces.
2. We can reframe the negative forces as challenges to solve. For instance:
   "In what ways might our product be perceived as superior?"
   "In what ways might we add value to the product to further justify its price?"
   "In what ways might we make up for the poor presentation?"
   "In what ways might we improve our relationship with the customer?"
3. Add more positive forces, such as customer service, packaged financing, bring in support personnel to help obtain the sale, and so on.

In Tug-of-War, maximizing strengths is the punch; minimizing weaknesses is the clever footwork. Consider how Steven Jobs and Stephen Wozniak created Apple Computers. In 1976, their principal strength was a unique design for a personal computer; their principal weakness was an utter lack of capital—between them they had $1,300.

- Jobs maximized their principal strength by selling fifty as-yet-unbuilt computers to a string of computer hobby stores, based on their unique design.
- He minimized their weakness by securing credit to buy parts, based on sales of unbuilt computers.
- He added a positive force by using the profits gained from the sale of

the first six hundred computers to start work on the enormously successful Apple II.

Apple went public at the end of 1980 and, after three weeks, its shares were worth more than Ford Motor Company shares.

SUMMARY

Once there was a man who died and found himself in Hell, with the road to Heaven blocked by a huge mountain. Although indignant that he was in Hell, the man assumed he could do nothing to change his situation and settled down to an eternity of suffering. He never discovered that the mountain was on wheels—to reach Heaven he needed only to push the mountain aside.

Once you identify the forces operating in your challenge, they become as negotiable as a mountain on wheels. You can either learn to live with the negatives by limiting your options and compromising your goals, or you can change their position and neutralize their impact.

CHAPTER ELEVEN

IDEA BOX

"In battle there are only the normal
and the extraordinary forces, but their
combinations are limitless;
none can comprehend them all."

SUN TZU

In poker, the highest possible hand is a straight flush—five cards in sequence in the same suit.

If you are allowed to keep the cards you wanted, discard others, and continue to draw cards as long as you wished, you would eventually draw a straight flush. Within a set number of cards there is a vast number of combinations, some good, others useless. The more combinations you create, the greater your likelihood of getting a winning hand. This is, in essence, the principle behind the Idea Box.

The Idea Box is modeled after the *morphological box,* credited to Dr. Fritz Zwicky. It is a way of automatically combining the parameters of a challenge into new ideas (parameter here means characteristic, factor, variable, or aspect). You choose the number and nature of the parameters for the challenge; what's important is to generate parameters and then list variations for each parameter.

Think of the parameters as card suits (hearts, spades, clubs, and diamonds), and the variations as the different cards within each suit. By coming up with different combinations of the variations of the parameters, you create new ideas.

BLUEPRINT

1. *Specify your challenge.*

2. *Select the parameters of your challenge.* To determine whether a parameter is important enough to add, ask yourself, "Would the challenge still exist without the parameter I'm considering adding to the box?"

3. *List variations.* Below each parameter, list as many variations as you wish for that parameter. The number of parameters and variations will determine the box's complexity. Generally, it is easier to find new ideas within a simple framework than a complex one. For instance, a box with ten parameters, each of which has ten variations, produces 10 billion potential combinations.

4. *Try different combinations.* When the box is finished, make random runs through the parameters and variations, selecting one or more from each column and then combining them into entirely new forms. You can examine all of the combinations in the box to see how they affect your challenge. If you are working with a box that contains ten or more parameters, you may find it helpful to randomly examine the entire box, and then gradually restrict yourself to portions that appear particularly fruitful. It's like hunting for stars in a box.

Let's look at an example.

NEW LAUNDRY HAMPER

Situation: I'm a marketing director for a company that produces laundry hampers. The market has matured, and the company needs a new design to capture the customer's imagination. My challenge is: "In what ways might I improve the design of laundry hampers?"

Description: I analyze laundry hampers and list their basic parameters. I decide to work with four parameters (material, shape, finish, and position) and plan to use five variations for each.

Idea Box: I construct my box with the parameters on top, leaving five

IMPROVE DESIGN FOR LAUNDRY HAMPER			
	MATERIAL	SHAPE	FINISH	POSITION
1	WICKER	SQUARE	NATURAL	SITS ON FLOOR
2	PLASTIC	CYLINDRICAL	PAINTED	ON CEILING
3	PAPER	RECTANGLE	CLEAR	ON WALL
4	METAL	HEXAGONAL	LUMINOUS	CHUTE TO BASEMENT
5	NET MATERIAL	CUBE	NEON	ON DOOR

boxes beneath each parameter for the variations. To generate the variations, I ask myself:

What *materials* could be used to make hampers?

What *shapes* can hampers be made in?

What *finishes* can be used on hampers?

What are the *positions* for hampers?

Under each heading I list five alternatives.

Idea search: The next step is to randomly choose one or more variations and connect them to create new possibilities. These random combinations may trigger new ideas or potential solutions.

After making any random runs through the box, one combination of variations for the parameters provoked an idea for a new design.

The idea: Using the random combination of net material, cylindrical, painted, and positioned on the door, I came up with a laundry hamper fashioned into a basketball-type net, approximately 40 inches long, attached to a cylindrical hoop and hung on a backboard that is attached to a door. This allows kids to play basketball with dirty laundry as they fill the hamper. When it is full, a tug on a drawstring releases the clothes.

Five alternatives for each parameter generates a possible 3,125 different combinations. If only 10 percent prove useful, that would mean 312 new ideas. In theory, a perfectly constructed Idea Box contains all of the possible solutions to a specified challenge. In practice, the box may be incomplete; a

NEW BUSINESS EXTENSION FOR CAR WASHES				
	METHOD	PRODUCTS WASHED	EQUIPMENT	PRODUCTS SOLD
1	FULL	CARS	SPRAYS	RELATED PRODUCTS
2	SELF	TRUCKS	CONVEYORS	NOVELTIES
3	HAND	HOUSES	STALLS	DISCOUNT BOOKS
4	MOBILE	CLOTHES	DRYERS	EDIBLE GOODS
5	COMBINATION	DOGS	BRUSHES	CIGARETTES

critical parameter or variation may not have been included. When you feel this may be the case, you should reconsider and adjust the parameters or variations accordingly.

New ideas and inventions are merely new combinations of existing bits and pieces. The Idea Box snaps existing information together into provocative new patterns, and the ideas appear, almost by accident, out of nowhere. When the ideas appear, you'll grin like a kid who has caught his first fish.

NEW BUSINESS EXTENSION FOR CAR WASHES

A car wash owner fell on hard times. To survive, he needed to find a new market, a new market extension, or a new idea. He analyzed "washing" and decided to work with four parameters: method of washing, products washed, equipment used, and other products sold.

He constructed a box with the four parameters on top; under each parameter he listed five variations. Then he randomly chose one or more items from each parameter and connected them to form a new business.

The random combination of self, dogs, brushes, stalls, sprays, dryers, and related products sparked the idea for a self-service dog wash. This dog wash has ramps leading to waist-high tubs where owners spray their pets, scrub them with brushes (provided free of charge), shampoo, and blow dry them. In addition, he sells his own line of dog products, such as shampoos and conditioners. Pet owners wash their dogs while their car is going through the full-service car wash.

In the figure below, we see the dot to which the arrow is pointing as part of the diagonal line, even though it is actually closer to the vertical line. We tend to ignore the relationship with the vertical line and see the dot *only* as a continuation of the diagonal one. This illustrates the principle of *common fate:* Events that *seem* to be continuous are likely to be seen as a single entity rather than as discrete events. This explains why we tend to perceive the elements of a challenge as a continuous whole rather than as separate items.

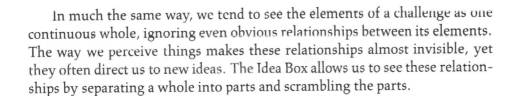

In much the same way, we tend to see the elements of a challenge as one continuous whole, ignoring even obvious relationships between its elements. The way we perceive things makes these relationships almost invisible, yet they often direct us to new ideas. The Idea Box allows us to see these relationships by separating a whole into parts and scrambling the parts.

NEW PRODUCTS FOR PUBLISHER

A publisher who is looking for new products decides to work with four parameters: kinds of books, properties of books, processes of publishing, and forms of information.

Under each parameter, he lists ten variations, allowing 10 × 10 × 10 × 10 or 10,000 possible combinations. Assuming a 10 percent yield of truly useful ideas, this gives him a possible 1,000 good ideas jumping over and around him like fleas.

Connecting how-to cooking book, odor, advertising, and premium, our publisher created a scratch-and-sniff cookbook for a major food company to use as a premium. All of the recipes featured the company's products, and each

IDEA BOX FOR PUBLISHING				
	KINDS	PROPERTIES	PROCESSES	FORMS
1	FICTION	SOUND (AUDIO BOOKS)	ACQUIRING MANUSCRIPTS	COFFEE TABLE GIFT BOOKS
2	NONFICTION	COLOR	MANUFACTURING	NEWSLETTER
3	CLASSICS	TEXTURE	MARKETING	ANTHOLOGIES
4	HOW TO BOOKS (COOKING, HOME CARE, ETC.)	SOCIAL RESPONSIBILITIES	DISTRIBUTION TRADITIONAL OR NONTRADITIONAL	SOFTWARE
5	BUSINESS	ILLUSTRATIONS	WRITING SOFTWARE	HARDBACK
6	TEXTBOOK	SUBSTANCE: PAPER OR FLOPPY DISK	REMAINDERING	PAPERBACK
7	CHILDREN	ODOR	ADVERTISING	PREMIUM
8	RELIGION	EXERCISES, GAMES OR PUZZLES	TIME FROM MANUSCRIPT TO FINISHED PRODUCT	MAGAZINE
9	MYSTERY	TASTE	KNOWLEDGE OR ENTERTAINMENT	LOOSE-LEAF
10	SPORTS	SHAPE, LARGE, SMALL OR ODD STRUCTURE	DESIGN AND FORMAT	PACKAGED WITH OTHER PRODUCTS

was accompanied by an illustration so that the reader could tell not just how the dish would look, but how it would smell as well.

The publisher then connected nonfiction, social responsibilities, advertising, acquiring manuscripts, nontraditional distribution, and hardback to create a new publishing concept. He intends to pay leading authors $60,000 each to write one-hundred-page hardback books on socially responsible topics. He will sell advertisement space within the books to finance publishing and printing, and distribute them free to 150,000 prominent people. The publisher will eventually sell the original book in stores and also sell reprint rights to paperback publishers, and license some of the books to foreign publishers.

The same publisher had a several-year-old book of standard speeches that had a miserable sales record. He decided to find an innovative way to sell this book. After analyzing how books are marketed, he selected four parameters: packaging, distribution, promotion, and selling.

Under each parameter, he listed ten alternative variations and randomly played with the various combinations until he came up with a new idea.

He combined packaging as a function, to be distributed through other retail outlets, provide free articles to newspapers, and selling using own direct force and got the idea to package the book's speeches as scrolls in a cardboard can, called *Canned Speeches.* This new product was sold in office supply stores as well as standard retail outlets. The publisher then wrote and sent articles about this novel package to major newspapers, thereby getting a good deal of free publicity. A mediocre collection of standard speeches became a smashing bestseller.

In the publishing examples, we could generate a possible 1,000 combinations. The more imagination you use in thinking up parameters and variations, the more possible combinations you can create. For instance, suppose you choose five parameters with twenty alternative attributes. This would give you $20 \times 20 \times 20 \times 20 \times 20$ or 320,000 possible combinations, all without spraining your brain.

Sometimes the best ideas are the result of fortuitous flux. Ideas large and small often occur as a result of a chance combination. An automobile salesman designed an Idea Box and played with it every day. One day he randomly connected odor, air-conditioning, operator-controlled, and new car smell.

This chance combination led to the idea of a fragrance-control system for cars. With a touch of a button, drivers can choose from jasmine, mint, a fresh leather smell, or perfume scents, all blowing through the air-conditioning system. The soft aromas will, according to the salesman, improve ride comfort. He intends to sell his patent to an automobile manufacturer.

SUMMARY

When you write a poem, you discover that the very necessity of fitting your meaning into a specific form requires you to search your imagination for new meanings. You reject certain ways of writing and select others, always trying to arrange the words in a new and imaginative way. Form is an aid to finding

IDEA BOX FOR MARKETING A BOOK			
	PACKAGING	DISTRIBUTION	PROMOTION	SELLING
1	COVER: HARD OR SOFT	TRADITIONAL DISTRIBUTORS AND WHOLESALERS	ADVERTISING	DIRECT SALES FORCE
2	FLOPPY DISK	DISTRIBUTE WITH OTHER PUBLISHERS	BOOK REVIEWS	DIRECT MAIL
3	PACKAGE WITH OTHER ITEMS	DISTRIBUTE AT EXHIBITS AND CONVENTIONS	TALK SHOWS	SPECIAL SALES: PREMIUMS AND INCENTIVES
4	PACKAGE TO ADAPT TO SEASON	COMPUTER STORES	BONUS INSERTS, COUPONS	TELEMARKETING
5	GIFT ITEM	OTHER RETAIL OUTLETS	VIDEOS BASED ON THE BOOK	DOOR TO DOOR
6	SOLO OR SERIES	CHAIN STORES	TIE-IN WITH CHARITY	INDEPENDENT REPS
7	PACKAGE WITH POPUS OR DIE CUTS	DIRECT TO CONSUMER	FREE ARTICLES TO NEWSPAPERS	SELL TO SCHOOLS AND LIBRARIES
8	PACKAGE WITH BUILT-IN GIMMICK SUCH AS A BOOK HOLDER	THROUGH MANUFACTURER OF RELATED PRODUCTS	SEMINARS AND WORKSHOPS	SALES KITS
9	CREATE PACKAGE TO SERVE SOME FUNCTION SUCH AS A DOORSTOP	SELF	TIME DISCOUNTS	AUTHOR CONNECTIONS
10	PACKAGING AS AN ALTERNATIVE ADVERTISING VEHICLE	THROUGH HOME PARTIES	CONTEST	SELL FOREIGN RIGHTS

new meaning, a stimulus to discovering the essence you wish to express. Think how much more meaning Shakespeare could put into his plays because they were written in blank verse rather than prose, or into his sonnets because they were limited to fourteen lines.

Fitting your challenge in an Idea Box simplifies and condenses it in a similar way. It forces you to find new connections and new meanings; your imagination must leap to fill the gaps and make sense of the whole. Imagine a mime impersonating a man walking his dog. The mime's arm is outstretched as though holding the dog's leash. As he jerks his arm back and forth you *see* the dog straining at the leash to sniff this or that. The dog and the leash become the most real part of the scene, even though there is no dog or leash. With the Idea Box, you may see a connection (the mime and his arm) that will provide the stimulus for your imagination to fill the gaps (the dog and the leash) and create a new idea.

CHAPTER TWELVE

IDEA GRID

"Therefore the skillful commander takes up
a position in which he cannot be defeated and
misses no opportunity to master his enemy."

SUN TZU

There is a vast order in the universe. Every time I throw a coin in the air, it returns and hits the floor. Because there *is* a vast order, things can be separated and understood. When NASA sends up four rockets one-half second apart, their afterimages are approximately simultaneous. We can say that we see four rockets "at the same time." This is the illusion of simultaneity. To see order, we attempt to comprehend spontaneously things that are non-spontaneous.

In the figure below, the two horizontal lines are the same length, yet the top one appears to be longer.

This is known as the Ponzo illusion and is explained by the fact that we attempt to comprehend the image as a whole and are led by our experiences to see the vertical lines as if they were railroad tracks receding in the distance.

The only way to comprehend what is really there is to examine each line individually, as a separate "event."

The universe of business is also composed of separate events, yet we say things like "that is a good business" or "that market is solid," as though all of the events were appearing as a singular entity at the same time. To find opportunities, you need to look at the separate events that make up the universe of business and understand their relationships. An Idea Grid is designed to let you do just that.

BLUEPRINT

The basic grid is the FCB Grid, a powerful tool that enables one to compress large amounts of complex information. It was first developed in 1978 by Richard Vaughn, a research director of the worldwide advertising corporation Foote, Cone & Belding.

High involvement represents perceptions of expensive products such as cars and boats.

Low involvement represents less costly products such as ordinary household products.

Think represents verbal, numerical, analytic, cognitive products for which the consumer desires information and data. For example, automobiles, boats, computers, cameras, and so on.

Feel represents products that appeal to a consumer's emotional needs and desires, such as travel, beauty, cosmetics, and so on.

You place your product on the grid by researching both the product and its potential market. For instance, life insurance would fall in the High/Left quadrant, insecticide in the Low/Left, and costume jewelry in the Low/Right quadrant.

Once the product is placed, you have a powerful basis for generating ideas. You can read and understand the grid immediately because the visual language used in placement is intuitively understood. It's like seeing the ocean for the first time: You learn as much about the vastness of the ocean from your first moment's glance as you would in a month of study.

The FCB Grid allows you to:

- Identify holes in the market.

FCB GRID

	THINK	FEEL
HIGH INVOLVEMENT	1.	2.
LOW INVOLVEMENT	3.	4.

- Predict the demand for new product ideas.
- Formulate an advertising strategy.
- Reposition your business or product by:
  Positioning it so it is the minimum distance from the competition you want to master.
  Positioning it so it is the maximum distance from the competition for maximum differentiation.
  Leaving the position unchanged and attempting to change customer perceptions.

When using grids, keep your analysis simple, clear, and expressible in only a few lines. If your grid is elaborate and takes a lot of time to communicate, it will lose its meaning. Think of the grid as a piece of rope which takes on meaning only in connection with the things it holds together.

USING THE GRID TO GET IDEAS

People think of a balloon as a continuous solid skin that holds air. But if you look at the skin of a balloon with a microscope, you'll find that it is not continuous at all; it is full of holes. The balloon is a kind of net in which the holes are so small that the air molecules cannot get out. There is, in fact, no such thing as a continuous solid skin, or a "solid" or "continuous" anything in the universe.

So there certainly can be no such thing as a "solid" company, or a market with no holes, or a "solid" anything in business. One way to get new ideas is to locate the holes in a market, an industry, or a business. The Idea Grid makes this easy.

A major publisher was confronted with the challenge: "In what ways might we publish a unique book on gardening for children ages four to twelve?"

He first researched six major publishing firms in the usual ways—surveys, questionnaires, sales records, and so on—and discovered that the major books on gardening for children were, basically, reasonably priced, straightforward, well-illustrated instructional books. He drew a grid and placed all six in various levels in the Low/Left quadrant as low involvement, thinking books.

He studied the grid and determined that his basic choices were:

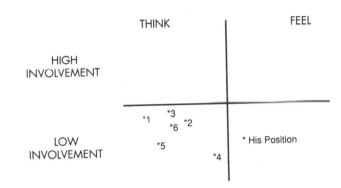

1. *Low/Left quadrant:* He could position his book against the existing books as a low involvement, thinking book.
2. *High/Left quadrant:* He could create a high involvement, thinking book, such as an encyclopedia or other reference book.
3. *High/Right quadrant:* He could create a high involvement, feeling book. Examples of this might include art books and books packaged with fairly expensive objects.
4. *Low/Right quadrant:* He could create a low involvement, feeling book, such as a coloring book or a book packaged with less expensive objects.

The publisher surveyed all the options and decided to focus on the Low/Right quadrant.

Using the grid to look for holes in the market, he found the idea he was looking for, floating like a flower in a bowl.

The idea: A coloring book titled *Growing Vegetable Soup.* The book

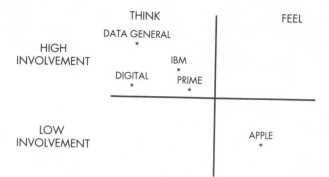

describes a delicious vegetable soup, then leads the reader through the actual work: planting the seeds, watering, weeding, and digging up the vegetables, and finally making the soup and eating it. The book was a bestseller.

USING THE GRID TO APPLY IDEAS

A new idea usually requires imagination and effort to get results. For instance, the essence of competition is differentiation; creating something better than and different from the competition. However, sometimes even an obvious functional difference doesn't sell unless you look for an imaginative application.

Look at Apple Computers. Their unbelievable success was not because of the product's small size or low price. After all, why would anybody buy a sophisticated piece of hardware that looked like a child's toy from some unknown company? There was no way Apple could claim superiority over IBM, Digital Equipment, Data General, or Prime, especially given the horror stories about the computer market at that time. Instead, Apple provided an imaginative application of their idea.

First, they graphed the computer environment as above.

Apple's genius was to avoid positioning themselves with the crowded cluster of giant competitors in the High/Left quadrant. Challenging these giants in their own quadrant would have been like challenging a school of piranhas to a game of water polo.

They avoided that position by not calling themselves a minicomputer or a microminicomputer. They did something different. They positioned themselves in the Low/Right quadrant as far away as possible from the giants and developed a marketing and advertising strategy that emphasized:

- A new and entirely different computer intended for the average person rather than computer experts.

- The term "personal computer" as opposed to minicomputer.
- Being part of a whole new generation of computers.
- Being user-friendly.

Apple went after the Low/Right quadrant—an enormous risk at the time. Was there really a market for a toy-like personal computer for the average person? There was. By using imagination in positioning their idea, the founders made billions as they captured the market they saw on the grid.

Summary

The grid helps you navigate the tricky seas of the marketplace. The waters are neither dull nor pretty, but a code that needs interpretation. The grid tells you everything or nothing, depending on how you read it. Make the right soundings, and patterns will emerge like a safe harbor out of the mist.

THE TOOTHACHE TREE

132

"What is difficult about maneuver is to make
the devious route the most direct and to turn
misfortune to advantage."

SUN TZU

In this illustration, the diagonal lines that are interrupted by the rectangular shapes appear to be three separate lines.

In reality, there is only one line. (Placing a ruler against the line will confirm that they are segments of one straight line.)

You could say that the rectangles prevent you from seeing the straight line. However, you could also say that the rectangles outline the way to see the straight line, since you know there are two obstacles distorting your perception, and you know they have to be removed before you can see the line. In the same way, obstacles outline the path to achieving your goal. When you have a challenge, identify the obstacles that stand in your way and remove them one at a time.

The late Charles Kettering, General Motor's head of research, almost broke his arm cranking his car one morning. A few days later, a friend of his was killed while crank-starting his car. Sad and angry, Kettering sat down and listed ten major obstacles that would have to be overcome before cars could be started automatically. He arranged them from the simplest to the most complex and began to solve them—and others as they developed—one at a time. The result was his first invention: the Delco self-starter. The Toothache Tree can help you overcome obstacles in a similar fashion.

BLUEPRINT

1. *State your challenge.*

2. *Identify and list the major obstacles to overcome.*

3. *Order your obstacles according to degree of complexity.*

4. *Draw a vertical line to represent a tree's trunk.* Write the challenge on this "trunk."

5. *Draw horizontal lines to represent branches.* Write your obstacles on the branches, with the simpler ones at the bottom and the most difficult at the top.

The tree can be simple or elaborate. The point is to express your obstacles in tangible forms, making them easier to deal with than abstract thoughts or notions. Each obstacle becomes a specific tree branch that must be removed in order to achieve victory.

A textbook publisher decided that his major challenge was to increase university textbook sales by 20 percent (the usual annual increase had been from 4 to 6 percent). To accomplish this increase, his managers listed as many obstacles to textbook sales as they could conjure up. The group prioritized them and then decided to devote their energies to overcoming the ten most pressing obstacles.

After the obstacles were defined and accepted by the group, they agreed to focus on removing as many obstacles as possible. Committed to a positive goal, with obstacles outlined, they had no choice but to charge through the obstacles and attain the goal—either that or publicly embarrass themselves.

The publisher illustrated the challenge on the Toothache Tree shown on the next page, giving the managers added incentive to attack the obstacles that were now visually displayed, an everyday reminder of their challenges.

Starting with the bottom branches, the managers worked on one obstacle at a time throughout the sales year. At each weekly sales meeting, the group discussed their progress, and as each obstacle was overcome, the publisher would hold a celebration to commemorate the removal of the branch.

At the celebration, the publisher would provide the background information about the tree branch (obstacle) that was removed from the Toothache Tree, and introduce the person or persons responsible for coming up with the "big idea" that overcame the obstacle. Those responsible would then erase the

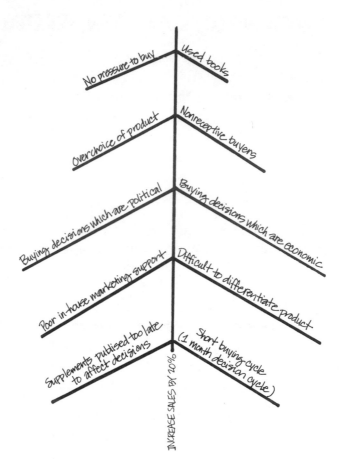

branch. They would discuss what they did and how they did it, and the publisher would detail what it meant to the corporation in terms of profitability. These stories made the rounds in the company because they were real stories about real people doing memorable things.

The sales in that one division increased by 32 percent. By focusing on one obstacle at a time, the managers were able to direct all of their energy toward specific ways to overcome specific obstacles. As each obstacle was removed, they moved closer to their general objective. Eventually, they solved nine of the ten most pressing problems and exceeded their goal.

After the nine tree limbs had fallen, the publisher said:

It was as if we returned to a plainer sense of things. It was as if we had come to a beginning of our imagination. It is difficult to choose the adjective for this feeling, this feeling of achievement. We were like baby gorillas who didn't know our own strength.

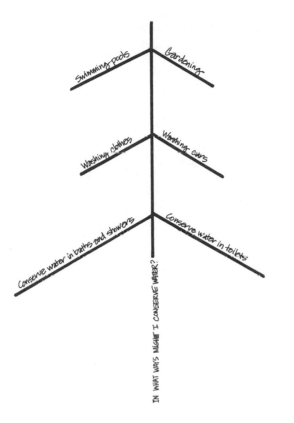

Obstacles can also inspire ideas for new products and services. When you concentrate on specific obstacles, you are forced to look for solutions.

Suppose your major goal is to conserve 15 percent of the water now being used by the general population. Some of the major obstacles to water conservation are:

- Water in toilets
- Baths and showers
- Washing clothes
- Washing cars
- Swimming pools
- Gardening

Arrange them on a Toothache Tree. Then frame each obstacle as a specific challenge.

The first branch represents the amount of water each toilet consumes, a major obstacle to water conservation. Convert this into a challenge: "In what ways might I conserve the amount of water a toilet consumes?"

Focusing on this one branch of the tree, you direct your energies on a specific solvable challenge. Its resolution will be one step toward your goal of reducing water consumption by 15 percent. One possible solution is to redesign the toilet.

The idea: A combination toilet-sink to eliminate water waste. The toilet would have a handle that when turned left would create a full tank flush and when turned right a half-tank flush. Rather than refilling automatically, the tank would be refilled with the runoff from a small sink atop the toilet, thus recycling the water that would otherwise be lost when you washed your hands. Such a toilet, would also save space and simplify plumbing.

The next branch of the tree is the problem of conserving water in baths and showers. Convert this into the challenge: "In what ways might I conserve the amount of water baths and showers consume?"

The obstacles to water conservation are no longer blurred problems; the Toothache Tree keeps them all visible. Because they are tangible, an idea to resolve one obstacle may help resolve others as well.

The idea: Invent a lightweight plastic reservoir to collect and conserve used shower and bath water for reuse in gardening and washing cars. A small electric pump would recycle the used bath water to the reservoir for storage until it is reused for other purposes. Thus, conserving water in baths and showers helps conserve water for gardening and washing cars as well.

By concentrating on one branch at a time and converting the obstacle into a challenge, you encourage yourself to search for ideas to conserve water. Ultimately, by concentrating on obstacles, you create new ideas that collectively or individually could lead to the achievement of your goal.

The block of granite that is an obstacle in the pathway of the weak becomes a stepping-stone in the pathway of the strong.

Whenever Mort, a diabetic, gave his presentation about financial services to high-powered executives, he would shake slightly. He would then imagine that the executives thought he was too nervous, too young, or not confident enough to himself or his product and then would literally freeze up and stumble through the presentation. A coworker nicknamed him Frigor Mortis. Frigor Mortis was on the verge of getting fired.

The major obstacle he had to overcome was the physical shaking he exhibited. Incredibly, he used this obstacle as a stepping-stone to success.

He developed a presentation that started like this: "I have what is politely called a health problem. I have had it since I was a child. I started losing weight. One week I lost twenty pounds. The next week I lost ten. The doctor said I would never gain those pounds back. The doctor gave me one of these."

He would then reach under the podium and remove a hypodermic syringe. With shaking hands, he punched the needle into the top of a blue vial

and drew the plunger upward. Holding the filled needle up for all to see, he said, "The reason I am shaking so badly is that I haven't had my insulin injection yet today. I'm late. But I wanted you to see exactly what I have to do."

Rolling up his sleeve, he positioned the needle halfway up his arm, then pushed down the plunger. The executives sat there electrified.

Then he went on to talk about how diabetes had changed his life. "I probably look at life a little bit differently than you do," he would say. "I see each day as a gift, as a bonus—and this needle and this shaking are my friends."

In a quiet, intense voice he continued: "If you have diabetes, or have ever wondered about it—I'd like to talk to you, to tell you what it's done for me after my presentation. Everything in my life is important, including my company and its financial services. I only work for those things I believe in, and now I would like to tell you why I believe in our services."

The audience would sit there, stunned and silent. They had become a different audience, having shared an almost therapeutic experience, and there would be murmurs of agreement and understanding as he presented his program. He achieved instant credibility whenever he gave this presentation.

Frigor Mortis became the superstar in his company by transforming a major career obstacle into a dramatic presentation tool.

SUMMARY

Identify the quantity and quality of the major obstacles you need to overcome to achieve your goal. Arrange them according to degrees of complexity on a Toothache Tree. Convert them into challenges and overcome them one at a time.

There is an old Greek myth of Theseus and Ariadne. Theseus says to Ariadne, "I'll love you forever if you can show me a way out of this labyrinth." So she gives him a ball of string, which he unwinds as he goes into the labyrinth, and then rewinds to find his way out.

Sometimes we look for some great power to guide us out of the labyrinth of our challenge, when all we need is that piece of string. The string shows us the pathway out. In the same way, obstacles show us the pathway to solutions.

PHOENIX

"The general who wins a battle
makes many calculations in his temple before
the battle is fought."

SUN TZU

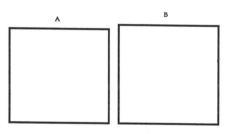

Which figure is a perfect square?

If you chose A, as the majority of people do, you are wrong. B is the perfect square. People tend to overestimate the lengths of vertical lines in comparison to horizontal ones. Consequently, they see the vertical lines of A as the same length as its horizontal lines.

If you had asked yourself the following questions, you would have selected the correct square:

- What is a perfect square?
- How can I determine which figure is a perfect square?
- Can I visually determine which is the perfect square?
- Should I use a measuring device?

Questions help you estimate your challenges; they give conscious direction to your thinking. When you ask yourself a question, you have to think about it. And when you ask yourself the right question, you have to think *up* as well as think *about* something.

Columbo, the famous television detective played by Peter Falk, did not investigate crimes by looking for clues. Instead, he engaged suspects in conversation, seeking, chiefly by questions, to induce them to talk and explain. He claimed no knowledge except of his own ignorance, and was apparently willing to learn from anyone. The inevitable result of such questioning, however, was that the suspect was reduced to a state of irritation and, finally, a confession of guilt.

Columbo did not solve his crimes with one or two questions, but by asking a long series of them. Asking one question would be like hoping to understand the wheel by examining one spoke. It takes many spokes, as well as a hub and a rim, to make the thing called a wheel, and we need to see the whole thing to comprehend it. In the same way, to understand a challenge, you need to ask a series of questions, not just one or two. To do this, use a question checklist.

A checklist of questions helps you make sure that no aspect of a challenge is overlooked. Read the following string of digits at the rate of about one per second then, look away and try to recall the digits in order:

7 9 1 4 0

Now do the same with this string of digits:

2 6 5 8 9 3 1 4 7 0 5 3 9

Most likely, you recalled the first string completely but recalled only part of the second string, perhaps about seven digits. This is because our memory span is usually limited to about seven items, give or take two. Even though you might think you know all the questions you should ask about any situation, you cannot produce them when you have to.

Unless your challenge is extremely easy to solve, you need to know what to ask.

Phoenix is a checklist of questions developed by the Central Intelligence Agency to encourage agents to look at a challenge from many different angles. Using Phoenix is like holding your challenge in your hand. You can turn it, look at it from underneath, see it from one view, hold it up to another position, imagine solutions, and really be in control of it.

Use the Phoenix checklist as a base on which to build your own personal checklist of questions. Note good questions when you hear others ask them, and keep adding them to your own checklist. With the right questions, you can solve a challenge the way Columbo would solve a crime; i.e., ask a number of questions, then suddenly ask the question that turns everything around. When that happens, you might say you "Columboed the challenge."

BLUEPRINT

1. *Write your challenge.* Isolate the challenge you want to think about and commit yourself to *an* answer, if not *the* answer, by a certain date.
2. *Ask questions.* Use the Phoenix checklist to dissect the challenge into as many different ways as you can.
3. *Record your answers,* information requests, solutions, and ideas for evaluation and analysis.

THE PHOENIX CHECKLIST

THE PROBLEM

- Why is it necessary to solve the problem?
- What benefits will you receive by solving the problem?
- What is the unknown?
- What is it you don't yet understand?
- What is the information you have?
- What isn't the problem?
- Is the information sufficient? Or is it insufficient? Or redundant? Or contradictory?
- Should you draw a diagram of the problem? A figure?
- Where are the boundaries of the problem?
- Can you separate the various parts of the problem? Can you write them down? What are the relationships of the parts of the problem?
- What are the constants (things that can't be changed) of the problem?
- Have you seen this problem before?
- Have you seen this problem in a slightly different form?
- Do you know a related problem?
- Try to think of a familiar problem having the same or a similar unknown?
- Suppose you find a problem related to yours that has already been solved. Can you use it? Can you use its method?

- Can you restate your problem? How many different ways can you restate it? More general? More specific? Can the rules be changed?
- What are the best, worst, and most probable cases you can imagine?

THE PLAN

- Can you solve the whole problem? Part of the problem?
- What would you like the resolution to be? Can you picture it?
- How much of the unknown can you determine?
- Can you derive something useful from the information you have?
- Have you used all the information?
- Have you taken into account all essential notions in the problem?
- Can you separate the steps in the problem-solving process? Can you determine the correctness of each step?
- What creative thinking techniques can you use to generate ideas? How many different techniques?
- Can you see the result? How many different kinds of results can you see?
- How many different ways have you tried to solve the problem?
- What have others done?
- Can you intuit the solution? Can you check the result?
- What should be done? How should it be done?
- Where should it be done?
- When should it be done?
- Who should do it?
- What do you need to do at this time?
- Who will be responsible for what?
- Can you use this problem to solve some other problem?
- What is the unique set of qualities that makes this problem what it is and none other?

- What milestones can best mark your progress?
- How will you know when you are successful?

Try using the question checklist to solve this difficult problem, known as the Greek Cross. On a table, arrange ten coins to match the following illustration. Move just *two* coins to another position to form two rows, containing *six* coins each when added up either horizontally or vertically.

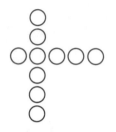

The solution can be found in this chapter's summary.

Suppose you defined a "rose" as a red, pink, or white flower one gives to a beautiful woman, a pleasant hostess, or a deceased friend. The tagging of a complex flower with the single label (rose) and one description would not inspire your curiosity. However, if you asked a series of questions about roses, you could better describe the flower, how it is grown, its thorns, its blossoms, its fragrance, how others have used it, and how to best package and use it.

Tagging any subject with a single label and description dulls curiosity and limits imagination. Consider the steel industry. Executives tagged a complex process with a single label (big steel) and one description (the integrated process) and suffered for years with an uneconomical industry. Finally, a group of young men asked a series of questions that changed the industry.

The integrated steel process had been uneconomical since it was invented in the 1870s—it involves beginning with iron ore, creating very high temperatures four times only to quench them, and transporting masses of metal over great distances. The only time the industry performed well was in times of war—it was a lump in America's gravy.

A group of new young managers asked aggressive questions about every step of the steel-making process and discovered that the integrated process contradicts basic laws of economics.

What they discovered was that since the early 1970s, the demand for steel had been going up. However, for integrated mills to meet the demand they had to add new units, which required a substantial investment. Since demand rises in small steps, the expansion would not be profitable until the demand reached the mill's new capacity. If a mill chose not to expand, it would lose its customers. In the steel business, if you can't deliver orders on time, customers don't wait. Faced with this choice, companies expanded. Consequently, companies were profitable for only that time when the demand reached the new capacity. When the demand exceeded that capacity, the integrated mills would be forced to expand again. This discovery led to the solution.

The idea: The young questioners proposed a shift from the giant, ever-expanding "integrated" plant to a "mini-mill." The end uses are the same as the integrated mill, only the costs are substantially lower. A mini-mill can be built for one-tenth the cost of an integrated plant, uses heat only once and does not quench it, starts with steel scrap instead of ore, and ends up with one final product (for example, beams, rods, etc.). The mini-mills offer modern technology, low labor costs, and target markets.

An executive stated that if these young men had not asked the right questions, we would still be making steel the old-fashioned way.

A question checklist also helps you increase your observation and association abilities.

A car alarm didn't stop thieves from shattering the window of one entrepreneur's Porsche and stealing his radio. Using the question checklist, he decided that the real challenge was disguising the radio, not finding a failproof alarm system. The question: "Suppose you find a problem related to yours and solved before, can you use its methods?" led him to think of how the military camouflages items it wants to disguise and hide. This association inspired his idea.

The idea: A fake front showing splayed wires and a gashed frame. Attached with Velcro over the real radio, it creates the illusion that the radio has already been stolen.

SUMMARY

The Greek Cross solution:

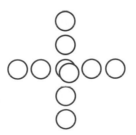

This problem can only be solved by moving one coin from the right arm to the left arm and moving the extra coin at the bottom to a position on top of the center coin.

Most problems like this are solved by sliding coins back and forth, but to solve this one you had to work in three dimensions.

The checklist questions that may have helped were:

- What are the boundaries of the problem? (Nothing prevents you from working in three dimensions.)
- Do you know a related problem? (The Dot Problem in "False Faces," page 44.)
- Can you intuit the result? (After sliding the coins around, you may sense that it can't be solved in two dimensions that may lead you to thinking about the third.)
- What is the unique set of qualities that makes this problem what it is and none other? (You're working with coins which can be stacked as well as moved.)

Solving a challenge is like walking a tightrope. If the rope is too slack, you will fall; if it is too tight, it has no resiliency, and you will also fall. The rope must be continually adjusted and supported at its weakest point. In the same way, asking questions will constantly adjust and support lines of speculation as you tiptoe toward a solution.

The Great Transpacific Airline and Storm Door Company

"If the army is confused and suspicious,
neighboring rulers will cause trouble. This is
what is meant by the saying: 'A confused army
leads to another's victory.' "

Sun Tzu

We do not see the stars in motion, though they move at speeds of more than a million miles per day. We do not see the trees grow, or notice ourselves aging each day. We do not even see the hands of a clock in motion. We tend to think statically and are surprised, often uncomfortably and sometimes fatally, by the constant changes in our world. This also applies to the world of business: It is difficult to shake our static notions of business and markets. This is why so many businesses seem to belong to an obsolete yesterday.

Static companies become frustrated and confused about the nature of their business; they often try to become all things to all people. Few things are less effective than those companies, like the apocryphal Great Transpacific Airline and Storm Door Company.

To get effective new ideas for your business, you must know what your business is *and* what it should be. Only by knowing these things can you apprehend the changing business world.

What Is Your Business?

On the face of it, nothing may seem simpler or more obvious than to know what a company's business is. A railroad runs trains, a publisher produces books, an automobile company manufactures cars, and so on. Actually, "What is our business?" is almost always a difficult question, and the right answer is often anything but obvious. Consider Bell Telephone. What could have been more obvious than the telephone business in the late 1800s?

Theodore Vail was fired by Bell Telephone in 1890 when he dared to ask top management "What is our business?" He was called back a decade later, when the consequences of the lack of an answer had become evident—that is, when the Bell System, operating without a clear definition, had drifted into a severe crisis and was being threatened by a government takeover.

Theodore Vail's answer was: "Our business is service, not telephones." That answer brought about radical innovations in Bell Telephone's business policy. It meant employee training and advertising that stressed service. It meant a new financial policy that assumed the company had to give service whenever it was demanded, and it was management's job to find the necessary capital and to earn a return on it.

Waiting until you or your industry is in trouble is like playing Russian roulette. Look at television. Simply put, Ted Turner showed the networks that their days of oligopoly were over. For quite some time, network executives sat around like smug sacred cows feeding each other a steady line of bull, while Turner, a Brown University dropout, parlayed his inheritance into cable television's most successful and influential programming company.

Among his innovations: cable TV's first national superstation; CNN, one of television's most successful networks; and Turner Network Television, an entertainment station with the largest initial viewership ever on cable TV. The major networks forgot to ask what is it that they do, and what it is they should do. Turner didn't. If you don't know what your business is you may end up on the wrong end of the business food chain.

How Should a Business Define Itself?

Is a company that pays for medical expenses in the insurance business or the healthcare business? Are combination gas stations and food stores in the grocery business or the convenience business? Is an NFL football team in the sports business or the entertainment business?

Businesses can define themselves according to products or services, markets, functions, or technologies.

IBM had long defined themselves as a data processing business. When the computer arrived, and with it a new technology that IBM knew nothing about, IBM top management realized that data processing would now have to mean computers, and asked "What should our business be?" They redefined their business from data processing to the new technologies of computer science and got on computers and software like wrinkles on a cheap suit.

On the other hand, life insurance companies have lost considerable ground to mutual funds and pension funds. At one time, they had access to the largest inventory of financial customers in the country and a virtual monopoly on their money. When inflation changed people's attitude toward life insurance and savings, the insurance companies had the resources, marketing, and financial expertise to retain customers. What they lacked was the ability to see the changes in the market.

Look at the illustration in the margin. It appears to be a static design. However, if you move the book in circles, spokes will appear and rotate within the design. If you make a copy of the design and move it in circles near the illustration in the book, spokes will appear and rotate in both.

Once you knew how to look for the motion, you saw it. It is the same with business and markets. They may appear to be static, but changes are inevitably occurring. Once you know to look for the changes, you'll see them.

BLUEPRINT

1. *Ask "What is our business?" and "What should our business be?"* These questions focus your attention on where to look for new ideas.

2. *Define and organize your business according to* products or services, markets, functions, and technologies. For instance, the key descriptors for a business book publisher would be:
   Products or services: Books.
   Markets: Books for the business professional.
   Functions: Books that provide business information.
   Technologies: Books based on the latest printing technologies.

3. *Under each variable, list the key words for the business:* Key words describe the products or services, markets, functions, and technologies in your industry.

A key word index for the business book publisher would be:

PRODUCTS | FUNCTIONS | MARKETS
hardback books | information | libraries
softback books | entertainment | bookstores
floppy disks | education | universities
cassettes | training | industry
electronic networks | resource | military

TECHNOLOGIES | SERVICES
print | professional discounts
electronic | book clubs
audio | newsletters
modular | seminars
video | information services

4. *Mix and match* your products, markets, functions, services, and technologies in various ways to explore new ideas.

A business book publisher might connect the following key words to create a new idea: cassettes, training, industry, audio, and seminars.

The idea: Produce audio cassettes about sales training. The cassettes would be based on the publisher's backlist of books on selling and would be sold directly to corporations. The publisher would provide sales training seminars by the authors as part of the package.

Or, connect electronic networks, information, resource, print, and information services to produce another idea.

The idea: An electronic data bank containing all the information from the publisher's backlist business books. The information would be sold as a business resource by way of a computer information network for businesses. Printed reports could also be purchased.

Close your right eye, stare at the X, and move the book back and forth about twelve inches from your eye until you find the point at which the break in the line magically disappears.

You are experiencing how your brain fills in missing information, trying to make some sense out of what it sees. Similarly, when you mix and match the key words for your business, your brain will fill in the missing information and create new ideas.

Consider what happened with the Prudential Home Company. One of the many things that buried savings and loan institutions was mortgage lending. Ten years ago, mortgage lending was dominated by the local savings and loan—a drab brick building on Main Street where an applicant could fill out forms between 9 A.M. and 3 P.M. In 1982, the Prudential Home Company asked the obvious: "What should our business be?" and came up with these key words.

Key Word Index

PRODUCTS	FUNCTIONS	MARKETS
mortgages	assumable	mortgage brokers
	shared appreciation	corporations
	renegotiated rate	real estate agents
	wraparound	other third parties
	bartering	

TECHNOLOGIES	SERVICES
telephone	24-hour
fax	speed
computers	profitability by pricing
electronic mail	control
electronic banking	processing

They mixed and matched the key words and filled in the blanks to arrive at the answer: The mortgage business should be selling convenience, speed, and personal attention, and protecting profitability through pricing.

They created a service that does business only by toll-free telephone lines, fax machines, and modem. They have become famous for speedy delivery, courteous service, and rigorous controls. Dealing exclusively through third parties—corporations, mortgage brokers, and real estate agents—they have created a mortgage company with no offices and whose speed of delivery is legendary.

In 1986, the service's business came almost entirely from corporations helping employees get mortgages. By the end of 1988, more than half of its

business came from mortgage brokers who match home buyers with mortgage lenders. When the mortgage business flattens out, Prudential plans to rent its entire processing service—from taking phone calls to closing the loan—to other lenders.

While other companies were devastated by rapid interest rate changes, Prudential thrived and has become the fastest-growing mortgage broker in the U.S. They constantly look at the key words in their business: the markets, products, functions, technologies, and services.

As a testament to their success, witness the following story from the chief executive, Marvin Moskowitz: "One of my favorite responses from customers came from an American businessman returning to Chicago from Japan. He said very flattering things about how our courteous service and speedy approval made it the smoothest house closing in his experience. What really impressed him was the fact that he had done the whole thing, application through closing, by telephone from Tokyo."

SUMMARY

An essential step in deciding the nature of your business is a systematic analysis and combination of the key words that describe existing products, services, markets, functions, marketing, and technologies. Are they still viable? Will they remain viable? What can be connected to produce a new idea?

Think of your business as a pot with two handles. One handle represents the nature of your business today, the other represents what your business will be in the future. To hold the pot steady, you have to grasp both handles by asking: "What is the nature of my business?" and "What should my business be?"

FUTURE FRUIT

> "In peace prepare for war, in war
> prepare for peace."
>
> **SUN TZU**

One thing is certain: We are all traveling toward the future at sixty minutes per hour, no matter who we are or what we do, and we are all going to arrive there no matter what. The first scratch on a new car is a stinging little reminder of the inevitability of a coming future. What is the future of your business? How can one prepare for it?

All human experience is expansive and omnidirectional, including the future. Because the future is not linear, you cannot prepare for it with one single plan. To harvest profits in the future, you should have several alternative plans based on improbable as well as probable future events. Think of future profits as future fruit. Having only one scenario is like planting one strawberry instead of a whole field of possible strawberries. Scenarios, like strawberries, may spoil. If you have only one scenario and it spoils, you have a problem.

In 1973, the world was hit by an oil shortage and a sudden rise in prices. Oil companies were caught with their pants down—except The Royal Dutch Shell company. They had realized that improbable events can take place without warning, and that such events demand swift and sure management, ideas, and decisions. They had prepared several different future scenarios, from "boom or bust" to "constrained growth," to address any economic eventuality.

A period of constrained growth did, in fact, follow the oil shortage, and their "constrained growth" scenario positioned The Royal Dutch Shell company to exploit the shortage. The Royal Dutch Shell company grew from number eight to number two during the 1970s by taking quick advantage of unexpected opportunities.

Exxon, by contrast, looked like a horse on ice after the oil spill in Alaska. Exxon, the state of Alaska, and the U.S. Coast Guard had only one scenario for a possible oil spill, and it was totally inadequate. When the Exxon *Valdez* went aground in Prince William Sound in March of 1989, it caused the largest oil spill in U.S. history. Exxon, the state, and the federal government were paralyzed for two days, as oil spilled into the sound from the ruptured hull. Their plan did not consider a spill of that magnitude, the utilization of personnel to handle such a spill, a breakdown in communications between the state and the federal government, or the possibility of not being allowed to use certain chemicals to disperse the oil.

In the end, the Exxon *Valdez* became a tragic symbol of the consequences that are suffered when companies and governments bet on one future scenario and have only one plan. Exxon's strawberry spoiled.

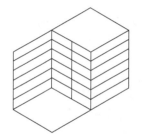

It is one of the strange facts of experience that when we try to think into the future, our thoughts also jump backward. Our mind seems to behave like the white diamonds in the above figure. The white diamonds alternately jump in and out so that either the top right or bottom left can be seen as closer to you.

It may well be that nature has some fundamental law by which opening up the future opens up the past to an equal degree. When you think of your death, for example, you automatically think about how you lived your life.

When you think into the future, your forward-looking and backward-looking thinking combine like two twists of rope, and twine inextricably around each other. Therefore, when you think about the future of your business, you also force yourself to think about what is happening in your business now and what has happened in the past.

BLUEPRINT

The procedures for preparing for the future are:

1. *Identify a particular problem in your business.*
2. *State a particular decision that has to be made.*
3. *Identify the forces (economic, technological, product lines, competition, and so on) that have an impact on the decision.*
4. *Build four or five future scenarios based on the principal forces.* Use all the available information and develop scenarios that will give you as many different and plausible possibilities as a pinball in play.
5. *Develop the scenarios into stories or narratives* by varying the forces that impact the decision. Change the forces (interest rates escalate, a key performer quits, need for your product or service disappears, etc.) and combine them into different patterns to describe the possible consequences of your decision over the next five years.
6. *Search for business opportunities within each scenario.* Then explore the links between opportunities across the range of your scenarios, and actively search for new ideas.

Suppose you are worried about future competitive trends in your business.

1. The problem is "What competitive trends are developing in terms of competitors, technology, and pricing?"
2. A particular decision that has to be made is one of pricing.
3. The forces that have an impact on pricing are profits, return on investment, cash flow, capitalization structure, competition's pricing, and so on.
4. You can now build four or five different, plausible scenarios around the forces you have identified.
   Scenario 1. Nothing changes. Everything remains the way it is today.
   Scenario 2. Your major competitor reduces prices by 25 percent.
   Scenario 3. A major technological breakthrough prices out your major product line.

Scenario 4. The country is hit by a deep recession and customers postpone purchasing indefinitely.

Scenario 5. The economy heats up and inflation drives interest rates up to 15 percent.

Each of these scenarios points to different actions you might take, and different business opportunities.

What future scenarios might a gasoline-service station owner develop? One might be: A major technological breakthrough makes gasoline obsolete.

Two very real possibilities are methanol and natural gas. Methanol is getting good PR as clean fuel, but its corrosive and toxic qualities require special handling. What if the handling problem is solved and methanol replaces gasoline? Or, consider natural gas which is clean, plentiful, and politically popular and is being used in Holland. So far, compressing natural gas is a cumbersome process, but what if someone solves this problem?

How can you position yourself now to take advantage of new opportunities which alternative fuels will bring? One thing you could do today is install a few methanol pumps for motorists who are willing to handle it and to make more frequent fill-ups.

Methanol will probably require larger automobile gas tanks. Another probable future opportunity will be in the design of the new tanks. Consider getting involved in the design and manufacture of methanol gasoline tanks for automobiles.

Another service station scenario could be predicted upon new technology that makes gasoline more clean-burning and cheap.

The problems with a cheap, clean-burning gasoline become pricing, competition, and service. To position yourself now to exploit future opportunities in this scenario, you could:

- Stress service. Install a car wash and provide free washes with fill-ups. Once they are built, car washes cost operators about 15 cents per car. Experts say washes can pump up gas sales by 25 percent.
- Provide an unusual service, such as hair cuts.
- Make your stations into "pit stops." This would appeal to harried commuters. You service the car and bring them their coffee, juice, cigarettes, and morning paper while they wait. You could also have a drive-by window where people who don't need gas can drive up and get coffee, a paper, or whatever.

Creating future scenarios pushes you to think about possible futures which, in turn, pushes you to generate ideas that will work now and give you the edge over your competition. You're thinking about getting into alternative fuels or the automobile design business, adding car washes, barber shops, and pit stops, while your competitor is still pondering whether to use air dryers or paper towels in his washroom.

Observe your reactions as you look at the figure in the margin.

Most probably, you immediately recognized the global letter (H), and hesitated a fraction of a second before you identified the local letter (S) that makes up the H. This is because processing the global letter interfered with processing the local one. This is the way we normally think. We go from the global to the local, and when we are even slightly surprised, we hesitate.

It is the same with the future. You may have some global notion of what the future may hold, but if you are surprised at what happens at the local level you may be paralyzed into inaction as you try to process the possibilities. You need specific scenarios which will enable you to deal with the local possibilities immediately. This is why many people who find themselves fired or laid off are unable to cope for a period of months. They were aware of the global possibility of losing a job and yet made no local plans about how to survive.

Henry Ford foresaw the global notion of an America on wheels. Still, the Ford Corporation failed to prepare scenarios for the future consequences, threats, and opportunities of this scenario. Consequently, the Ford Company was paralyzed for a number of years as they tried to process what had happened to their market. What would have happened if Ford had designed fuel-efficient autos or concentrated on quality enhancement before the Japanese and Germans?

In times of good business, scenarios enable you to prepare for the bad; and when business is lean, they help you prepare for the good.

Consider the case of tanning products and booths. Publicity about tanning's negative effects is becoming more and more strident. It's possible that at some point an aggressive Surgeon General may outlaw tanning booths and people in the tanning business will need something to replace their present products.

One tanning booth manufacturer working with this scenario put all their investment money into developing alternative tanning products. Their research produced a brand new product that will hit the market soon. *The idea:* A safe pill that can tan people overnight. People will look tan and healthy without any ill effects. By preparing for the worst, they invented a product that could be a breakthrough for safe tans.

The more possible futures you foresee, the more options you can create;

```
S         S
S         S
S         S
S  S  S   S
S         S
S         S
S         S
```

the more options you have, the greater your chances of finding the unexpected opportunity.

Summary

In 1888, Henry Heinz bet everything he had on a single future scenario and bought the entire cucumber crop from a 600-acre farm. A year later, he was bankrupt. "Bankruptcy changes the way a man views the future," he said. Within a few years, he was back in business. This time Heinz was a full-fledged futurist with "57 Varieties," several different scenarios, and strategies for his products in good times and bad.

Heinz took his "bracketed sets of opportunities" from his future scenarios and became one of the first to endorse the federal Pure Food and Drug Act, an unpopular stance in the food industry at the time. He also developed a model factory in an era when sweatshops were the norm. His workers enjoyed private lockers, a library, piano music, their own swimming pool, free medical care, and free manicures daily. Management from around the world studied his factory, including a delegation from Japan who signed the guest book in 1901.

If you do not plan for the future, you may end up like the farmer who overfarmed his land to the point that he couldn't even raise his voice on it.

Group C

These techniques reorganize information in ways that help you break away from the most obvious and reasonable perspectives. An obvious rearrangement of information is often too closely related to old, familiar patterns to provoke a big idea. The more dramatic your change of perspective, the greater your chance for an original insight or breakthrough idea.

Think about siphoning water from a bucket. You start by doing the unnatural and unexpected—sucking water *upwards* into a tube. Yet, once the water reaches a certain point in the tube, the siphon effect takes over and the water flows naturally out of the bucket. In the same way, a seemingly unnatural use of information can produce a perfectly natural idea.

BRUTETHINK

Technique: Random stimulation.
Profile: Forces a connection between two dissimilar concepts to create a new idea.

HALL OF FAME

Technique: Forced connection.
Profile: Produces ideas and insights by creating a relationship between your challenge and the words and thoughts of the world's great thinkers.

CIRCLE OF OPPORTUNITY

Technique: Forced connection.
Profile: Generates ideas by forcing a connective link between common attributes and your challenge.

IDEATOONS

Technique: Pattern language.
Profile: A way to get ideas by using abstract symbols instead of words.

CLEVER TREVOR

Technique: Talk to a stranger.
Profile: How to get ideas by increasing the number and kind of people you talk to about your challenges.

BRUTETHINK

"To foresee a victory which the ordinary man
can foresee is not the acme of skill."

SUN TZU

The pattern below appears to be a grid, but it is not. None of the lines touch each other, yet we see the empty spaces as circles or squares hiding the grid intersections. We connect the illusory figures to create a street-like effect out of empty spaces.

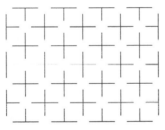

In order to get original ideas, you will always need a way to create new sets of patterns in your mind. One way to do this is to force yourself to see relationships between dissimilar things. When you can do this, you will see ideas where none existed before.

We all see relationships between those objects that we've been taught are related, such as chair and table, ham and eggs, bread and butter, brother and sister, teacher and student, work and money, and so on. In traditional thinking, we put things together because there is a reason to put them together.

In the world of art, however, it is common to put things together which have no obvious connection; the random juxtaposition of unrelated objects provokes new ideas. For example, a modern painting might portray a garbage truck with a sunset painted on it. From the juxtaposition come ideas of func-

tion, durability, and mundaneness contrasting with beauty and nature. One observer might feel the need to reexamine routine objects in his life for beauty, while another might look for more function in nature. It is not uncommon for an artist to come up with a unique pattern which scientists later find in nature.

Brutethink lets you learn from relationships that might not occur spontaneously by pairing two things that have nothing in common and seeing what emerges. Trying to define the process is a little difficult, somewhat like trying to bite your own teeth. What would happen, for example, if you paired rectangular black-and-white tiles with parallel lines?

Combining these two elements creates the famous "cafe wall" illusion. The tiles seem to be wedge-shaped, but the lines are in fact parallel, and the tiles are perfectly rectangular.

One breakthrough idea reached by this method is distortion-free glass.

Alastair Pilkington, production chief of the glassmaking firm of Pilkington Brothers, Ltd., had been working for years on developing a way to rid glass of distortion. At the time, the best technique was to pass molten glass through rollers and then polish away the imperfections, which was costly and not very effective. Glass experts thought the solution lay in developing superior grinders and polishers.

One foggy October evening, Pilkington was washing dishes in his home in northwest England. His mind clear and free, he daydreamed as he watched a bar of Ivory soap float in the greasy water. He visualized glass floating like a bar of soap, and suddenly conceived of an idea that revolutionized the five-thousand-year-old glass industry.

He made a connection between two dissimilar concepts—floating soap and distortions in glass—and invented float glass. In this process, the glass is made in an oven floating in a tub of molten tin. The glass cools and hardens before the tin; it is then rolled into a special annealing chamber without any damage to its finish. No grinding or polishing is needed. Distortion-free glass is now produced cheaply and efficiently, because one individual washing dishes saw a connection between a bar of soap and a whole industry.

Forcing connections opens your mind as wide as a village priest's Bible. You will find that as you develop this thinking tool you will become more open to outside influences. Indeed, you will seek out such influences.

One workshop had the challenge of reducing the very high turnover rate for telephone operators on a toll-free 800 line. They selected a word at random—"prison"—and searched for similarities, connections, and associations between "prisons" and "turnover of telephone operators." After generating many novel ideas, the one they adopted and implemented was to use prisoners to handle their 800 calls.

The idea: They test minimum-security and outside trustee inmates, and offer a two-day training course to the best qualified. Graduates can handle responses from TV, radio, catalogs, dealer referrals, and magazine subscriptions on a toll-free line. Thirty percent of their operators are now prisoners, and the results have been spectacular.

The inmates can earn up to $6 an hour, substantially more than prison pay. They are allowed to keep a portion of their earnings for personal use, a portion goes to a victims' restitution program, and the rest is held in a fund until they are released. In addition, they are considered for full-time employment upon release from prison.

A company spokesman says that they would never have come up with this idea without Brutethink.

WHY BRUTETHINK WORKS

In tetherball, a ball is fastened to a slender cord suspended from the top of a pole. Players bat the ball around the pole, attempting to wind its cord around the pole above a certain point. Obviously, a tethered ball on a long string is able to move in many different directions, but it cannot get away from the pole. If you whack at it long enough, eventually you will wind the cord around the pole. This is a closed system. Like tetherball, human thought tends toward a closed system.

The human brain cannot deliberately concentrate on two separate objects or ideas without eventually forming a connection between them. No two inputs can remain separate in your mind no matter how remote they are from each other. Eventually, like the tetherball, you will wind one around the other. The trick is to hold both of them in your attention and to *look* for relationships and connections between the two. Your attention is the restraint that helps make this a closed system. Once you become aware you will routinely see connections between dissimilar things.

Many of these connections will be less than complete. The figures below are easily perceived as a triangle, a face, and a circle, even though none of the figures is complete. The brain tends to fill in the gaps in order to perceive complete forms, and to fill in the missing information to make a relationship whole.

The connections will provide you with new information about your challenge: a different perspective about the problem or perhaps an analogy that has its own line of development.

Imagine your challenge is: "In what ways might I improve my relationship with my manager?" You randomly select the word "pencil." You might think the relationships and connections between your challenge and a pencil are:

1. *Eraser.* We both keep bringing up past failures. We need to erase them.
2. *Shaft.* He gives me too much to handle. I'm getting the shaft in my territory because of office work. I need help.
3. *Yellow.* I don't have the courage to confront him and have a heart-to-heart conversation about my career. Perhaps I could do it informally after work?
4. *Lead.* Get the lead out. His support and follow-up are always late and this is hurting me financially. Can I get support from other areas?
5. *Gold circle.* He doesn't think I'm going after the lucrative accounts. How can I demonstrate my commitment?
6. *Cheap.* Our commission plan is not equal to others in the industry. Should I propose a new plan?
7. *Six sides to a pencil.* The six most important things to work on are: improve communications, have a heart-to-heart about my career, propose new commission plan, prioritize accounts, improve time management, and create new ways to follow-up on accounts.

You can now identify many issues and many ways to respond to the challenge of trying to improve your relationship. A chain of ideas stretches out from the random word to link up with the challenge. Some of the links may be helpful, others not. The purpose of using a random word is to generate a large number of different ideas in a short period of time.

The random word "pencil" is used to get things going, to get your creative juices flowing. The key is to do *something*. Nothing happens until you start thinking. You know that empty feeling that comes from stating a challenge and not being able to produce a single idea. You feel like a dead atheist all dressed up in your best suit with no place to go.

BLUEPRINT

1. *When you are looking for a fresh approach to a challenge, bring in a random word.* The word you bring in must be truly random, and not selected for any relevance to the stated challenge. Random words will spark a fresh association of ideas in your mind. Like pebbles dropped in a pond, they stimulate other associations, some of which may help you to a breakthrough idea.

Random words from unrelated contexts are a rich source of connection-making material. There are several ways to select a random word. Among them are:

- *Soap, Soup, and Sand.* At the end of this chapter is a list of random words—close your eyes and point to one of them with a pencil. Do *not* read the list and select the most likely word for your purposes.

- Retrieve a random word from a dictionary by opening it, by chance, to any page. Make a point of using only one word per challenge per day. Just knowing that you are going to use another word can defeat the effectiveness of this Thinkertoy.

- Use a table of random numbers to select a page in the dictionary, and perhaps the word on the page as well. You can also just make the page and word numbers up off the top of your head.

- You can use any other method so long as you do not deliberately select a word.

The best words are simple and familiar, words you know well enough that it is easy to visualize the objects they represent. *Soap, Soup, and Sand* is an excellent collection, because the words are:

Simple: You have used these words repeatedly throughout most of your life.

Visual: They easily evoke images.

Connection-rich: Each word will trigger other words and images. For example, "soap" might make you think of baths, showers, sinks, public restrooms, bubbles, lard and other ingredients that make up soap, laundry, soap commercials, slipping on a bar of soap, other products that soap manufacturers make, and so on.

2. *Think of a variety of things that are associated with your chosen word.* Suppose you randomly select "bottle." What are the characteristics of a bottle? What does a bottle do? It contains. What can you do with a bottle? Cork it. Fill it. Empty it. Bottles have labels. Bottles are transparent. Bottles are made of glass and plastic. Bottles bring refunds. Bottles are functional and sometimes are aesthetic as well. Beer bottles are packaged in six-packs. You can buy single bottles, packs of bottles, or cartons of bottles.

3. *Force connections.* Make a forced connection between your random word and the challenge you are working on. Suppose your challenge is:

"In what ways might I increase sales this month?" You select "bottle" as your random word. Draw a picture of a bottle and think about the similarities, connections, and associations between "bottles" and "increasing sales."

- Bottles can be filled up. How much are we listening to the customers? Should we devise a program or programs that would allow customers to fill us up with their true needs and desires?

- Six-packs. Can we repackage our goods and services in a new and novel way to differentiate ourselves from all others? Can we make the package part of the product's form?

- Point of purchase. Beverages can be bought singly, in packs, or in cartons. Should we offer different packages for different customer needs?

- Bottles bring refunds. Should we develop a creative financing program that gives rebates for repeat purchases? Should we give rebates when we replace goods or services with newer ones?

- Empty bottles make noise. How much of my work is useful and profit-oriented? Can I develop an index to rate my activities in terms of profit and potential and then discontinue the empty activities?
- Bottles have labels. Should I look for ways to label our goods in such a way that we are easily differentiated from competitors? Labels list ingredients and expiration dates. Should we price our goods and services with a certain time frame to encourage early purchases?
- Empty bottles are sometimes used for holding flowers, or as aesthetic fixtures. Can we develop other uses for our packaging that would add value to our goods? Can the package be made functional? Can we find other uses and markets for our used goods and services?
- Bottles come in various shapes and sizes. Should we develop a greater array of options? Low-end and high-end markets? Different prices for different packages based on customer needs? How many different ways can we reshape our goods and services?
- Bottles are useless when empty. Salespeople continue to work, even when drained of techniques, energy, and ideas. Perhaps some kind of peer jury should examine salespeople once a month to keep them motivated and fresh.
- Bottles break. When a bottle slips from your hand it falls to the floor and breaks. How can we prevent the factory from slipping up on orders and causing lost sales?

4. *List your ideas.* Otherwise, you won't remember them. Not recording your ideas is like sitting in a shower of gold with nothing but a pitchfork.

Allow yourself five minutes for this exercise; this should be ample time. You will find that connections and ideas are still occurring long after your five minutes are up. A good way to practice this technique is to use a random word on some problem for five minutes every day.

Imagine that the CEO of a company is reluctant to make decisions. Other people often can not act until he makes a decision, yet he delays and waffles for days about even minor matters. The challenge is: "In what ways might we get the CEO to make decisions?"

I randomly select the word "rotating spit." I draw a picture of a rotating spit and think of links, relationships, and associations between "spits" and "indecisive CEOs."

The attributes of a rotating spit could be:

1. Active way to cook.
2. Self-basting.
3. Expensive current.
4. Cooks all the time with constant turning.
5. Put items on in a certain order and take them off in a certain order.
6. Cooks different objects.
7. Heat source, timer, and control are all on same unit.
8. Objects being cooked appear and then disappear from sight.

What connections can you make between the challenge and the attributes listed above? What solution would you propose to the challenge of the reluctant CEO?

My proposed solution would incorporate ideas generated by attributes 1, 4, 5, 6, and 8. Proposal: Consider forming two or three panels that represent different areas, such as manufacturing, marketing, and accounting (cooks different objects). The panels would be comprised of people the CEO respects.

The CEO makes a fast initial decision and gives it to the appropriate panel for review. The panel gives their opinion and sends it back to the CEO who finalizes it or changes it (active way to cook; cooks all the time with constant turning; cooks different objects; items put on in a certain order and taken off in a certain order; objects being cooked appear and then disappear from sight).

This encourages fast initial decisions because the panel review minimizes risk to the CEO, encourages fast analysis because people on the panel need a decision in order to act, and engenders fast, final decisions because the panel shares the risk.

In the end, the final idea of having different panels assist the CEO is much like putting the decision on a rotating spit:

1. Active way to make decisions.
2. Decisions being made all the time with constant turning of topics.

3. Decisions are put on in a certain order and taken off in a certain order.
4. Decisions are made on different topics.
5. Topics being decided appear and then disappear from sight.

Ultimately, you will not use most of the connections you come up with, but you can't prejudge which lines of thought will be fruitful—let alone which lines of thought will lead to a big idea, like a wondrously painted Easter egg waiting for someone to part the grass and find it.

Recently, I purchased a stale candy bar from a vending machine. Obviously, people were not patronizing the machine. I selected as my challenge: "In what ways might I improve business for vending machines?"

I randomly selected the word "casino." Among the things the word made me think about were gambling and roulette wheels. These two thoughts merged with my challenge to create a new idea for vending machines.

The idea: A vending machine that would tempt passersby with a roulette-style game. You insert your coin, make your selection, and a roulette wheel starts spinning; if it stops on the lucky number you get your selection free.

Sometimes searching for ideas is like being a mosquito in a nudist colony. You know what you want to do, but don't know where to begin. Forcing connections between random words gives you one starting point, but there are some other useful ways to stimulate the random juxtaposition of ideas.

VERBS AND NOUNS

Play with noun and verb relationships to think up new and useful ideas, goods, and services. For instance, take the sales problem for which we randomly chose the word "bottle." Consider the words bottle and sales as both nouns and verbs: "bottling sales" and "selling bottles." Bottling sales suggests looking for ways to close sales; selling bottles suggests looking at ways beverages are sold and distributed.

PACK RAT

Collect the store ideas like a pack rat. Keep a container (coffee can, shoe box, desk drawer, file folder, or the like) of ideas and idea starters. Collect interesting advertisements, quotes, designs, ideas, questions, cartoons, pictures, doodles, words, and other intriguing items that might trigger additional ideas by association.

When you are looking for a new idea, shake up the container and pick one at random, then see what intriguing connections you can discover between the item and your challenge. You may find a diamond shining in the trash.

MAGAZINES

Randomly pick up a magazine and read one article, no matter how remote its subject is to your challenge. Then contemplate the connections between the article and your challenge; try to generate some new ideas. Any such exercise is extremely valuable in helping you set up and cultivate habits that encourage random input.

SHAPES

Select a shape, such as a circle, and focus on that shape for a day. When you enter a room, pay attention only to objects that are circular, and try to make connections between those objects and your challenge.

Here is another way this can work: Assume I want to open an unusual restaurant. I select the circle as my shape and decide to focus on three circular things: oysters, the shape your mouth makes when you say "Owww," and Dante's circles of Hell.

The idea: A restaurant called "The Cruel Grill." The restaurant could feature a grill where patrons could watch the food being prepared. The menu would feature items such as oysters, which could be placed on a grill while still alive. As they fry, their shells would open and shut, making sounds. Shrimp, lobster, and other shellfish could be broiled alive. You could advertise it as the restaurant that serves cuisine from Hell. Such restaurants are already quite popular in Japan.

SUMMARY

Looking for ideas using Brutethink is like sleeping under a too-short blanket. You pull it up and your toes rebel, you yank it down and your shoulders shiver; but cheerful folks always manage to yank and pull until they get it just right and sleep in comfort. *Your* comfort results from yanking and pulling on dissimilar objects until you come up with new ideas.

SOAP, SOUP, AND SAND

The words that follow are simple, visual, and connection-rich. They are designed to be used with this Thinkertoy for solving challenges.

bench envelope broom radio landlord cashier toast soup soap beer shoe egg
meat cup umbrella hook door window roof lake violin candy gutter
computer paint man glue water bottle neon light shaft prison bag chain
torpedo ladle insect rose fly fossil butter nut twig bird sword motor
monster dog field gun acid stamp beetle sun summer ice dust Bible drum
fog football bridge rope pulley toe woman plow mattress sunset gate clock
rash car road zoo museum painting sand menu index book ashtray lighter
hip mouse poster aisle milk horse tide knot seed weed bruise toilet closet
shirt pocket pipe rubber cancer plane pill ticket tool hammer circle needle
rag smoke referee sky ocean pepper valve triangle thermostat tube octopus
hook magnet spaghetti disco thumbtack tie sink bifocals television
Jell-O eye pot wedding ring wine taxes pig hoe mouse wok gondola
coconut telephone sleet toll notebook dictionary file lobby clouds volcano
suitcase fish lamp library university fulcrum barbecue canister chimney
rotating spit toxic waste coffee ashes groundhog ribcage parking lot lungs speech
math war brunch sailboat mirrors burdock sludge wastebasket watch flag
helmet eye cactus cowboy tavern butterfly cube X-ray money magazine
screwdriver VCR stereo ink ditches razor tea eyedropper actor homeless
queen artist storm Indian snake fox lobster Satan balloon sauce acne crystal
shrimp army beet brick prostitute catsup explosives diamond camel leaf train
lunch meat liquor pilot lipstick caviar perfume gum cheese flame fruit ham
highway lingerie jelly bean bubble choirboy penis pet hair dye eraser bikini
canyon cards button riot jacket film runway flamingo police White House
lava rainforest island sunrise plastic Hindu clay gourmet roast heat limo
campfire fireworks tomato tongue fracture watermelon Christmas politician
quail handball AK-47 donut madman peanut dance song congress arrow
honey bath igloo tub ruler nomad subway mass missing link vein truck
monk dinner label laboratory sandpaper wedge sundial squirrel mustache
organ molar ghetto bag lady ghost athlete herd flute rod constitution
handkerchief key trophy zodiac turkey surf refrigerator dragon turtle seaweed
goulash mud ostrich vine worm planet opera chameleon wart olive map
coupon foam nosebleed mushroom gasoline music recess rain hockey eel
rocket barge trash pyramid dome chapel thunder caterpillars jaguar firefly
wasp moon moss panda stomach brush gland intestine roach exhibition
holocaust ax lamb doorbell marble knot pump umpire shark onion garage
rum attic fireplace deli knapsack circus ant clamp wrench bum software star

crown curb fingerprint guerrilla iodine jam silver microscope nail piston
priest doctor salt mouth horizon griddle candle banjo anteater tent funeral
gear carpet windsurfer champagne salmon underwear diaper lugnut microphone
paperweight griddle rifle paperclip EKG copier desk vibrator earrings shower
podium Scotch hat jet soda stoplight confession roulette spaceship judge
explorer dice electrical outlet nose drain bookmark torch tomb can gold
spear beans sparkplug bat lawnmower pothole bookends fly cufflinks belt tile
piano skyline creek snow biology cow cowboy bandage calendar calculator
cake fence toothbrush rainbow apartment wagon magnifying glass wire dock
rock top cursor tire drawer sock taxi zebra elevator stairs branch ladder bus
toy hair rubber band pond dream pencil steak template compass tattoo
insulation wheat legs bread paper soda insurance pennant chess stew waiter
goose sandwich sneakers chair gutters zipper want ads vest crab lottery rake
soldier disk necklace flashlight monument dam teacher bank China fan
steering wheel silk earthquake supermarket leash teabag noodles theater mast
cabin bone buffalo kite hoop archer hunter ballet shotgun dirt cream skin
spoon swing skates curtain wax hose golf fortune cookie change atlas
phonebook cuffs vacuum courthouse chips blindfold teeth flowers whale
chocolate mantle ball bearings lock terrorist dishwasher laundry toolbox
chopsticks bathrobe conscience chalk pool table jar bracelet satellite boot
helicopter fishing pole rice puddle wind comic roller mat Volkswagen safari
lightning sculpture board keyboard fig pole oceanfront townhouse angel drill
orange tobacco myth journey child eagle costume Heaven brain minnow
society examination Genesis sin shadow cells fetus hand sex fire poem blood
castle psychology Grail symbol globe mow cross intersection parent blueprint
forest wigwam iceberg snail jungle syrup parachute pudding parsley ape
sidewalk vodka suicide maid comb picture frame jeep Rolex mailbox shampoo
pendant rail megaphone skyscraper skyline hubcap carton sugar match
deadbolt steam saucer remote control boxing glove noose jeans aerial crayons
pipe cleaner ribbon pencil sharpener battery wheel baton orchestra suspenders
brassiere tractor candlestick newspaper secretary salesman wallpaper tower
kitchen magnifier garden general eyebrow chapter catalog bonnet butcher
dinette bed locker professor cereal cotton brochure mime elbow medal
fountain fingernail beard student thumb basket purse arch cloak jazz block
screen vase basement logo torso pickle pigeon whip lint meatball tape coffin
meadow cyclone lips watermelon knee swamp furnace bingo weeds paper

studio patch bleach cord pliers magician faucet mason jewels lap sweater
band frost girdle stove hotel nipple telescope RV grandfather clock cruiseship
stage binoculars audience fur juice buffet husband bacteria spirit sauna
Monopoly mold teenager handcuffs Tinkertoys chess scaffold easel flood
cockroach frying pan crewcut Hell miracle palm tree choir frankfurter trivia
crust oasis stream hostage dandruff rib popovers dope frog pilot milkshake
wheelbarrow level aunt pimple pizzeria balcony Communist hedge thesaurus
workshop cheesecake gang shelf celebrity rectum leather snowflake salad
senator bomb airport cornmeal cornstalks manure cur trumpet cone
temperature sauna howitzer rally merchant box willow stick canteen gourd
polyester Stetson minute IRA office wand graph amplifier line bagel beef
floor barn dolphin aircraft carrier submarine reef casino revolution bow
kneecap borscht raincoat dawn steam engine cliff seam tumor zone office
psychology Easter scar dancer hero fear hamburger welfare Vaseline media
laughter principal script contract forecast grid herring warrior occult putter
bush tugboat bonds glove compartment wig deodorizer news display interest
leopard team staple hearing aid expressway breeze postcard beets photograph
scalp cremation network scripture anchor cauliflower pack rat cult dime
robotics engineer tar maple classroom Pope statistician bomber textbook border
sagebrush aluminum shutter safety pin cargo lemon garter mustard seed
symbol logo United Nations grammar fertilizer feast cigar ornament disease
poppy horseradish group strip spinach dividend hospital tank sonar sardine
binding scab detective England dumpling prune poker gravy mulch poetry
nude trial traveler fraction sausage headhunter matchsticks fat rabbit duck
words cartridge dwarf mat shuttle DC-10 bulletin plum check checkers FAA
wildfires bluebells vinyl brakes cavity pornography landfill wages vacation dial
CIA mosquito cherry rattlesnake saxophone auditorium timer dill cork condom
microwave rhinoceros marshmallow scarecrow beam scallop pumpkin plumber
lizard lounge official eggshell Peace Corps fugitive gully Hawaii lantern sulfur
alligator cobra cattails giraffe ranch vampire emerald confederacy cradle
alphabet lettuce reindeer paintbrush dynamite beam supertanker Astrodome
cheetah Olympics trout scissors dune forehead Jerusalem muffler résumé
chuckhole jellyfish liver shield fuel Japan lacrosse parakeet hock excrement
vines

HALL OF FAME

"And therefore only the enlightened sovereign
and the worthy general who are able to use
the most intelligent people as agents are
certain to achieve great things."

SUN TZU

Imagine a man jumping from one boat to another. At the outset, the boats are more or less parallel to one another. As the man jumps from the stern of one boat, it turns and whirls in reaction to his motion. When he lands in the stern of the other boat, it whirls toward the first boat. Rather than going in opposite directions, the boats run into each other.

This is the way your mind works; for every action there is a reaction. When looking for ideas, picture yourself jumping from your challenge to a quotation or great thought. The quotation, like the boat, will turn and crash into your challenge, sparking a new idea.

Hall of Fame helps you gain new insight into your challenges by consulting the world's great minds, both real and fictional. Quotations contain seeds and principles of ideas that can be applied to a variety of challenges, and when you find the seed of one idea you find many ideas.

RESOURCES

To use this Thinkertoy, you'll need quotations. Some suggestions:

- Two of the best reference books are Bartlett's *Familiar Quotations* and Edward's *Dictionary of Thoughts*, but there are countless other reference books containing quotations and thoughts from the world's great thinkers.
- Collect your own quotations and thoughts from books, biographies, the Bible, the Talmud, newspapers, magazines, cartoons, movies, and television. Record and collect any quotation that appeals to you. You can categorize them according to subject, or randomly. Some of my favorites come from the Talmud:

    "He who walks with butter on his head should not walk in the sun."

    "Don't hitch a horse and an ox to the same wagon."

    "One coin in a bottle rattles; the bottle filled with coins makes no noise."

    "Woe to him who makes a door before he has a house or builds a gate and has no yard."

    "If two logs are dry and one is wet, the kindling of the two will kindle the wet one, too."

    "Just as wheat is not without straw, so no dream is without some nonsense."

- Some of my other favorite quotations:

    "Ruling a big country is like cooking small fish."—Lao Tsu

    "Where the telescope ends, the microscope begins. Which of the two has the grander view?"—Victor Hugo

    "There are two ways to spread the light, to be the candle or the mirror that reflects it."—Edith Wharton

    "God is a geometrician."—Plato

    "Handle your tools without mittens; remember that the cat in gloves catches no mice."—Ben Franklin

"The perfection of art is to conceal art."—Quintilian

"Not only strike while the iron is hot, but make it hot by striking."—Oliver Cromwell

"And I must find every changing shape, to find expression."—T. S. Eliot

"When you eliminated the impossible, whatever remains, however improbable, must be the truth."—Arthur Conan Doyle

"Form ever follows function."—Louis Henri Sullivan

BLUEPRINT

1. *Create your personal Hall of Fame.* Select those people, living or dead, real or fictional, who appeal to you for one reason or another. Following are some of the members of my personal Hall of Fame:

Ben Franklin	Sherlock Holmes	Jesus Christ
Bill Moyers	Diogenes	Julius Caesar
Mark Twain	Ralph Waldo Emerson	Plato
Clarence Darrow	Andrew Jackson	William Shakespeare
Rupert Murdock	Sigmund Freud	Aristotle
George Patton	Peter the Great	Robert Frost
John F. Kennedy	Leonardo DaVinci	Eugene O'Neill
Dorothy Parker	Pearl Buck	Aldous Huxley
W. Somerset Maugham	Adlai Stevenson	Sun Tzu
	Albert Schweitzer	Thomas Jefferson
Winston Churchill		

2. *When you have a challenge, consult your Hall of Fame.* Select an adviser and choose a favorite quotation.

3. *Ponder the quotation.* Write down your thoughts, regardless of appropriateness to the challenge. If you think it, write it, and try to use these thoughts to generate more relevant thoughts. The basic rules are:

> Strive for quantity.
> Defer judgment.
> Freewheel.
> Seek to combine and improve your thoughts.

4. *Choose the thought or combination of thoughts that holds the most promise.* Then restate it.

5. *Allow yourself five to ten minutes to come up with new ideas.* If you produce nothing significant, select another quote or go to another adviser. Keep consulting your Hall of Fame until a quote or passage provokes a train of usable ideas.

Suppose my challenge is: "In what ways might I increase my repeat sales?"

I raid my personal Hall of Fame and select Robert Frost to act as my working consultant on the challenge. I look up Robert Frost in Bartlett's *Familiar Quotations* and review various passages, finally selecting:

> "The woods are lovely, dark and deep.
> But I have promises to keep,
> And miles to go before I sleep."

You can review all of Frost and then select one passage, or pick one at random. I chose this one because there seemed to be some link between this passage and my challenge of improving repeat sales.

I record the thoughts and ideas that the quote elicits from me, without censoring. There are no wrong answers. I write whatever comes to mind, and end up with:

- What does the customer see as important? How can I deliver?
- Can I go the extra mile for the customer? Will it make a difference? Will they become loyal purchasers? What can we do?
- Woods are full of trees. Trees are customers. How are trees tended? Cared for? Harvested? What similarities are there between trees and customers? Can I nourish customers daily? Weekly?
- What are the customer's deep and dark desires? Can I discover them?
- Should I work harder? Longer?
- Should I make company promises in writing?
- Should we rewrite our guarantees?
- What can I do so the customer perceives me as honest and hard working?
- Wood comes from trees. Wood builds. In what ways can I build better relationships with customers? More establishment? More service? Problem solving? Provide information?

- Robert Frost made personal appearances. Should we have executives make personal calls? Seminars?
- Trees are pruned. Do I have too many customers? Should I prune the unprofitable accounts so I can devote more time to our profitable ones?

The thought that seems to hold the most promise for me is the insight into building better relationships with customers. I restate it as: "How can I build profitable relationships with customers?"

The resulting ideas for building better customer relationships are:

- Analyze the customer's problems and provide the best and most current product information possible to help them address their problems.
- Entertain customers more with the idea of finding out what's important and what is not to the customer.
- Ask key customers to work for me as consultants.
- Help the customer do more business by supporting their endeavors more. Suggest and initiate marketing programs for key customers.
- Inform them about what their competition is doing. Become a clearinghouse of information about the customer's competition.
- Make sure that salespeople are compatible with their accounts; if not, switch accounts to ensure compatibility between salespeople and customers.
- Give loyal customers preferential treatment. Larger discounts, a special service line, guaranteed response time, better credit terms, and so on.

Ideas that come from the words and thoughts of others often come through a new route in the imagination by a new and express train of associations.

For years, I was bothered by the ugly speakers that came with my stereo. Finally, I decided to do something about it. I formulated my challenge: "In what ways might I improve the appearance of my speakers?"

I selected Henry David Thoreau for my advisor, looked up Thoreau in *Bartlett's*, and randomly selected:

> "I am a parcel of vain strivings tied
> by a chance band together."

I free-associated from this thought, writing down everything that came to mind. Two of the ideas were significant:

- "Band together"—combine speakers with some other item or items.
- "Vain striving"—make speakers something aesthetic.

I restated the challenge to: "In what ways might I combine my speakers with an aesthetic object?"

I hired a designer to disguise my speakers as ceramic vases. She was so intrigued with my idea that she started a new business that disguises speakers in a variety of aesthetic objects.

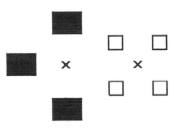

Quotations will give you a new perspective on your challenge. For a graphic demonstration of the difference perspective can make, cover the white squares above and focus on the X next to the black rectangle for thirty seconds. Then, look at the X in the center of the white squares. The vertical distance between the left-hand pair of squares will now appear greater than that between the right-hand pair.

By concentrating on the black, you changed your perspective and created movement of the left-hand pair of squares. When you concentrate on a quotation, your perspective on your challenge will be changed, which will move your imagination to think of new things.

An inventor read about an elderly woman who was so desperate to take her arthritis medicine that, unable to get the child-resistant cap off, she chewed through the bottom of the plastic bottle. He formulated the challenge: "In what ways might I make drug caps more accessible to older people?"

He reached into his box of quotations for something to stir his imagination and pulled out:

"It is always good when a man has two irons in the fire."—Francis Beaumont

His significant thought centered on "two irons." A drug bottle has two tops, the safety cap and the regular cap. The number "two" also provoked him to look for solutions that were not part of the bottle. The bottle + a tool = a solution.

The idea: He developed a pliers-like tool that can cut through or pull off the safety cap mechanism, leaving only the regular cap underneath.

A dead coal can be rekindled when a live coal is placed next to it. When your creative fire has gone out, place a quotation or great thought in your mind to rekindle it. For variety, you may wish to try another way of consulting advisors: Create your own personal, imaginary Board of Directors.

BOARD OF DIRECTORS

The Board of Directors is a fantasy board of powerhouse business leaders and innovators who will assist you in overcoming your business challenges. Imagine having at your disposal the experience, wisdom, and know-how of Thomas Edison, Douglas MacArthur, Alfred Sloan Jr., Lee Iacocca, Thomas Watson, John D. Rockefeller, Bernard Baruch, Sam Walton, Andrew Carnegie, J. P. Morgan, Henry Ford, Donald Trump, Ted Turner, or whomever you admire most, living or dead.

BLUEPRINT

1. *Select the three to five business movers and shakers, living or dead, whom you admire most.*

2. *Get photographs of your Board (these could be photocopied from magazines),* and pin them on your wall in a prominent spot. These photographs will constantly remind you of the talent at your disposal.

3. *Research your heroes:* Hit the library, read their biographies and autobiographies, read what their critics say about them; in short, read everything about your heroes that you can get your hands on.

4. *Take notes on your favorite passages,* perhaps about obstacles and how they overcame them, or anything that strikes you as relevant and interesting. Pay particular attention to

the creative techniques they employed to solve problems, their secrets, what made them stand out, what made them extraordinary, and so on. Keep a separate file on each hero.

5. *When you have a challenge, consult the members of your board and imagine how they would solve it.* How would Henry Ford resolve a labor problem? Can you think of the ways Thomas Edison would suggest to look for new products or services? How could you use Thomas Watson's sales techniques?

CONSULTING THE BOARD

The sales manager of a tire company was concerned about flat sales. His challenge was: "In what ways might we improve tire sales?" He consulted his file on super salesman Thomas Watson. Watson's history inspired him to consider ideas about better motivating *all* employees to sell, not just salespeople. Watson's question became his: "How can I get the people to put their heart into the business and the business into their heart?" Turning to his next adviser, David Packard, he noted the quote "by having overall objectives that are clearly stated and agreed to." He also became intrigued by the entrepreneurial atmosphere Packard created at Hewlitt-Packard. Now, in addition to motivation, he considered the entrepreneurial spirit and agreed-to objectives.

His challenge became: "In what ways might we clearly state objectives that everyone agrees to; objectives that will foster an entrepreneurial attitude and will motivate all employees to participate in selling tires?"

The idea: The objective everyone agreed to was for all employees to participate in selling tires. Our sales manager asked each employee to chip in one dollar a week to finance promoting the tires with shopping mall displays and cards left on windshields. This small contribution gave employees a sense of ownership (entrepreneurial attitude). To get the employees excited and give them a new sense of purpose (motivation), he exhorted them with speeches, songs, and slogans (such as "We make them, we can sell them"). He asked all employees to sponsor and participate in a tire-selling campaign.

SUMMARY

"As is your sort of mind,
So is your sort of search; you'll find
What you desire."

Robert Browning

Have someone hold up a newspaper just far enough away that you cannot read the headline. Ask the person to tell you what the headline says. As soon as they do, you will actually be able to read it. This is known as the newspaper headline illusion, and it is based on expectation. You read the headline because you *think* you can read the headline because you *expect* to read it.

If you expect to find ideas in the thoughts and words of others, you will believe you can, and you will.

CHAPTER NINETEEN

CIRCLE OF OPPORTUNITY

"The flavors are only five in number
but their blends are so various that
one cannot taste them all."

SUN TZU

Landing a plane is a delicate, dangerous operation requiring exact timing, so air traffic controllers only land one or two airplanes at a time. If traffic is heavy, inbound flights "stack up" above the airport, waiting for clearance. Getting ideas can be delicate as well. Circle of Opportunity randomly isolates one or two attributes of your challenge for comprehensive consideration—all the other attributes stay "stacked up," allowing you to comprehend or "land" a new idea.

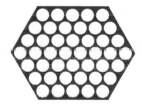

If you concentrate long enough on the figure, the circles will begin to appear hexagonal. Prolonged viewing also causes triangular, hexagonal, and rhomboid groupings of the circles to emerge.

By using selective concentration, you allow your brain to process the circles into a variety of new and different shapes, assigning them new meanings.

Concentrated study of one or two randomly selected attributes will allow your brain to process existing information into new relationships and meanings, which leads to original ideas and insights.

BLUEPRINT

To play Circle of Opportunity, you need a pair of dice.

1. *State the challenge you want to solve.*
2. *Draw a circle and number it like a clock (1 through 12).*
3. *Select any twelve common attributes,* or choose twelve attributes specific to your challenge. (Think of attributes

as the various aspects of a subject.) Write the attributes next to the numbers on your circle.

Common attributes include substance, structure, color, shape, texture, sound, taste, odor, space, and density; marketing, selling, manufacturing, function, and time; responsibilities, politics, and taboos.

4. *Throw one die to choose the first attribute to focus on.*

5. *Throw both dice to choose the second attribute.*

6. *Consider the attributes both separately and combined.* Free-associate about the individual attributes and the combination.

Free-associating is a great way to release creative energy. Start with your first idea about the attribute and keep making connections until you trigger an idea or the beginning of a line of speculation. Free-associating should feel like driving a car around a long, gentle curve until you arrive at something worthwhile. In the figure below, the attribute "yellow" spreads into a number of associations.

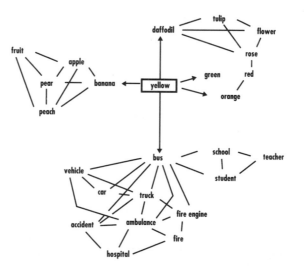

The spread of association resembles what happens when you drop a stone into a pool of still water. The magnitude of the disturbance depends upon the size of the stone and the amount of time elapsed since the rock entered the water. The spread of associations depends upon the strength of the initial attribute, and the amount of time since you did the exercise. When the links are strong, the associations will spread far and fast; when the links are weak, the spread will be slow and restricted.

Write down the associations as they occur to you.

7. *Search for a link between your associations and your challenge.* Ask yourself:

- What associations can I make?
- What do the associations remind me of?
- What analogies can I make from the associations?
- What are the relationships between the associations and the challenge?
- Any new insights?

An advertising agency wanted to create a novel promotional campaign for an airline. They drew up this Circle of Opportunity:

The creative director threw the dice and got 4 (green) for the first attribute and 9 (mobile) for the second.

She free-associated the following thoughts: green lawns, green eyes, green emeralds, travel, tourists, in transit, green "flash" at sunset in the Florida Keys, peas, green islands in the sun, money, green apples, and several others.

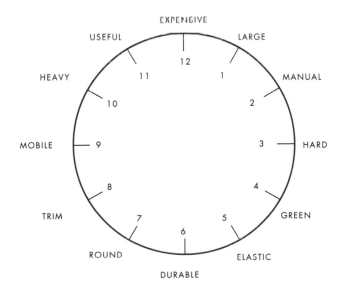

She combined green eyes, travel, and tourists to produce the idea for the campaign.

The idea: People with green eyes get 50 percent off their fare on vacation flights to the Caribbean. The airline, hoping there aren't that many green-eyed people, plans to offer the eye-catching promotion for one year.

When you find an idea using the circle, it's like finding one of those tiny, exclusive French restaurants that have no sign. You find it almost by instinct.

A retailer looking for new ways to make money at his airport gift shop tried the Circle and rolled "round" and "elastic." He free-associated and originated a novel way to make money. He developed a simulated golf game in which players hit golf balls into an elastic net as a diversion for travelers who are delayed or stuck.

Let's construct another Circle of Opportunity with a different set of common attributes. Imagine that we are trying to come up with a new package design for a product. Instead of randomly selecting attributes, this time we'll use attributes that pertain to packaging: inexpensive, loud, rectangle, light, selling, exotic, blue, strong, words, porous, sharp, and conservative. Our circle would look like this.

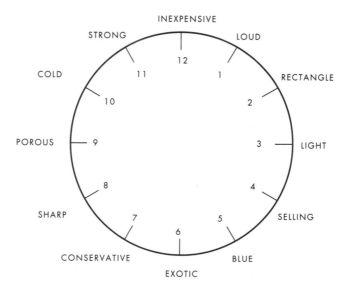

I toss the dice and get 6 (exotic) for the first attribute and 4 (selling) for the second. When I consider "exotic" and "selling" separately and combined, the associations I call up are tropical shirts, tropical islands, exotic music, quality photos of exotic locations, selling exotic things, selling my product, selling the package to the company, selling the package, selling packaging, selling exotic packaging, selling something exotically packaged, and so on. I take the material that I conjured up and, in spite of its seeming irrelevance to my stated challenge, look for ideas.

Trying several different ideas, I settle on selling packages. At first I thought of selling my idea for packaging a product to the manufacturer. Then I thought about selling exotic packaging services. And then it occurred to me: Packaging is a statement, so why not make it your own? Why not just sell packaging?

The idea: Many people tape music for their friends. Produce an audio cassette cover kit so people can package the audio tapes as gifts. The kit would contain everything to customize tapes, such as high-quality photos of exotic places with adhesive backing, a mailing envelope for sending it to a friend, and press-on lettering.

SUMMARY

The Circle leads you to explore associations and links that would not ordinarily be brought to bear on your challenge. It increases your probability of perceiving the challenge in a new way. Like mangrove trees that make their own soil, you make new ideas from within a closed circle of common attributes.

CHAPTER TWENTY

IDEATOONS

"Therefore, when I have won a victory I do not
repeat my tactics but rearrange them to
circumstances in an infinite variety of ways."

SUN TZU

Although written language evolved from pictures and symbols, it is not necessarily more advanced—after all, the latest advance in computer technology is the graphic symbol. Many professions rely on graphic languages: Physicists draw diagrams, executives use charts, football coaches draw Xs and Os, and corporations are known by their trademarks.

Visual and verbal thinking complement one another. As you focus on the figure below, you will notice lines A and B interchanging places. First, A will be in front, then B. Then A will be in front again, and so on.

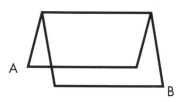

This is how visual and verbal thinking work. What we call verbal thinking is always on the outside. But the visual thinking is always there, on the inside, and when we turn our thinking inside-out, we call that thinking, too.

Consider a rubber glove with a red exterior and green interior. When the red side is out, it fits your left hand. Strip it off, turning it inside out, and it fits the right hand. First the red was visible and the green was invisible, then vice versa.

There is no right or wrong way to wear this glove; both the red and the green are equally functional. In the same way, verbal and visual thinking coexist in your mind. There is no reason to believe that one is better than the other, but we tend to rely too heavily on the verbal. Ideatoons show you how to liberalize your thinking by turning it inside out.

Visual thinking helped physicist Niels Bohr, who found language simply inadequate to describe what goes on inside the atom. Bohr reported that he originally worked out his complex atomic models not with classical mechanical notation but with pictures. Later, he translated the visual to the verbal.

Pattern language is a visual thinking technique. It was originally invented by architects Alexander, Ishikawa, and Silverstein to help create new building designs. The visual, flexible nature of pattern language makes it a useful creative device for seeing new and different relationships between attributes.

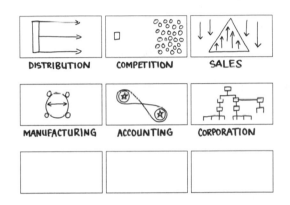

This language consists of a number of abstract visual symbols, which you create to substitute for words. Do not dwell on drawing expert symbols; your drawing skills are not relevant. Remember that one blade of grass of your own raising is worth more than a wheelbarrow of roses from your neighbor's garden. The only consideration is what the graphic representations mean to you.

Some business symbols I have used are illustrated above.

BLUEPRINT

1. *Divide your challenge into attributes.*
2. *Describe each attribute by drawing an abstract graphic symbol.* Each drawing should represent a specific attribute and be on a separate index card. Draw whatever feels right for you. Allow the image of the attribute to emerge in its own way—to state what it wants to say. On the back of the card, write the attribute.

You can make pattern language as simple or as complex as you wish. One possible technique is to use a different color for each parameter of the challenge in addition to the graphic symbols that describe the attributes. For instance, in marketing a product you might have four parameters: packaging, distribution, promotion, and selling. You could draw the appropriate graphics on red cards for packaging, yellow for distribution, blue for marketing, and white for selling.

3. *Place all of the file cards on a table with the graphic symbols facing up.* Group and regroup the symbols randomly into various relationships. Try letting the cards arrange themselves without conscious direction, as if they were telling you where they wanted to be. Mix and match the symbols to provoke ideas.

4. *Look for ideas and thoughts that you can link to your challenge.* Try to force relationships. Try free-associating. Record the most idea-provoking arrangements.

5. *When stalemated, you may want to add other Ideatoons* or even start an entirely new set. A New Hampshire banker who wanted to solve the problem of stolen checks used several different sets of Ideatoons to search for a solution. Finally, the act of using pictures *itself* prompted him to think of the answer.

The idea: He invented a system that lets banks print customer's pictures on their checks.

Many people are trying to save money these days by selling their own homes. Some of their problems are:

- Not being home to show the house to a serious prospect.
- Identifying serious buyers.
- Getting key information about the house to serious prospects.

Let's work on the challenge: "In what ways might we provide a product or service to assist homeowners in getting key information to serious buyers?"

I take the whole, "the process of selling houses," divide it into attributes, and describe each attribute with a symbol.

Grouping, shuffling, and regrouping the cards, I link mailbox (from the one in front of the house), house data (taxes, selling price, points, etc.), commission (which reminded me of coins to use in vending machines), and contract (which reminded me of a roll of paper). This new set of images—a mailbox, things that dispense, house data, and rolls of paper—inspires an idea.

The idea: The "house data box." A box shaped like a mailbox that could be placed in front of the house for sale. In the box would be a roll of tear-off sheets listing information about the house such as asking price, various taxes, how long owned, points, special features, etc. The prospect would drive up, pull out an information sheet, and drive away, and the serious ones would call back for an appointment. This should considerably reduce the number of missed prospects and save homeowners from wasting time saying the same thing over and over. The house data box could be manufactured and sold or rented to homeowners.

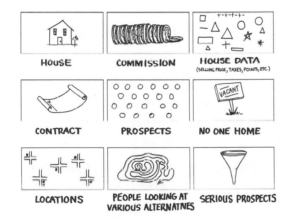

Physically rearranging your cards will invent new relationships and provoke new ideas. Try turning your symbols upside down and sideways to generate new patterns. Juggle the symbols and test the limits of your imagination.

An advertising executive who specialized in small billboard-type ads on buses framed the challenge: "In what ways might I create ads that once seen are never forgotten?"

He separated his challenge into several attributes. Among them were: billboards, high traffic, buses, unique, media, and memory. Using pattern language, he drew the symbols on the following page.

His abstract symbol of a bus reminded him of a cow. Shuffling the cards again and again, he came up with the idea of billboard advertising on cows. He located farms near high-traffic areas, such as airports, and convinced the farmers to rent him space on their cows for two-by-three-foot pieces of oilcloth carrying advertising messages. For an extra fee you can rent a cowbell to attract attention. Also, if the cow gives birth while carrying your sign, you get a sign on the calf for free. Billboards who have babies. What a value. Ads are commonplace, but people who see a billboard on a cow will remember it for the rest of their lives.

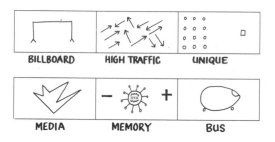

Ideatoons is a device that allows you to express, see, and think about your business challenge in a different and unique way by seasoning your challenge with the sauce of pictures.

A travel agent looking for ways to increase business drew Ideatoons to represent practically everything he could think of that is a component of travel. He drew symbols representing airplanes, travel agencies, travel books, globes, boats, travel videos, travel audio cassettes, desks, chairs, airport lounges, and so on. He grouped and regrouped his cards. Finally, the idea bounced up and hit him.

The idea: He created a new design concept for travel agencies: A travel center with lounges for viewing travel videos, private suites for discussions, and a gift shop selling books, cassettes, and globes. His concept won a design award.

SUMMARY

Creative businesspeople have begun using pattern language to increase their capacity to divide wholes into parts, and regroup the parts into a variety of new patterns. Symbols also help you develop a deeper insight into any situation. One major advertising agency in New York tests pattern language abilities in job applicants with the following exercise:

A delegation of Martians has just landed in Central Park. They do not understand any Earth languages—only graphic symbols. Prepare a short speech composed of graphic symbols to welcome them and tell them just what kind of a place Central Park is.

Take a few minutes to compose such a graphic speech for the fun of it. How did you do?

Sometimes when your imagination has been warmed by verbal techniques––many, too many times—it ends up like coffee that has been microwaved too often. You need to change your techniques and alter the way you use them to keep your imagination fresh-perked. Pictures permit you to look at challenges with a pair of fresh eyes. With fresh eyes, you may see the idea bouncing around on your desk like a chicken trying to avoid becoming Sunday dinner.

CHAPTER TWENTY-ONE

CLEVER TREVOR

"He who exercises no forethought but
makes light of his opponents is sure
to be captured by them."

SUN TZU

My friend Clever Trevor once said: "When a distinguished and successful expert states something is possible, he is almost certainly right. When he states something is impossible, he is very probably wrong." Some famous experts and their opinions:

Charles Duell, director of the U.S. Patent Office, in 1899: "Everything that can be invented has been invented."

Grover Cleveland in 1905: "Sensible and responsible women do not want to vote."

Robert Millikan, Nobel prizewinner in physics, in 1923: "There is no likelihood man can ever tap the power of the atom."

Lord Kelvin, president of Royal Society, in 1895: "Heavier-than-air flying machines are impossible."

The King of Prussia who predicted the failure of railroads because: "No one will pay good money to get from Berlin to Potsdam in one hour when he can ride his horse in one day for free."

Sometimes it seems that the test of a truly brilliant idea is whether or not the "experts" discount it. Often these are the ideas that later seem obvious—even to the experts.

There are as many stories about experts failing to understand new ideas as there are keys on a piano. In 1861, Philip Reis, a German inventor, built an instrument that could transmit music and was very close to transmitting speech. Experts told him there was no need for such an instrument, as "the telegraph is good enough." He discontinued his work, and it was not until fifteen years later that Alexander Graham Bell patented the telephone.

Some social scientists believe that the more expert you become in your field, the more difficult it is to create innovative new ideas—or even obvious ones. This is because becoming an expert means you tend to specialize your thinking. Specializing is like brushing one tooth. You get to know that one tooth extremely well, but you lose the rest of them in the process.

When experts specialize their thinking, they put borders around subjects and search for ideas only within the borders of their expertise. This can be illustrated by the following figure of two gray squares. The square on the right of the shaded border appears brighter than the one on the left.

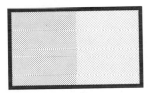

However, if you cover the border between the two squares with a pencil, you will discover that there is no difference; the illusion of brightness is created by the border itself.

This is what happens when experts think. They put borders around subjects and events, creating the illusion of right and wrong classifications where none, in fact, exist. Consequently, they dramatically limit their possibilities by failing to investigate the whole

Nonexperts do not have enough expertise to draw borders. As a result, they look everywhere for ideas. This is why breakthrough ideas are usually found by nonexperts.

This is the principle that prevented the "experts" at Univac from seeing the huge business market for computers. The computer, they said, was designed for science, not business. The same thinking, in 1905, led the German manufacturer of Novocain to wage a furious national campaign to prevent dentists from using it because their company "experts" developed the drug for doctors, not dentists. And the same borders explain why virtually every "delivery expert," including the U.S. Postal Service, unanimously declared Fred Smith's concept for Federal Express unworkable, as people would not pay a fancy price for speed and reliability.

Very much aware of how experts think, Sir Clive Sinclair, the British inventor of the pocket calculator and the flat-screen television, has said that when he enters a new field, he reads "just enough to get a base, just enough to get the idiom" of the field. Anything more and he would start drawing borders.

Clever Trevor's all-time favorite story about experts is about Xerox. Chester Carlson invented xerography in 1938, but more than twenty major U.S. corporations, including IBM and Kodak, showed an "enthusiastic lack of interest" in his system, as Carlson put it. No major corporation or office-supply expert saw a market for xerography. After all, who would buy a copy machine when carbon paper was so cheap and so plentiful?

To get ideas, talk to people (nonexperts) outside your field.

BLUEPRINT

1. *Talk to someone who is outside your field and from an entirely different background.* The more casual the relationship, the more likely he or she will give you a unique perspective. If you're looking for ways to increase sales, ask a priest, teacher, doctor, bartender, or Girl Scout for ideas.

    Frank Perdue (the "it takes a tough man to make a tender chicken" man) was told by the chicken experts that a chicken is a chicken is a chicken—consumers bought by price and price alone. Perdue went to work as a clerk in a supermarket and talked to housewives about chicken. He discovered what the experts and their market research did not—that the color of a chicken and unplucked feathers were more important than price.

    Recently, a gynecologist developed a new birth control device. He perfected the new design in a casual discussion before a dental exam. The dentist came up with the new shape and form almost immediately after the gynecologist described his challenge.

2. *Seek out idea-oriented people.* Surround yourself with people who love ideas and use them in their businesses and lives. They will fire up your imagination. Who is the idea person in the figure on the next page.

    Surround yourself with people:

- Who are creatively alert—people who are always offering alternatives, ideas, and suggestions about anything and everything.

- Who have a keen interest in life and are excited about being alive.
- Are naive about your business, but not stupid or ignorant.
- Who have a great wit and see the absurdity in things.
- Who have different value systems than yours.
- Who travel and pay attention to what they observe.
- Who are voracious readers.

Make a list of friends, neighbors, and relatives who stimulate your creativity and arrange to spend more time with them. Discuss your challenges and ask them for their ideas.

A steel company executive was finding it harder and harder to locate people to work in his plant. He discussed the challenge with his minister, who suggested recruiting at local churches. They formed a network of three local churches to search for qualified parishioners, and the executive has hired every candidate the ministers have sent his way. He's thrilled with the results. "The ministers sift out the best candidates," he observes. "They don't send loafers or drifters, just solid citizens with strong families and work ethic."

3. *Draw out the creativity in strangers you meet casually.* Everyone has at least one idea that might be useful to you. H. J. Lawson got his revolutionary idea for using a chain to power the bicycle from a waiter at his favorite restaurant.

An executive of a major motel chain was conversing casually with his garbage man about the motel business when the garbage man said, "If I were you, I'd sell pizza in my motels. You can't believe the number of pizza boxes we pick up in the trash at motels and hotels." The executive installed pizza ovens in his chain with great results. Once the garbage man said "pizza," the executive realized that they were missing out on a big market.

4. *Listen.* Joseph Kennedy withdrew his money from the stock market before the 1929 crash after listening to numerous strangers (including his bootblack) on the street warn about stock speculation. At the same time, the experts, including leading Yale economist Irving Fisher,

were saying that stocks had hit a "permanently high plateau."

Frieda Caplan listens. She is the chairperson and founder of Frieda's Finest, a celebrated and thriving produce company. In a field dominated by generic products and devoid of new ideas, she's created a brand identity and persuaded millions of Americans to buy fruits and vegetables they never heard of. How? By listening. Her cardinal rule: "Always have an open door; always listen to what anyone has to offer."

She listened one day when a stranger asked if she had ever heard of a fruit called the Chinese gooseberry. She had never seen one, but promised to keep an eye out. Six months later, by sheer coincidence, a broker stopped by and offered a load of Chinese gooseberries. The gooseberries were fuzzy, green, wholly unappealing little fruit.

What the fruit needed was some good PR. She gave the fruit a new name, one suggested by another stranger: Kiwifruit, derived from the kiwi bird of New Zealand. She convinced local restaurants to serve kiwi desserts and developed posters that explained to shoppers what a kiwi was and how it could be used.

By listening to a stranger, Frieda changed American cuisine.

LISTEN UP

Here are two simple tests that allow you to rate yourself as a listener. There are no correct or incorrect answers.

1. Circle the term that best describes you as a listener.

   Superior   Excellent   Above Average   Average

   Below Average   Poor   Terrible

   On a scale of 0–100 (100 = highest), how would you rate yourself as a listener? _____

2. On a scale of 0–100, how do you think the following people would rate you as a listener?

   Your best friend _____

Your boss _____
Business colleague _____
A job subordinate _____
Your spouse _____

Eighty-five percent of all people rate themselves as average or less. Fewer than five percent rate themselves as superior or excellent. On the 0–100 scale, the average rating is 55.

When comparing the listening self-ratings and projected ratings of others, most respondents believe that their best friend would rate them highest as a listener—and that rating would be higher than the one they gave themselves.

People usually think their bosses would also rate them higher than they rated themselves. We tend to listen to our bosses better . . . whether it's out of respect or fear doesn't matter.

The grades for colleague and job subordinate are just about the same as the listeners rate themselves . . . around 55. But when you get to "spouse," something really dramatic happens. The score here is significantly lower than the 55 average. And what's interesting is that the figure goes steadily downhill. Newlyweds tend to rate their spouse at the same high level as their best friend. As the marriage goes on, the ratings fall. So in a household where the couple has been married fifty years, there could be a lot of talk. But maybe nobody is listening.

Following are ten keys to better listening that are the heart of developing better listening habits that could last a lifetime.

TEN KEYS

1. *Find areas of interest.* Ask "what's in it for me?"
2. *Judge content, not delivery.* Skip over a speaker's errors.
3. *Hold your fire.* Don't judge until you've heard everything.
4. *Listen for ideas.* Try to discern the central themes.
5. *Be flexible.* Use four or five different systems to help you remember the content.
6. *Work at listening.* Work hard, keep your body alert.
7. *Resist distractions.* Fight or avoid distractions; tolerate bad habits and know how to concentrate.
8. *Exercise your mind.* Use difficult expository material to keep your brain working.
9. *Keep your mind open.* Interpret color words; do not get hung up on them.

10. *Capitalize on the fact that thought is faster than speech.* Challenge, anticipate, mentally summarize, weigh the evidence, and listen between the lines to tone of voice.

Most people are inefficient listeners. Tests have shown that immediately after listening to a ten-minute oral presentation, the average listener has heard, understood, properly evaluated, and retained approximately half of what was said. Within forty-eight hours, that drops off another 50 percent to a final 25 percent level of effectiveness. In other words, unless you work hard at listening, you will probably only retain one-quarter of what you hear.

SUMMARY

Multiply your ideas by multiplying the number and kind of people you talk to about your challenge.

How would you describe the following figure?

There are so many things in our world that we take for granted, noticing them only when they are brought to our attention. Why, for example, do we only see the figure as three groups of two lines each, rather than six single lines? It is because we have become experts at perceiving nearby elements as a group instead of as a row. We only realize this when it is pointed out that the lines can also be perceived as six single lines in a row.

In much the same way, we take so many things for granted in our fields that we can only notice this state of affairs when it is brought to our attention by someone outside our field.

A salesman for Panasonic hosted a birthday party for his son at which the children all played with sample camcorders. The salesman discussed the merits of the camcorders with some of his son's friends and asked for their suggestions as to how they could be improved. One of his son's friends said: "The camcorders are great, but where can I get one for left handers?" An obvious question, but apparently no one had marketed a camcorder with a viewfinder that swivels to accommodate both right-handed and left-handed people. Panasonic does now. It immediately came out with a camcorder called "The Switch-hitter."

By talking to strangers outside your field, you'll get the kind of creative fiber you can't get from your breakfast cereal.

PART TWO

INTUITIVE
THINKERTOYS

Intuitive Thinkertoys allow you to tap into your unconsciousness and find the ideas that you already have.

Tilt the book slightly, and examine the figure on the previous page under a moderate light. Many people are able to see impressions of light pastel shades of colors, organized in small hexagonal cells at right angles to the diagonal lines. This is called the Luckiesh-Moss figure and was first introduced in 1933. You see the colors. Yet, no matter how hard or long you study it, you just can't explain how it works. No one has been able to explain why the colors appear in this figure.

In the same way that the mysterious colors are contained within the black lines, the answers to all our challenges are within our unconsciousness. We need only to know how to see them.

A person is sitting around minding his own business, and suddenly—flash!—he understands something he didn't understand before. As Einstein put it:

> The supreme task . . . is to arrive at those universal elementary laws from which the cosmos can be built up by pure deduction. There is no logical path to these laws; only intuition resting on sympathetic understanding.

To solve a problem, you have to believe that you already have the answer in your unconscious. It is as if you misplaced your watch somewhere in your house; if you keep searching, you will eventually find it. This is a different perspective from, "Is there a watch anywhere in this house?" The knowledge that the watch is there will lead you in your search to find it. The theory behind intuitive techniques is that at some level you already know the answer to your challenge. Once you make this assumption, you need only know how and where to look for it. This is a different perspective from, "Is there a solution?"

Increasingly, companies and universities are probing for ways to cultivate intuitive skills. In our era of rapid change, intuitive skills are more important than ever. The International Institute for Management in Lausanne, Switzerland, recently studied top managers from the United States, Europe, Japan, and Brazil. According to their findings, successful managers claim to use intuition in most major business decisions. They describe intuition as a flash of brilliance coming from an unknown source.

This section contains intuitive techniques that show you how to take advantage of your right-brain capability to perceive insights and "whole" solutions, all at once, from your unconscious. You should eventually learn to use all the intuitive techniques described in this section. Favoring only one or two techniques is like trying to learn the rules of chess by observing moves made in one small corner of the board.

Profiles

CHILLING OUT

Technique: Relaxation.
Profile: Relaxation techniques designed to clear your mind.

BLUE ROSES

Technique: Intuition.
Profile: Ways to use intuition, and how to develop it.

THE THREE B'S

Technique: Incubation.
Profile: Describes incubation and demonstrates how to use it.

RATTLESNAKES AND ROSES

Technique: Analogies.
Profile: How to use personal, direct, symbolic, and fantasy analogies to originate ideas.

STONE SOUP

Technique: Fantasy questions.
Profile: Coaches you to direct your imagination with fantasy questions and how to use the fantasies to generate ideas.

COLOR BATH

Technique: Creative visualization.
Profile: How to use colors, money, and other objects to invoke desired qualities and energies.

DREAMSCAPE

Technique: Dreams.
Profile: How to capture the ideas in your dreams.

DA VINCI'S TECHNIQUE

Technique: Drawing
Profile: How to use free-hand scribbling, doodling, and drawing to inspire ideas.

DALI'S TECHNIQUE

Technique: Hypnogogic imagery.
Profile: How to originate surrealistic imagery, and how to find the associative link between the images and your challenge.

NOT KANSAS

Technique: Imagery.
Profile: How to direct your imagination with guided imagery scenarios to find ideas in unlikely places.

THE SHADOW

Technique: Psychosynthesis.
Profile: How to create your own spiritual adviser to help you solve your challenges.

THE BOOK OF THE DEAD

Technique: Hieroglyphics.
Profile: How to find ideas in the hieroglyphics from the Egyptian Book of the Dead.

CHAPTER TWENTY-TWO

CHILLING OUT

"He who is prudent and lies in wait for an
enemy who is not will be victorious."

SUN TZU

Stars cannot be seen during the day, because their faint points of light are overwhelmed by the sun. In a similar way, some ideas cannot be discovered, because their faint points of light are overwhelmed by your brain's active beta waves, which are as noisy as a goose eating dominoes.

In the illustration, the problem is to get the beetle inside the box. Resolution seems impossible. However, if you relax, clear your mind, and stare passively at the box for a minute or two, something strange will happen: The problem will solve itself. It sort of turns inside out, and you'll see the beetle inside on the checked floor of the box. You become the medium through which the problem solves itself.

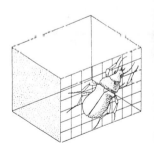

You can become the medium through which *any* problem solves itself by using relaxation and meditation. These techniques produce alpha brain waves that are slower and deeper than beta waves. Alpha waves quiet your mind so you can see the solutions that are already there.

One champion of alpha waves is financier Wayne Silby, founder of the Calvert Group, which today manages billions of dollars in assets. Silby, whose business card reads "Chief Daydreamer," occasionally retreats for inspiration to a sensory deprivation tank where he floats in warm water, sealed off from light and sound. "I went into the tank during a time when government was changing money-market deposit regulations, and I needed to think how to compete with the banks. Floating in the tank, I got the idea of joining them instead. We wound up creating an $800 million program. Often we already have the answers to our problems, but we don't quiet ourselves enough to see the solutions bubbling just below the surface."

Alpha waves are promoted by four simple things:

1. *A quiet environment.* A quiet room or a pleasant, quiet place outdoors.

2. *A specific mental technique.* If you already have a favorite technique for relaxing deeply or entering into a meditative state, practice it and use it frequently. Otherwise, use one of the techniques described in this chapter.

3. *A passive attitude.* Empty your mind. Do not dwell on thoughts as they pass through your consciousness.

4. *A comfortable position.* Select a position that will allow you to remain still for at least fifteen minutes without falling asleep.

RELAXATION TECHNIQUES

TRIPPING IN THE PAST

Recall the time when you were most relaxed and at peace with yourself and the world, in as much detail as possible. For instance, it might be a past vacation where you remember relaxing in the sun. Feel the sun and the sand. Experience the warm breezes. The seagulls. The boats. The more incidental details you remember, the deeper your relaxation will be. The experience might be a tranquil scene in the mountains, a drowsy afternoon in front of the fireplace, a crisp fall evening, or a Key West sunset. The more you practice conjuring up your most pleasant past experience, the more you will strengthen the link between the image and total relaxation.

Affirm the pleasantness you feel every time you conjure up your images. Say, "This, or something better, now manifests for me in totally satisfying and harmonious ways for my good and the good of all concerned." Trip in the past only so long as you find it enjoyable. It could be three minutes or thirty minutes. Repeat it every day, or as often as you can. The more you trip, the more you will imprint the pleasant relaxing experience upon your mind; the stronger the imprint, the more relaxing the trip becomes. With practice, this technique will help you become as cool as the other side of a pillow.

THE JELL-O SYNDROME

This is a deep-muscle relaxation technique.

Get comfortable. The basic technique is to relax your body by relaxing each muscle in turn, from your toes to your scalp. Imagine that as each muscle relaxes the tension flows out of your body. Try to relax each muscle group sequentially without exerting too much conscious effort. Let go a little at a time, stop frowning, let your arms, hands, shoulders, and jaw go. By systematically relaxing your muscle groups you can achieve a state of deep relaxation in which the conscious is subdued and quieted, and that still, small voice from the unconscious can come through.

If you have trouble relaxing your muscles in sequence, imagine that your body is a series of inflated rubber balloons. Two valves open in your feet, and your legs begin to collapse until they are two deflated rubber tires lying flat. Next the valve in your chest is opened, the air escapes, and your entire trunk goes limp. Continue with your arms, neck, and head.

When your body is totally limp, breath deeply and slowly from your stomach. Fill your lungs with air. Breath in, whisper "re-e-e-e-e" (pause), then exhale whispering "la-a-a-a-a-ax." Do this until you feel totally free and relaxed.

A slightly different way to achieve the Jell-O Syndrome also begins with your lying down, as comfortable as possible. Then, systematically tense each muscle group. (The groups are listed in the exercise below). Focus on the tension in the specific muscle group, then relax. Focus on the experience of feeling the tension leave the muscle group.

Tape the following script so you can listen to it as you perform the exercise. Give yourself plenty of reminders to focus on the feelings of tension and letting go. Remember, you tense, pause, and let go.

> Close your eyes. Think of deeply relaxing all of your muscles . . . now clench your fists . . . relax them . . . flex your hands toward your shoulders . . . relax them . . . place your hands on your shoulders . . . flex your biceps . . . now relax your arms by your sides . . . shrug your shoulders . . . frown . . . relax your face . . . close your eyes tightly . . . relax them . . . push your tongue against the roof of your mouth . . . relax . . . press your lips together . . . relax . . . push your head back . . . push your head forward . . . relax your neck . . . arch your back . . . relax . . . suck your stomach in, tensing the muscles . . . relax . . . tense your buttocks . . . relax them . . . flex your feet . . . relax them . . . curl your toes . . . relax them . . .

Now repeat this exercise, letting go of even more tension in each muscle group. Remember, the key to the Jell-O Syndrome is to concentrate on the tension in the muscle group and then to experience the tension leaving your body.

When your muscles are deeply relaxed, breathe from your center. Breathe through your nose, and become aware of your breathing. As you breathe in, whisper the syllable "re." Pause. Breathe out, whispering the syllable "lax." Let the air flow slowly and naturally: r-e-e-e (pause) l-a-a-a-x. Continue for ten to twenty minutes.

When you are totally relaxed, you will sense yourself drifting deeper into another level of peacefulness and spaciousness. Do not worry about whether you are successful in achieving a deep level of relaxation. Be passive and allow relaxation to occur at its own pace. Soon you'll be lying there without a care in the world like a shivering tub of Jell-O.

TRUMAN'S FOXHOLE

President Truman bore up under the stress and strain of being a wartime president better than any previous office-holder. Despite a multitude of problems, the office of the presidency did not age him or exhaust his vitality. When asked by a reporter how he managed, Truman's answer was, "I have a foxhole in my mind." He explained that, just as a soldier has a foxhole for protection, he would retreat to his own mental foxhole, where he allowed nothing to bother him.

You can create your own inner sanctuary, and you can create it any way you want.

Close your eyes and relax as deeply as you can. Visualize yourself in an ideal environment, any place that appeals to you, such as a forest, by the sea, on a mountain, in a meadow, a cave, a foxhole, a desert, or wherever. Create a vivid mental picture of your sanctuary. It might have a house with a fireplace, a grass shack by the ocean, a spaceship orbiting Earth, or just a peaceful place surrounded by a soft light.

This is now your special place, where you can go just by closing your eyes and wishing to be there. Retreat to your own inner sanctuary whenever you wish peace and tranquillity.

Sixteen-year-old Denise Parker is one of the top archers in the world. She creates what she calls her "happiness room," a place to which she withdraws to visualize an upcoming match. She described it this way in a *New York Times* article:

There's stairs leading up to it and these big doors you go through. It has brown wall-to-wall carpeting, a king-sized waterbed, stack stereo, a big-screen TV and a VCR, posters of Tom Cruise and Kirk Cameron on the wall, and a fireplace that's always blazing. That's where I go when a meet's coming up. I drive up to it in a Porsche, go inside, lie down on the waterbed and watch a tape of myself shooting perfect arrows. Later, when I get to the tournament, everything seems familiar. Even at the Olympics, I was calm as I began to shoot.

HOT AIR BALLOON

Close your eyes and breathe deeply and slowly as you count backwards from 10 to 1. Gradually allow yourself to feel deeply relaxed.

Imagine a giant blue hot-air balloon moored in the middle of a lush meadow. Picture it as vividly as you can. Now, picture yourself placing all your worries in the basket. When the compartment is fully loaded, imagine the hot-air balloon being released from its mooring and floating away from you. There is nothing more you need do as the balloon carries your mental baggage into the distance.

LETTING GO

You can catch a monkey by burying a narrow-mouthed jar of nuts in the ground. A monkey comes along, puts his paw into the jar, and grabs a handful of nuts. But the mouth of the jar is too narrow to let him withdraw his clenched fist. The monkey is unwilling to let go of the nuts and so is trapped. You too can be trapped by not letting go—of your beliefs, opinions, worries, and anxieties.

If you are experiencing a mental block of some kind, try this exercise. Imagine that your mental block is physically represented by something you are wearing, such as a ring. Then take off the ring, and you will feel tremendously relieved and relaxed.

WARM STONES

Autogenic training teaches you to move through a series of bodily states that correspond to shifting states of consciousness. For instance, many people find it difficult to think of an abstract notion such as relaxation; they find it easier to think about warmth and heaviness. By thinking of making your hands warm and your limbs heavy, you can induce a state of self-hypnosis that enables you to relax.

Picture yourself lying stretched out on your bed. See yourself lying there with heavy stone legs and arms. See how the mattress sinks down under your heavy, inert weight and the pressure you are exerting on it. The mattress sags close to the floor from the weight. Close your eyes, breathe deeply and relax for a few minutes, then repeat silently: "My hands are warm, my legs and arms are feeling heavy like stone." Feel the warmth creep into your hands. Feel your arms and legs grow heavier. And heavier. And heavier.

AUM

The brain, by its nature, is constantly chattering. When you are striving to become deeply relaxed, stray thoughts may arise to distract you. To quiet the ongoing chatter of consciousness, some Eastern mystics focus on a specific *mantra*, a special sound or word repeated over and over to clear the mind.

"AUM" is a popular mantra that represents to our ears the sound of the energy of the universe, which is manifested in all things. You start in the back of your mouth "ahhhh," and then "oo," you fill the mouth, and "mm" closes the mouth. All vowel sounds are included in the pronunciation. Consonants are regarded as interruptions of the essential vowel sound. All words are fragments of "AUM." AUM is a symbolic sound that puts you in touch with the universe; the AUM of being in the world. It is called the four-element syllable. A-U-M—the fourth syllable is the silence out of which AUM arises. One need only hear the chanting of Tibetan monks chanting AUM to appreciate the meaning of this word.

A Harvard study found that mantras were very useful for reducing hypertension in patients. (They used one-syllable words like "one," "me," "yam," and "oh" to avoid the religious connotations of a traditional mantra.)

An anonymous Catholic monk wrote in the fourteenth century:

Choose one word of one syllable such as "God" or "Love": Choose whichever one you prefer, or if you like, choose another that suits your tastes, provided it is one syllable. And clasp this word tightly in your heart so that it never leaves it no matter what may happen. This word shall be your shield and your spear whether you ride in peace or war. With this word you shall beat upon the cloud and the darkness, which are above you. With this word you shall strike down thoughts of every kind and drive them beneath the cloud of forgetting.

SLEIGHT OF HEAD

Describe the figure in the margin.

If you see an old woman in full profile looking down, a slight change in focus will allow you to see a young woman looking away. (You can see the tip of the old woman's nose as the young woman's chin.) If you first saw the young woman, with a slight change in focus you can see the old one.

With a slight change in focus, you cleared your head of your initial inferences about the figure and changed the nature of the illustration. In the same way, you can clear your head of inferences about a challenge by changing your focus of attention. When you clear your head of inferences, you allow yourself to think in a more free and relaxed way. You do this by pretending to walk away from the problem.

Great ideas sometimes come when you pretend to walk away from your challenge. This technique is called "sleight of head," and it is a favorite of creative consultants for getting a group to clear their minds. While working on a particular problem, the consultant will ask clients to pretend to work on something else.

One consultant took her shoe company clients on a "pretend" excursion—a conscious walk away from the problem. One manager imagined he was on a tropical island walking on the sand in his bare feet. One of the marketing people became intrigued, and the group focused on what people enjoy about walking around without shoes. They decided it was lightness and the ability to pivot. These two attributes led to the design of a highly successful new shoe with an innovative two-piece sole that makes it easier to pivot.

In another group, engineers were wrestling with the challenge of identifying uses for a new semiconducting polymer. The consultant took the engineers on a "pretend" excursion into their favorite hobbies and sports. One of the engineers recounted a tennis game that was decided by a dubious out-of-bounds call. The engineers focused on the problems of making in-bound calls for tennis matches and suddenly came up with an imaginative new use for the polymer.

The idea: A touch-sensitive boundary for tennis courts. They created a wafer-thin material out of the polymer that will ring tennis courts. The material will record precisely where a ball lands. Not even a John McEnroe will be able to dispute the calls that will be made by this material.

SUMMARY

Learning how to chill out takes time. If you're uptight six days a week and you really try to relax on the seventh, then maybe the next six days aren't going to be quite as stressful. These exercises will, with practice, relax you and clear your mind. When that happens, you will begin to think the way a child skips rope, the way a mouse waltzes.

BLUE ROSES

"It is according to the shapes that
I lay plans for victory, but the multitude
does not comprehend this."

SUN TZU

213

In ancient times, an emperor declared that his daughter would marry the first suitor who brought her a blue rose. The emperor's daughter was as wise as she was beautiful and various suitors tried to win her, one with a sapphire rose, another with a dyed rose, and a third with a porcelain tea cup on which a blue rose was painted. One evening, she met a minstrel outside the palace and fell in love. When he returned the next day, he brought a common white rose. The emperor's daughter declared that it was, indeed, a blue rose, and the wedding took place.

The emperor's daughter made her choice by relying upon her intuition. Using intuition means paying attention to your feelings and knowing their accuracy, and how well you apply them. An important assumption when using intuition is that you already know the answer.

George Washington solved his most difficult problems during the Revolutionary War with intuition. He would instruct his orderlies not to let anyone disturb him while he relaxed and intuited decisions. In fact, the founding fathers thought intuition was so important that they tried to remind us of its power on the back of the dollar bill. There is a picture of an unfinished pyramid with an eye above it. The pyramid is not complete until the seeing eye is settled in the capstone position. Or, until the intuitive component of the mind plays a major role in developing ideas or making decisions.

A number popped into Conrad Hilton's head when he was bidding for the Stevens Hotel in Chicago. He offered the number and won the world's largest hotel by $200. A number popped into Henry Heinz's head and that number,

"57," became one of the most successful trademarks of that time, despite the fact that Heinz had many more than 57 fine food products. George Eastman, founder of Eastman Kodak, said that the legendary Kodak trademark "K" came to him out of the blue.

Successful managers have more than a sardine of intuition. Present an intuitive manager with a company's financial report and he or she will make an accurate assessment of the firm's strengths, weaknesses, and future. Present the same manager with a personnel problem and he or she will assess the problem and intuit the solution and/or possible courses of action. Present the same problems to managers with no intuitive skills, and you will most likely get answers scraped out of the dog dishes of business textbooks.

FIVE WAYS MANAGERS USE INTUITION

Harvard business professor Daniel Isenberg studied sixteen senior managers in major corporations. He spent days observing them as they worked, interviewing them, and having them perform various exercises designed to figure out what made them successful.

Isenberg identified five different ways that successful managers use intuition:

1. To help them sense when a problem exists.
2. To rapidly perform well-learned behavior patterns.
3. To synthesize isolated bits of data and experience into an integrated picture.
4. To check on the results of rational analysis. They search until they match their "gut" feeling and their intellect.
5. To bypass in-depth analysis and come up with a quick solution. Charles Merrill of Merrill Lynch once said that if he made decisions fast, he was right 60 percent of the time. If he took time, analyzed a situation and made a decision carefully, he would be right 70 percent of the time. However, the extra 10 percent was seldom worth the time.

One manager at a film company sensed that productivity was down because of low office morale. His gut feeling led him to initiate a sports betting pool. The pool had a tremendous unifying effect on the office workers, bringing everyone from librarians to executives together. They now publish a humorous weekly update on the results, hold an end-of-the-season party, and winners routinely buy colleagues a drink. Morale and work performance have soared. The manager was able to *sense* the problem and to *feel* what would unify the office.

Intuitive people develop superior insight that enables them to perceive whole situations in sudden leaps of logic. John Mihalasky and E. Douglas Dean at the New Jersey Institute of Technology discovered that 80 percent of the CEOs whose profits doubled over a five-year period had above-average intuitive powers.

Consider George Foerstner, founder of Amana Refrigeration, Inc., and the marketing of the microwave. We had the microwave technology from the early 1940s, and many people were aware that it could be used for cooking. Yet, they believed that the consumer market didn't understand or care about microwave cooking. Foerstner didn't give a damn what the experts thought. His gut told him that it could be produced and consumers could be convinced that they need microwaves.

Foerstner demanded a microwave oven shaped like a box with a $500 price ceiling, and he persuaded consumers that they needed it. His intuitive decisions on design, price, and marketing made the microwave oven a household reality.

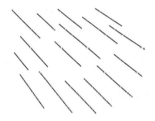

Look at the lines above. All of them originate at a point off the page on your lower right. Turn the book clockwise so that this point is directly in front of you. Tilt the book slightly away from you and close one eye. The lines will magically "pop" straight up from the paper.

Once you know how, you can make the lines pop up from any position. In much the same way, once you know how to use your intuition, answers and insights will pop up in your mind.

BLUEPRINT

The two basic principles of intuition are: It must be *developed*, and it should be incorporated with reason.

1. *It must be developed.* You can not fly like an eagle with the wings of a wren. Strive to be aware of your intuition on a daily basis. How do your intuitive impulses feel? When do they occur? Practice your intuitive skills by making guesses before a situation is fully analyzed.

   To condition your intuitive mind, try asking yourself some "yes" and "no" questions to which you already know the answers. For instance: birthdates, the name of the company where you work, the names of brothers and sisters, and so on. Observe how you get the answers. You may hear a yes or no in your mind, you may *see* a yes or no, or you may see flashes of color (green for yes, and red for no). However your answer comes, concentrate on getting future answers in the same way.

   Do the same with choices. Start by thinking about a choice you have already made, and imagine the options you had when you made the choice. As you think of the choice you have already made, observe the word, phrase, image, or symbol that represents that choice. Concentrate on how you got the answer, and focus on getting future answers in the same way. Continue to re-make choices you have already made, and continue to concentrate on how the response appears. Try making a few simple choices you *haven't* made before.

2. *Combine intuition with reason.* Jonas Salk, the scientist who discovered the polio vaccine, said in an interview:

   > I'm saying we should trust our intuition. I believe that the principles of the universe are revealed to us through intuition. And I think that if we combine our intuition with our reason, we can respond in an evolutionary sound way to our problems. Effective creative conceptualization requires that one incorporate reason and logic, as well as intuition and feeling.

Like a marriage counselor bringing a separated husband and wife back together, these exercises will reintroduce you to your intuitive senses. Some simple ones are:

TELEPHONE CALLS

When the phone rings, before you answer it, ask yourself the following questions:

1. Is the call for you or someone else?
2. Is it a male or female?
3. Is it a routine call? Or is it from someone you haven't heard from in quite a while?
4. Is it long distance or local?

After the call, intuit the answers for the next call and write down the answers by the phone.

WORK

If you're in sales, think about the following before you go out on calls:

1. How many sales will I close today? This week? This month?
2. Select one customer and decide what color he or she will be wearing. Solid or print? Dark or light? What mood will the person be in? Happy or depressed? Will they buy now? Later?
3. Where will you park? Near the business? What street? What is the location in relation to the office?
4. What objections do you feel the customer will raise during your presentation?
5. What will customers buy and what won't they buy?

MAIL

Before the mail arrives, ask yourself:

1. How many pieces of mail will there be? How many bills? How many pieces of junk mail? Personal letters? If personal, happy news or sad? Business mail?
2. Will there be any extraordinary mail such as an announcement that you won a prize?

MEETINGS

Before a meeting, try to predict the mood of other people who will be there. Will they be happy or depressed? How will they be dressed; i.e., what colors,

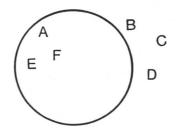

formal or informal, etc.? Who will be positive? Who will be negative? Who will be the best prepared? Intuit the positions of each participant on issues before issues are raised, and the results of the meeting.

Sam Walton, the founder of Wal-Mart, understood how to combine intuition with reason. Sam felt in his gut that one could build a retailing empire by ignoring major cities and offering cut-rate prices to the heartland of America. His intuition told him to bring a down-home spirit to retailing, call his employees associates, treat them like team members, and lead the cheerleading. There isn't a single graduate school of business that teaches this.

Starting with one store in 1962, he now has a 1,300-store empire with revenues in excess of $25 billion. If you had invested $1,000 in this man's intuition in 1970 when he held a public offering, it would be worth more than $500,000 today.

PROBLEM SOLVING

Professor George Turin, of the University of California at Berkeley, states that the components of solving problems with intuition are:

1. The ability to know how to attack a problem without knowing how you know.
2. The ability to relate a problem in one field to seemingly different problems in unrelated fields. The ability to see links, connections, and relationships between ideas and objects.
3. The ability to recognize the crux of a problem.
4. The ability to see in advance a general solution to the problem.
5. The ability to recognize solutions because they feel right. The ability to focus on what *may be* rather than what is.

People who are expert at the intuitive problem-solving approach can rarely provide an accurate account of how they obtained their answers and may be unclear on just what aspect of the problem they focused on.

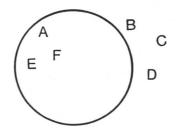

Consider the illustration on the previous page. See if you can determine the system being used to place either inside or outside the circle all the letters of the alphabet. A goes inside, B goes outside, C goes outside, D goes outside, E goes inside the circle. Where do the rest of the letters go? Can you determine the system?

Did you solve it? If you assumed there was some complex intellectual system involved, you probably failed. The solution is in the simple shape of the letters themselves. Letters with curved lines go outside the circle, letters with only straight lines go inside. If you have strong intuitive skills, you probably saw the shape of the answer immediately.

The owner of a travel agency funded a complex and costly advertising and marketing program to bolster his struggling business. The program failed and he sold his business. One cold snowy day in January, the new owner's intuition told her that the way to sell travel was to be where the people had to go in bad as well as good weather—the grocery store. She immediately approached a supermarket chain and opened fifty-three travel centers throughout the chain. Sales went through the roof. Once she saw the shape of the problem, she intuited a simple solution.

BRAINWRITING

Brainwriting is a way to solve problems using intuition. Find a quiet spot and get relaxed. Write out your particular challenge and concentrate on it for a few minutes.

Write down some pertinent questions about your challenge: What is in my best interest? What should I do? What are other alternatives? What alternative is preferred? And so on. Then wait for the answer. It may come as a voice in your mind, or it may seem that you are communicating with someone else. Write down your answers as they come. Don't analyze or think. Write whatever occurs to you. Keep asking questions, and keep writing the responses until the responses stop. Finally, read and review what you have written. The answer to your challenge may be there.

The owner of a diet center framed the challenge: "In what ways might I develop a new diet product?" She tried brainwriting. Two of her responses were:

- People drink a lot of water when they diet.
- People exercise with weights as they diet.

These two thoughts sparked an idea. The idea: One-pound water-weights that carry liquid in plastic bottles for exercise now and refreshment later.

SUMMARY

In intelligence work, agents often lack the time to make a detailed analysis of a dangerous situation; they must make fast decisions and accept the consequences. One agent makes decisions by flipping a coin: heads is yes and tails is no. If he feels comfortable with the result, that is his decision; however, if he feels uncomfortable with the result he will make the opposite decision. This is not a waste of time. However the coin falls, the decision is ultimately made by his intuition. This agent also told me: "When your life is on the line, about the only thing you trust is your gut instinct."

CHAPTER TWENTY-FOUR

THE THREE B'S

"To wait at ease while the enemy
is toiling and struggling, to be well fed
while the enemy is famished—
this is the art of husbanding one's strength."

SUN TZU

A well-known physicist once said that all the great discoveries in science were made in one of the three B's—bus, bed, and bath. Many successful people report that their best ideas come when they are not thinking about solving problems. This is because of the principle of incubation.

The most famous example of this principle involves Archimedes, the Greek mathematician. A king, suspecting that a golden crown contained more silver than gold, asked Archimedes to devise a method for determining the metal's purity. Archimedes wrestled with the problem for many days. Finally, he decided to put it out of his mind and relax in a hot bath. While sitting in the bathtub, he noted that the bathwater was overflowing—and suddenly an ingenious solution occurred to him. He realized that a pure gold crown would displace a different amount of water than one made of alloy. According to legend, Archimedes was so excited by his discovery that he rushed naked into the streets of Syracuse shouting, "Eureka!" (I've found it!).

Incubation works because your subconscious mind is continually processing information. It usually involves setting your problem aside for a few hours, days, or weeks and moving on to other projects. This allows your subconscious to continue working on the original challenge. The more interested you are in solving a challenge, the more likely it is that your subconscious will generate ideas.

As Bertrand Russell wrote in *The Conquest of Happiness*:

I have found, for example, that if I have to write upon some rather difficult topic, the best plan is think about it with very great intensity—the greatest intensity with which I am capable—for a few hours or days, and at the end of that time give orders, so to speak, that the work is to proceed underground. After some months, I return consciously to the topic and find the work has been done. Before I discovered this technique, I used to spend time worrying because I was making no progress; I arrived at the solution none the faster for this worry and the worrying time was wasted.

Note that shadowy gray spots mysteriously appear at the intersections in this grid. However, when you concentrate on any specific intersection, the spot disappears.

Sometimes ideas, like the gray spots, mysteriously appear only when you are not concentrating on them. Modern science recognizes this phenomenon yet cannot explain why it occurs.

William Carrier, a twenty-five-year-old Cornell University engineering graduate, was waiting on a foggy railway platform in Pittsburgh. He had been working on the problem of regulating humidity for a printing company and had decided to give up for a while and take a vacation. Carrier gazed absent-mindedly at the mist surrounding the station and tracks, wondering how late his train was going to be. Suddenly, the answer to one of the most vexing problems of his time appeared to him out of the fog.

The answer was air-conditioning, which was the result of marrying two technologies, refrigeration and electricity. His idea was to blow air through a fine mist that would act like a condenser, drying out the air. Since air's moisture content varies with temperature—cold air is drier than warm—changing the temperature of the mist would also alter the humidity. His invention fathered an industry that brought prosperity and growth to the hot, muggy areas of the world.

By taking a vacation from his problem, he removed the artificial limitation of a deadline and solved his problem. Incubation will help you break the artificial limitations that you impose on yourself. Your mind will become less frantic and better able to deal with concepts, patterns, even the ridiculous combinations of thoughts that are such great aids to creativity. It's like the breaking up of a long, hard winter.

BLUEPRINT

1. *Identity.* Identify a challenge worth working on and think of the consequences of solving it. If you can envision a world in which your challenge is solved, you will be pulled subconsciously toward a constructive, creative answer.

2. *Prepare.* Collect and gather all available information and literature about your challenge. Read, talk to others, ask questions, and do as much research as you can. Consciously work on the challenge as intensely as you can, until you are satisfied that you have prepared as thoroughly as possible.

3. *Instruct.* Instruct your brain to find the solution to the problem. Close by saying: "Okay, find the solution to this problem. I'll be back in two days for the answer" or "Let me know the minute you work it out."

4. *Incubate.* Let go of the problem. Don't work on it. Forget it for a while. This period may be long or short. Take a walk or a shower, go to a movie, or sleep on it. Incubation has to occur and it will.

5. *Eureka!* It may take five minutes, five hours, five days, five weeks, five months, or whatever, but insight will occur.

Thunder is impressive, but it is the lightning that does the work. Long after the thunder of conscious thinking has faded from your mind, insight and creative ideas will arrive like flashes of lightning.

A stockbroker searched for months for a new business opportunity. He collected information and did considerable research about financial services. He then forgot about his challenge. A week later, while shopping for shoes, his idea suddenly arrived.

The idea: He created a one-stop IRA store in a high-traffic location. He saves consumers the trouble of shopping for an IRA and choosing among the many complex programs. He can charge a reasonable fee and make a commission from the IRA sellers as well. He is now opening branches in office buildings and other malls.

BENEFITS OF INCUBATION

Incubation helps you put the challenge in perspective. Edna Ferber wrote, "A story must simmer in its own juices for months or even years before it is ready to serve."

An architect was uncertain where to place sidewalks between buildings in an office complex. He did nothing for a period of time, letting the problem "simmer." One day, he noticed that people walking on the grass had left pathways between the buildings—paths that were perfectly sized for traffic flow. He paved the pathways, which directly met user needs in an aesthetic fashion.

You put your subconscious to work on the challenge. As a simple experiment, write the alphabet vertically on a piece of paper. Now write a sentence vertically next to the alphabet, stopping with whatever letter parallels Z. Now you have a row of initials. Think of as many famous people as you can (real or fictional) for each set of initials in ten minutes. If you couldn't come up with some names but then suddenly thought of them while you were working on other initials, you experienced your subconscious mind at work.

When you leave a problem and come back to it fresh, you will likely develop a different perspective on it. A volunteer in upstate New York faced the challenge of raising money for a certain charity. He considered the usual fundraising methods and then let go of the problem for some weeks. One day while he was fishing on the Genesee River, he remembered the challenge and wondered about ways of combining raising money with sport. This inspired the latest craze in fund-raising.

The idea: A plastic duck race. Three-inch-long plastic ducks are numbered and then tossed toward a finish line a mile down the river. Spectators pay $5 to bet on the ducks, and the first-place winner receives a prize. Volunteers follow the plastic ducks in rowboats, scooping up strays in hand-held nets. In addition, nets are strung across the river at the finish line so that the ducks do not contribute to pollution.

Incubation can help you realize your personal goals. Write down a goal that is important to you. It could be a short- or long-range goal. Then, write out the ideal situation exactly as you would like it to be when your goal is realized. Describe it in the present tense, as if it had already happened, in as much detail as possible.

When you have finished, write at the bottom of the page: "This or something better is now manifesting for me and will be manifested for me in a totally satisfying way." Then sit quietly, visualize the realization of your goal, put the paper away, and forget about it. Months or years later, when you find and read it, you may be surprised to find that the goal has somehow come into being in your life.

SUMMARY

One prominent French scientist observed that practically all of his good ideas came to him when he was not working on a problem or even thinking about a problem, and that most of his contemporaries made their discoveries in the same way. When Einstein was troubled by a problem, he would lie down and take a long nap.

When you have a case of the dooms about a challenge, incubate it. Then, when you least expect it, in perfect silence, the answer will come like a flock of birds breaking out of a tree, but you will feel as if the tree itself is breaking up, sending particles of ideas into the air.

CHAPTER TWENTY-FIVE

RATTLESNAKES
AND ROSES

"Now the shuai-jan is a snake found in the
Ch'ang mountains. Strike at its head, and you
will be attacked by its tail; strike at its tail,
and you will be attacked by its head;
strike at its middle, and you will be attacked
by head and tail both."

SUN TZU

Sun Tzu drew an analogy between the behavior of the shuai-jan and that of
soldiers in battle. To succeed in war, he observed, men must have tenacity and
unity of purpose and, above all, a spirit of sympathetic cooperation.

Analogies are comparisons of the similar features of two things—they are
also mental telescopes through which you can spy ideas. For instance, consider
the following inventions and their counterparts in nature:

Helicopters: The hummingbird can also hover and fly backwards.

Hypodermic needles: The scorpion uses the pointed tip of its tail to inject
poison.

Sonar: Bats used sonar long before man. They emit sounds inaudible to
the human ear that bounce off objects in their way.

Anesthesia: Many snakes use venom to paralyze and desensitize their prey before eating it.

Snowshoes: The caribou's feet are designed to skim over snow.

Tanks: The turtle is a virtually impregnable mobile unit.

Airplanes: Planes brake with flaps just as birds brake with tailfeathers.

Are there similarities between a telephone network and the human body? Bell is developing a new self-healing communication system based on an analogy with the human circulation system.

When important telephone arteries are damaged or cut, the system will pump phone service through new channels, keeping communications alive.

A bird's special gift is flight, ours is the imagination to make connections between two dissimilar areas of experience. For example, take the two nonsense words "maluma" and "tuckatee" and match them to the figures, A and B.

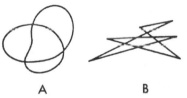

A   B

Gestalt psychologist Wolfgang Kohler used the above exercise to demonstrate that humans somehow make universal metamorphical-analogical connections. Kohler's patients would unerringly match "maluma" to A and "tuckatee" to B. Did you?

Suppose my challenge is to improve the common flashlight. I draw the following analogy between two dissimilar areas of experience:

"Improving a flashlight is like attending medical school to learn surgery."

Next, I describe what's involved in learning surgery:

1. I'll need textbooks and manuals.
2. I'll need to attend class and talk with professors.
3. I'll have to learn how to administer anesthesia.
4. I'll have to insulate myself from social demands while in school.
5. I'll practice surgery on cadavers.

I examine each item and see what ideas it might stimulate.

1. Package first-aid pamphlets with flashlights (from "textbooks and manuals").
2. Incorporate a radio transmitter and receiver (from "talk with professors").
3. Include a mace spray for protection (from "administering anesthesia").
4. Insulate flashlights to protect batteries from extreme temperatures (from "insulating from social demands").
5. Include a miniature tool kit (from "practicing on cadavers").

By making analogical connections between flashlights and learning surgery, I quickly came up with a number of unconventional ideas for improving the common flashlight.

When you use analogies to generate ideas, you'll find that analogies grow like plants, like trees, like children, like love. They go through a series of stages, finally maturing into something rich with ideas.

MAKING THE FAMILIAR STRANGE

Most of us are threatened by the strange and unfamiliar and have a need to understand it. When confronted with something unfamiliar, we tend to break it down and analyze the different parts to see if this will allow us to understand it or make it familiar. We also generalize by analogy, asking "What's this like?" Our minds compare the unfamiliar object with things that *are* familiar, and this process can convert the strange into the familiar.

Look at the collage of shadows in the above illustration.

Notice how your mind first perceives the shadows as strange, then searches for meaning. The search continues until your mind is satisfied that it represents the image of a bearded man in a white robe standing against a background of brush. Your mind searches for meaning until it makes the strange shadows into something familiar.

This tendency explains why *making the familiar strange* is a key to creative thinking. When you reverse the usual process, you push your mind to search for new connections and ideas.

Venturing into strange areas which seem totally unrelated to your challenge will increase your chances of seeing the challenge in a new context. You do this by using analogies.

The stranger the analogy (the greater the distance between challenge and example), the greater your chance of generating a unique idea. For instance, if your challenge is to improve the stamina of rose bushes, you are more likely to see the challenge from a unique viewpoint if you look at stamina in rattlesnakes instead of in other flowers or plants.

A new nightclub was having its grand opening, and the owners wanted to send out clever and amusing invitations. They worked with the following analogy: "An invitation is like an aspirin." In other words, they made the familiar strange. How can an invitation be like an aspirin?

This analogy forced them to search for connections and similarities between the two items. The search resulted in one of the year's most unusual invitations.

The idea: Make the invitation pill-like. The club sent out a blue pill nestled in a black velvet ring box. Instructions on the box read "Drop into warm water, stir, and let dissolve." When immersed, the capsule dissolved and a piece of cellophane with the time, date, and place floated to the top. The invitations cost $1.10 each, and the opening was a smash.

Using analogies allows one to dismiss all unrelated thoughts, as though parting the grass to find the path leading to a new idea.

The owner of a jewelry store needed to sell more high-end items, customers balked at high prices and had doubts about how the jewelry would look with their wardrobes. He made an analogical connection between high-end jewelry and paper dolls. With paper dolls, children cut out and play with paper wardrobes and jewelry. This stimulated his idea.

The idea: Paper cutouts of jewelry. He created punch-out paper representations of expensive jewelry, and sent the paper copies to prospective customers so they could try out the jewelry at home with various outfits. Once people modeled the paper cutouts, their doubts disappeared, and they came in and purchased his jewelry.

To satisfy hunger, you must take some kind of action. You cannot just sit there and expect your hunger to disappear—you have to make something to

eat or go to a restaurant. Similarly, you cannot just wish to have an idea. You have to act. One action you can take is to make the familiar strange with one of the four kinds of analogy: personal analogy, direct analogy, symbolic analogy, or fantasy analogy.

Of these four, the *direct analogy* is the most productive idea-getter and the only one that requires a detailed blueprint. The others are described in enough detail that you don't need a blueprint to understand and use them.

PERSONAL ANALOGY

This analogy involves identifying with some part of your problem and trying to see the challenge from its perspective. Imagine that you are trying to design a new clock. Ask yourself what it would be like to be the hands of a clock.

The personal analogy demands that you lose yourself in the object of the challenge. Wear the problem's clothes, talk its language, eat its food, sing its songs, recite its slogans and mottos. Become a kind of blood-hyphen with the object.

Look at this man.

Can you imagine him merging with a rat? This figure can be seen as either a man or a rat: The man's glasses are also the rat's ears, the man's nose is the rat's head, and his chin is the rat's tail. You should merge as completely as this with your problem.

The basic questions to ask yourself are: "How would I feel if I were. . . .?", or "What would it say to me if our positions were reversed?", or "What would it say to me if it could think and talk the way I can?"

T. A. Rich, a famous inventor at GE, describes how he comes up with his new ideas this way: "I put myself in the middle of a problem; try to think like an electron whose course is being plotted or imagine myself as a light beam whose refraction is being measured." Einstein imagined he was a beam of light hurtling through space, which led him to the theory of relativity.

A tiny company that markets wall coverings had the challenge of competing with enormous conglomerates. Fortunately for this tiny company, innovation is one of the few precious resources that can't be bought; the best ideas have always been simple enough to scribble on the back of a cocktail napkin, and the CEO knew this.

This CEO kept asking himself, "What would wall coverings say to me if they could talk?" "What would their concerns be?" "What would they worry about?" "How would I feel if I were a wall covering?" He asked himself these questions every day and was finally able to imagine himself as a wall covering.

One concern he imagined wall coverings would have is the fear of fire. Wall coverings are often made of vinyl, polypropylene, and other fabrics that are highly toxic when burned. The giant wall covering companies were all selling these potentially dangerous products.

The tiny company developed its own nontoxic, fire-resistant fiberglass material. This company then sent flyers to distributors, architects, and others who choose or buy wall coverings. The flyers detailed the high toxicity of the giants' vinyl and polypropylene wall coverings and emphasized the danger of litigation. In the event of fire, the victims or their estate could file a class action suit naming the property owner, the architect or engineer who specified the dangerous wall covering, the distributor, and the maker.

Suddenly the tiny company was getting orders from nursing homes, hotels, casinos, prisons, hospitals, schools, and major hotel chains. The giant companies were rocked to their heels. The distributors and designers they'd done business with for years were questioning their products and moved their business to the safe little company.

Suppose you own an outdoor advertising business and are looking for creative new ways to advertise. Imagine that you are an outdoor billboard. What would you feel? What would your problems be? How would you advertise your products?

If I was a billboard, I would like to talk to the passing motorists about my products; I would like a chance to sell them my products in person. This prompts an idea.

The idea: Display a provocative back view of a male or female model with a phone number to call. Callers would find themselves listening to real or taped sales presentations from the sexy models, extolling the virtues of the product and implying that the model could be found on a certain beach using the product.

DIRECT ANALOGY

The direct analogy is probably the most productive for generating ideas. With direct analogies, you can imagine comparisons and similarities between par-

$$+ \quad + \quad \times \quad \times$$

allel facts and events in different fields or "parallel worlds." "If X works in a certain desirable way, why can't Y work in a similar manner?"

Alexander Graham Bell observed the comparison between the inner workings of the ear and the movement of a stout piece of membrane and conceived of the telephone. Edison invented the phonograph one day, after developing an analogy between a toy funnel and the motions of a paper doll and sound vibrations. Underwater construction was made possible when someone observed how shipworms tunnel into timber by first constructing tubes.

Consider the story of George de Mestral, a Swiss inventor who went hunting one day in the late 1940s. He and his dog accidentally brushed up against a bush that left them both covered with burrs. When de Mestral tried to remove the burrs, they clung stubbornly to his clothes. This would be a minor annoyance to most of us, but de Mestral was curious about why the burrs were so hard to remove. After he got home, he studied them under a microscope and discovered that hundreds of tiny hooks on each burr had snagged to the threads of his pants. Burrs, he thought, would make great fasteners.

After several years of work, he finally succeeded. The result: Velcro fasteners, now used on millions of items, from blood pressure cuffs to tennis shoes.

The analogy does not have to be long or complicated. Stamp collecting is a specialized hobby yet its components can be compared to those of many businesses: supply and demand, information requirements, search procedures, rarity of certain items, utility of certain items, classification, marketing, word of mouth, value, value added, and so on.

In the above illustration, one plus one equals four or more. Of the two lines, one crosses the other horizontally in their centers, creating four arms. You can also, with imagination, see four rectangles, four triangles and four squares. By shifting the lines from the centers, you can also create several unequal and unique figures.

In the same way, your subject plus a dissimilar object will produce four or more ideas.

Assume my challenge is "In what ways might I become more creative at work?" I look into an unrelated field—home appliances—and decide that my analogy will be: Being creative at work is like being a toaster. One (being creative at work) + one (toaster) = four or more ideas.

Following are descriptors of a toaster. A toaster:

- is operated by pushing down a lever or bar.
- is plugged into a power source.
- takes bread in completely.
- concentrates its energy on the surfaces of bread.
- accepts different sizes and types of bread.
- may shock you if you tamper with it with a fork or knife.
- produces toast which is sometimes combined with butter or jam to improve it.

I examine each descriptor, and produce the following ideas on how to become more creative at work:

- I should push down negative thoughts about my creative abilities. (From pushing down the bar on a toaster.)
- I need to identify the real benefits to me of being creative. (From "power source.")
- I need to accept the challenge of being creative completely. (From "takes in bread completely.")
- I should concentrate my energies on ideas instead of digging for reasons to come up with ideas. (From "concentrates its energy on the surfaces of the bread.")
- I should try different kinds of creative techniques. (From "accepts different sizes and types of bread.")
- I should become a risk taker and try for the dramatic idea. (From "you may get shocked.")
- I should combine creative thinking techniques. (From "butter and jam.")

With a little imagination, the ordinary household toaster pops up a whole program for improving my creativity at work. One (improve creativity) + one (toaster) = seven ideas.

BLUEPRINT

The basic blueprint for using direct analogies is:

1. *State your challenge.* A lumberyard owner stated: "In what ways might I sell more lumber?"

2. *Choose a key word or phrase in the challenge.* He chose "sell."

3. *Choose a parallel or distant field.* The greater the distance the parallel world is from your challenge, the greater your chance of producing new thoughts and ideas. A business analogy to a business challenge is too close—analogies from television or cookery might be more likely to stimulate creative thought.

   The field selected for the challenge of selling more lumber was "computers."

4. *List the images that you associate with your chosen field, then choose one or more particularly rich ones.* Listing images will allow you to describe the analogy in as much detail as possible. Among the images evoked by the computer field are: science, multiple uses, user-friendly, hardware, software, add-ons, computer-aided design, schools, business uses, and recreational uses.

5. *Look for similarities and connections between the two components of your analogy.* Don't think of looking for connections as something arduous, or feel as though you were forcing yourself to swallow something unpleasant for your own good. Think easy. Let your thoughts come and go as they wish.

   The lumberyard owner looked at a number of connections between the images and his challenge of selling more lumber, ultimately discarding most of them. The final images he focused on were: computer-aided design (CAD), computer add-ons, and recreational uses.

   He combined and connected these three concepts with his challenge of selling lumber, stirring an idea.

   The idea: Use CAD to design backyard decks. Provide a computerized system in the lumberyard with which salespeople can design decks to a customer's specifications. One would set up a user-friendly kiosk with a large video screen and easy-to-use controls for the salesperson. The customer could specify the deck's size and the number of stairways needed, and select railings and spindles. The system would then design the deck from the ground up and calculate the cost. If the cost came out too high, the customer could change the dimensions. Once the price is right, the computer could print out full instructions. This free service would encourage more people to build decks, and the lumberyard will sell more lumber.

The "parallel world" you select must be something you know well, and you should use a specific object, situation, event, or example from that world. For instance: "The NFL Champion San Francisco Forty-niners" will make for a much more fruitful analogy than "football." The more detailed images you can record, the better. If you decide to use "restaurants," choose a specific, familiar restaurant.

Following is a sample list of different worlds, fields, and disciplines which parallel the business world. Use this list to get started, but do develop a unique list of parallel worlds that best suits your particular knowledge. When choosing a parallel world, examine four or five possibilities in order to select the one that best suits the general principles of your challenge.

Parallel Worlds

Accounting	Acupuncture	The animal kingdom
Architecture	Art	Astrology
Astronomy	Ballet	Baseball
Basketball	Biography	Biology
Birds	Cancer	Bowling
Calculus	Cartoons	Cardiology
Caribbean	Chiropractors	Chemistry
China	Composers	The civil rights
Comics	Dentistry	movement
Dance	Economics	The Civil War
Deserts	Entertainment	Computers
England	The fast-food industry	Department stores
Farming	Fishing	Education
Fine cooking	Funeral homes	Evolution
Football	Geology	Finance
Geography	Government	Flying
Golf	Grocery stores	Garbage collecting
The Great Depression	Hunting	Germany

History
India
Interior decorating
Journalism
Korea
Mafia
Medicine
Mining
The moon
Mythology
Oceans
Pharmacology
Physical fitness
Planets
Politics
Psychiatry
Religion
The Revolutionary War
Seminars
Soap operas
Space
Taverns
The steel industry
Tennis
Transportation
The U.S.S.R
Wall Street
World War I
World War II

The I.R.S.
Inventions
Jungles
Insects
Law
Law enforcement
Manufacturing
Meteorology
Monasteries
Movies
Nuclear physics
The old west
Philosophy
Physical therapy
Plumbing
Pornography
Psychology
Resorts
Sailing
Shakespeare's plays
Sociology
Special education
Television
The sun
Terrorism
The travel industry
The Vatican
Wholesalers
The Yukon

Great books
Hawaii
Hypnosis
Japan
Literature
Math
The military
Monuments
Music
Nutrition
The Olympics
Photography
Physics
Political science
Printing
Publishing
Restaurants
Sculpture
Skiing
South America
Stars
TV news
Talk radio
Television
Theater
Unions
The Vietnam War
Wine

Examine your parallel world for details and information that you can compare to your challenge. Work the analogy over like a Chinese chef who leaves hardly any part of the duck unserved.

Suppose you have a problem selling copiers. You select "Television," and then decide to focus on television evangelists. Next, you list the characteristics of television evangelists and then compare these characteristics to the principles of selling copiers. Your objective is to draw meaningful relationships which may lead to a productive idea. Take a few minutes and try it.

How did you do?

One could say that evangelists sell a product—their sermons. One could also say they sell hope, which is the product of the sermon. In other words, hope is the "product of the product" of the TV evangelist. What is the "product of the product" in selling copiers? Is it convenience? Service? Efficiency? If you promoted the product of your product, could you sell more copiers?

Now compare selling copiers to a full-service restaurant. You might discover that your menu (product line) is comprehensive but you have too many restrictions, which cloud the customer's mind. For example, your company may have specialized salespeople (waiters). Thus, customers can't order everything from one salesperson (waiter) but need to order beverages from the beverage waiter, salad from the salad waiter, potatoes from the potato waiter, fish from the fish waiter, meat from the meat waiter, and so on. In this case, one solution would be to consider ways of simplifying the product line and ordering procedures.

A friend of mine disliked the standard 20 × 40-foot rectangular swimming pool. He wanted an affordable pool which would allow a variety of water activities—swimming, diving, serious lap swimming, and horsing around—to take place simultaneously.

He decided to design his own swimming pool, but needed ideas. He selected the parallel world of golf and began to look for analogies. He considered course layouts, sand traps, fairways, the rough, golf clubs, golf clothing, and golf equipment. He eventually focused on golf equipment; in particular, the clubs.

He drew connections and relationships between the number one wood—the driver—and his challenge of designing a swimming pool.

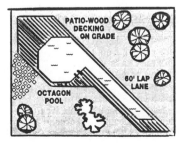

Above is the pool he designed.

His pool is a modified octagon. Six of its sides are 23 feet long, while one side extends to form a sixty-foot lap area. This allows all water activities to take place simultaneously. In addition, the pool takes up less room and uses one-third less water, which saves on pumping, filtration, and chemicals. Its unusual shape can be adapted to unusual sites and can even be wrapped around a house. It also has a zippered cover, much like a golf club cover.

My friend, who is strictly a meatloaf-and-yams man, explained: "Using the direct analogy with golf clubs I had twenty-four ideas that jumped between my ears. I grabbed the last one and designed my pool."

SYMBOLIC ANALOGY

A symbolic analogy is a representation of the key elements of a challenge in visual images. This technique works best when you disassociate yourself entirely from labels and words and just make mental pictures of the problem. One of the most famous examples of this technique was Fredrich von Kekule's discovery that benzene and other organic molecules are closed chains or rings—a direct result of a symbolic analogy in which he visualized snakes swallowing their tails.

To try this technique, close your eyes and picture your challenge or problem in your mind. Block out verbal thoughts. (This can be done by repeating a simple word such as aum, one, om, or so over and over, until it becomes meaningless.) The resulting visual ideas can be expressed verbally, drawn, or written down at a later time.

A group of engineers used symbolic analogies to invent a compact jacking mechanism that extends some three feet and can support up to five tons. Among the mental images the group produced were:

- The Indian rope trick in which a rope is at first coiled and soft, then becomes hard as it extends.
- The hydraulic principle of the erection of the penis.
- A steel tape measure.
- A bicycle chain with flexible links that stiffen as they are driven out of the jacking mechanism.

These images combined to provide a concept on which the design for the compact jack was ultimately based.

Try it. Imagine that your challenge is to create a unique design for directional signs that will mark major intersections within a housing development. Picture directional signs as your subject. Repeat a simple word, over and over, to block out your verbal thoughts. Write down what you visualized.

What did you get?

Among the images and associations I came up with are:

- *Images of landmarks.* People use landmarks to locate things. Association: Think of a sign as an artistic landmark.
- *Images of hunting dogs.* Dogs assist hunters by pointing to prey. Association: Use an animal cutout as a sign.
- *Colors.* People use colors to denote direction ("Turn right at the red house.") Association: Use different bright colors to denote major and minor intersections.

These images and associations produce a unique design idea: Mark major intersections with giant metal animals (perhaps a horse, steer, and wolf) that function both as art and landmarks. Mark secondary intersections with metal birds (roadrunner, owl, blue jay). Paint the signs with bright colors such as hot pink, yellow, and turquoise. ("Turn left at the blue horse and right at the pink owl.")

A salesperson confronted the challenge of getting druggists to display baby lotion in both the baby department and the adult section. He coaxed out a mental image of a diamond ring hidden behind aspirin bottles and interpreted this image into an effective sales promotion.

The idea: He built an entire campaign around the notion of "hidden profits." He listed all the ways you could make money by placing baby lotion in the adult section, in small print, on a leave-behind card with a little magnifier attached to it. This little gimmick was one of the most successful sales promotions in the company's history.

Think of symbolic analogies as imaginary mushroom clouds (destroying nothing, making nothing) rising from a blinding consciousness. It is your careful interpretation of the clouds that gives them meaning and value.

Fantasy Analogy

The fantasy analogy involves using your imagination without reference to objective reality. When faced with a problem, imagine the best possible world—one that would permit the most satisfying solution to the problem. This fantasy analogy will permit you to combine words, concepts, and assumptions with apparently irrelevant objects and events. The result is a rich treasure of associations; an imagination avalanche with whole mountains of ideas crashing down.

An artist can paint the world however he wishes but a businessperson is limited by tradition. Using a fantasy analogy allows you to imagine the best possible solution to a problem because you temporarily suspend all judgment. This allows a businessperson to create ideas like an artist.

Most of the business concepts we work with have been handed down to us by others, but we are expected to adhere to these prepackaged concepts. Creating your own world where these concepts do not hold enables you to think and act with a Maker's responsibility. This attitude modifies your view of the real world and nullifies the effect of traditional beliefs.

As Maker, you can visualize anything, not excluding even the wildest ideas; for example, training insects to perform small business tasks. It's like inventing a sky with new stars in it.

The Navy didn't think of training insects to perform routine tasks, but they did spend a lot of time thinking about training marine life in response to the challenge: "In what ways might we improve our security against saboteurs, reduce cost, and minimize risk to human life?"

Using fantasy analogies to generate ideas, a Navy problem-solving group developed a clandestine program to train and use dolphins to guard the Trident nuclear submarine base in Bangor, Washington. Dolphins are faster than Carl Lewis running the 100-meter dash and have better sonar than anything man has invented. This will be the first use of dolphins in domestic surveillance.

Putting aside traditional beliefs allows you to visualize a more coherent hypothesis than you might have thought possible. Push aside the ordinary laws of doing business and take a peek at the other side before the laws snap back into control.

A salesperson confronted the challenge: "In what ways might I discover the prospect's real objections to my product?" She felt that once she determined the real problems, she could overcome them.

Her fantasy analogy was to make her customers into judges who would bang their gavels every time they had an objection. This hatched the idea.

The idea: She began handing each prospect a gavel, saying, "You be the judge; if you have a question or an objection, bang the gavel!" She would then make her presentation on why the prospect should buy her product. She increased her closing ratio by 80 percent. It was a quick attention-getter that the customers enjoyed.

You may get the best ideas by combining types of analogy. Assume you sell law books direct to lawyers and would like more productive sales techniques. Start with a fantasy world, such as the following:

"Imagine a world in which lawyers line up outside your door and plead for your services, and you select which lawyers will have the privilege of buying your books."

You may then find yourself going from the fantasy analogy to the direct and then to the personal. For instance, a direct analogy for the above fantasy might be the medical field where patients come to an office and wait until the

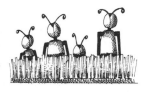

doctor has time to see them. A personal analogy would be imagining yourself as the lawyer or patient and empathizing with him.

Possible ideas to implement the fantasy analogy and get lawyers to come to you might be:

- *Selection of customers.* Provide a greater array of services for preferred lawyers. The longer they do business with you, the greater the number of services you provide. For instance, you could team up with a travel agent to offer "preferred lawyer" discount travel arrangements. You could also offer free reservation services for theaters and restaurants to big accounts.
- *Prestige.* Personal recognition is important to most lawyers. Invite lawyers to work with you as book reviewers, authors, coauthors, and marketing consultants.
- *Convenience.* One reason people visit doctors is because of the medical resources concentrated in one office. Concentrate legal resources in your office (i.e., books, videotapes, data banks, on-line computer services, a legal reference library, legal secretaries, journals, and so on) to motivate lawyers to come to you.

Just as soil needs some element to fertilize it, just as vitamin-starved sailors call for lemons, so too the imagination needs nourishment. The fantasy analogy feeds your imagination; it allows you to move through space by walking or flying, or stay still and watch the components of your challenge as they fly around you. Becoming an observer, will permit you to stand back from your challenge and obtain both physical and psychological distance. How important does any problem seem, for example, when viewed from Mars?

SUMMARY

Consider water. Civilization as we know it is based in part on running water—supplying it, distributing it, and turning it off and on when we need it. That overall system had to be well thought out. A similar sort of planning lets you design a waterworks for the mind.

Rattlesnakes and Roses is a utility, a commodity, a waterworks for your mind, the spigot that dispenses images and experiences when you turn the handle. But the system must be based on the fluidity of your thought. Thoughts, like water, go nowhere when frozen.

CHAPTER TWENTY-SIX

STONE SOUP

"When campaigning, be swift as the wind; in
leisurely march, majestic as the forest; in
raiding and plundering, like fire; in standing
firm, firm as the mountains. As unfathomable as
the clouds, move like a thunderbolt."

SUN TZU

A lion has to be a lion all its life; a dog has to be a dog. But a human being can play with and bring about one of a huge number of different identities; the one he finally chooses will be determined by neither reason nor common sense, but by imagination.

Consider the role the beggar's imagination plays in the following story, based on an old Eastern European children's fable.

The weather had grown cold and the trees had burst into color, the reds and yellows glowing as though the leaves had gobbled the light of the fall sun and were releasing it slowly. The fields were piled with golden pumpkins and russet squashes and trees with red apples so sweet you could smell the juice.

The barefoot beggar's clothing was torn, his hair tangled. He could smell roasting meat from the villagers' kitchens and his mouth filled with saliva—he had not eaten in two days. Desperate, he built a small fire at the edge of the village, put his pot on the fire, and placed a small stone in the pot. "Just suppose," he thought, "this stone could make a delicious soup." He sat on a box and imagined that he was really making soup.

The curious villagers came out and collected around his crackling fire. They asked him what he was brewing and he told them about the magical stone that made a delectable soup. "Stone soup tastes best when the frost is in," he told them. The villagers were fascinated with this soup and began to comment on its fine aroma. The beggar invited them to join him. The excited villagers said they would bring their own dinners to complement his gourmet soup.

They returned with vegetables, fruits, turkeys, hams, eggs, and sausages. "Now let us pray," the village priest said. The beggar thought, "I pray the food doesn't get cold before he finishes." Then the beggar dug in. He ate everything there was to eat, like there was no tomorrow. He broke apart four fried eggs with the tip of his knife and ate them with whole slices of fried ham. He cut two pieces of turkey, fork the meat into his mouth, and then add some boiled potatoes and beans—and then tear off a hunk of buttered bread and eat that too. He didn't seem to notice that the villagers sipped bowl after bowl of his wonderful soup while he ate everything in sight, including half of a strawberry pie.

When he finished, he sat there for a few moments as if stunned. Finally, he got up, packed his stone and left. He didn't look back.

By directing his imagination, the beggar was able to create the illusion of a wonderful soup. Once the villagers convinced themselves that it was, in fact, a wonderful soup, the beggar was able to feast on their food and thus accomplish his goal of getting a hearty meal. His imagination fed his belly. Your imagination can feed your business belly if you just ask "What if . . . ?" and "Just suppose . . . ?"

E. L. Doctorow told of having a writing block that lasted for three months. He was frantic for ideas. One day, he gazed absentmindedly at the wallpaper and wondered about the age of the paper, and then about the age of the house.

He pursued this thought and discovered his house was built in the early 1900s. "Just suppose," he thought, "I could be transported back in time to the date my house was built."

He imagined it. His imagination took him back to the early 1900s and he began the astonishing novel, *Ragtime*, which re-creates with stunning authenticity all the sights, sounds, aromas, and emotions of the time when his house was built. "Just supposing" created a bestseller.

Doctorow discovered what Einstein knew, which is that anything goes when you are limited only by your imagination. Einstein developed some of his early theories by speculating. "Just suppose bodies could be in motion and at rest at the same time." He asked, "What would that mean?"

Look at the four white arrowheads.

What if the arrowheads are black and the background is white? When you imagine the black arrowheads, they become as real as the white. Your sense of the arrowheads is now a product of your imagination.

Imagination is everything you have ever experienced. It so permeates the human condition that many people feel they have no imagination. Yet, imagination is the crux of every human perception. Your sense of time, space, and history, of planning for tomorrow are all products of your imagination. Without it, you would be as oblivious to your surroundings as a fish is to water.

"What-iffing" is a great way to learn to direct your imagination toward a desired goal. This technique lets your ego relax, and the playfulness of the ideas it generates will cause it to relax even more.

What if our attitudes about sex and food were reversed? Would this mean that people would engage in public sex acts in restaurants while fast-sex stores dotted the landscape? People would never eat in public, and children would be told not to say "knife" or "fork." Would all the eating be done behind closed doors, and might there be movie houses featuring "food flicks" for "perverts" who sneak food items into theaters under their raincoats?

Most humor uses imaginative possibilities to create new insights. For instance, take the story about the boastful Texan vacationing in Maine. The Texan, surveying a tiny farm, explains that back home on his ranch, he can get into his car and drive all day without ever crossing his own property line. The Maine farmer pauses for a moment to digest this thought, picks his teeth, and replies, "Ayuh. Had a car like that myself once."

At the point in the story where the two lines of thinking (property and cars) meet, the farmer's imagination creates a whole new perception of events by following the less obvious direction. "What-iffing" pushes you to produce something new. In the joke, we produced something funny. In business, you can produce the profound.

The figure on the next page is known to psychologists as the Penrose triangle. If you follow the white surface, it appears to go from being the outside of a three-dimensional triangle to being the inside. The three-dimensional figure is impossible; it cannot exist.

Like the triangle, individual genius sometimes comes from moments of absolute fiction that provide a ray of insight leading to an innovative solution. To achieve that ray of insight, one must take the imaginative chance, abandon the usual ways of looking at things, transcend the possible, and reach for the impossible.

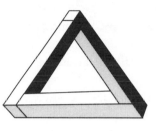

Following are some examples of general imagination-spurring questions:

- What if you had eyes in back of your head as well as the front?
- What if human beings never died? How would this affect our personal, business, and religious lives?
- What if every five years you experienced a natural sex change (if you're male, you become female; if you're female, you become male)?
- What if trees suddenly started to produce petroleum in great quantities?
- What if people slept twenty-three hours every day and were awake for only one hour?
- What if every worker in the United States had to adopt one homeless person and take care of that person for life?
- What if fashion were done away with and everyone, regardless of station in life or occupation, had to wear the same uniform?
- What if as you aged you became more beautiful and intelligent?
- What if international disputes were resolved by awarding victory to the country that could make the world laugh the hardest?
- What if our genitals were on our foreheads?
- What if you could eat clouds for breakfast?

After you ask the questions, try to answer them. What if a pill was developed that would do away with all prejudice and bigotry in all of its present forms? How would this affect TV talk shows? What would happen to all the political action groups? Would some sort of a new hatred replace bigotry; for example, would people become prejudiced against dogs or oak trees? Would our political institutions change? Would the court system improve? Would life be better, and, if so, how? Would global politics become more or less intense?

In trying to answer the questions, you find yourself developing new insights that may lead to new ideas. Suppose our question is: "What if people were like skunks and could repel attackers with odor?" Trying to answer it inspires an idea: Clip a plastic capsule that contains synthetic skunk oil onto one's clothing. If a person is attacked, he or she squeezes the capsule to release an odor so offensive it drives the attacker away. A concentrated deodorizer could be applied to neutralize the odor once the attacker has fled.

Playing "what if" games on a daily basis will free you from boredom and let you connect previously unrelated thoughts and experiences.

"What if you could lose weight by writing down the number of pounds you want to lose?"

The idea: A computer simulation that will motivate dieters by showing them what they will look like after losing ten to twenty-five pounds.

Once you understand how to direct it, your imagination will become a hard and inescapable reality instead of an escape from harsh reality.

BLUEPRINT

The easiest way to begin is by saying: "I need fresh and novel ideas to solve my challenge. I will suspend all judgment and see what free and easy ideas I can think up. It doesn't matter how weird or offbeat they are, since no one need know about them." Allow yourself the freedom to conceptualize without judging your ideas in terms of the real world.

1. *Stipulate your challenge.* One environmental dilemma is how to dispose of old porcelain toilets that are being dumped in already overloaded landfills. Our challenge is: "In what other ways might we dispose of toilets?"

2. *List as many "what if" scenarios as you can.* One scenario is: What if we simply threw all the old toilets into the ocean?

3. *Try to answer the questions posed by your scenarios.* Toilets would make ideal reefs for fish. Porcelain fixtures are just as good as rock as far as fish are concerned—they are just funny-shaped devices with lots of spaces for fish to hide. Toilets would make great reefs for the very reason they are terrible in landfills: A toilet lasts virtually forever.

To find radical solutions to old problems, it is essential to take the imaginative leap to produce an image or metaphor that you can grip and mold into a new idea. For instance, imagine you own a company that manufactures television sets in a country where only the rich can afford to own one. Your sets are outperformed in the city market by every competitor and you lack the resources to advertise nationally. What do you do?

Matsushita faced this problem in the early 1950s. They were outranked and outperformed by just about every competitor, in Japan and elsewhere. The executives knew, as everybody else did, that television was "too expensive for the Japanese." In 1955 the chairman of Toshiba said, "Japan is too poor to afford such a luxury." Toshiba and Hitachi made better sets at the time, but they only showed them on the Ginza in Tokyo and in big-city department stores, making it clear to the average Japanese that this product was beyond their reach.

The national sales manager at Matsushita said, "What if Japanese farmers were rich and could afford television?" and proceeded to devise a sales plan based on this fantasy. His salesmen sold televisions to poor farmers door-to-door, something no one in Japan had ever done with anything more expensive than cloth or aprons. The Japanese farmers could not afford the sets, but they bought them anyway. Those farmers wanted access to the outside world and were willing to make incredible sacrifices to get it.

Directed imagination focuses you on how to solve a problem instead of wondering if the problem can be solved. Once the sales manager imagined the farmers as a market, he set about to make it happen. Today, Matsushita is better known by its brand name—Panasonic. *The lesson:* In a land of withering grapes, imagination can make a raisin a king.

Suppose you own a company and your challenge is: "In what ways might I increase sales?" See how many "What if" scenarios you can create. These are mine:

- What if personal selling were outlawed by the government, and I had to find ways to get customers to come to me and ask to buy?
- What if I were selling a telephone to a Trappist monk? He must observe a strict rule of silence but can nod acceptance at the close. How would I sell it?
- What if I had to get a year's worth of sales in eight hours?
- What if I could read the customer's mind before I entered his or her office?
- What if dogs could be trained to sell my products?
- What if I had to use a set number of words in sales presentations? For instance, no more or less than forty-five words.
- What if all products, goods, and services cost the same amount? A car would cost the same as a pencil, a house the same as a hamburger, and so on.
- What if I couldn't speak? How would I sell?

Let's work with: "What if dogs could be trained to sell my products?" What are the characteristics of dogs and how can they be related to selling?

Characteristics of dogs include: You train dogs by using repetitious techniques with small rewards for good behavior; dogs bark when threatened; they are loyal, territorial, affectionate, and eager to please. Dogs bury bones and chase cats. Some people are afraid of dogs.

What connections can you make between the characteristics of a dog and the characteristics of selling? What ideas does this "what if" question inspire? What would it be like if dogs could sell?

Possible lines of speculation:

- *Dogs are rewarded for good behavior with small rewards.* Create an incentive plan that gives an immediate reward upon the closing of a sale. Pay commissions, or a portion of the commission, immediately.
- *Dogs bark when threatened.* Develop an early warning system to alert us to the defective goods or services that salespeople hear about from customers. Reward salespeople who spot new problems.
- *Dogs are loyal.* Create loyalty among salespeople by publicly petting workers for good and consistent performance. Give tangible symbols of recognition. Reward loyal customers with surprise gifts and/or discounts.
- *Dogs are territorial.* Redefine company policy to afford more autonomy to salespeople in their territory. The salesperson makes all

decisions regarding that territory and runs it as if he or she owned it. Involve the salesperson in every decision that affects the territory.

- *Dogs are affectionate and eager to please.* Develop a customer-oriented campaign. Create a system wherein you periodically call customers after a sale to find out how things are and what more you can do. Send every customer a birthday card with a personal note.

- *Dogs bury bones.* Create an options package for customers with buried benefits that are triggered throughout the year. Consider a sales commission plan that buries a portion of each commission in an investment program that salespeople can draw on at a later date.

- *Dogs chase cats.* Develop a training program that concentrates on identifying and aggressively overcoming objections during the sales presentation. Train yourself and others to enjoy the identification and the handling of objections. Record objections and keep a tally of "caught" objections. Have a contest to see who catches and overcomes the most objections during the week.

- *Some people are afraid of dogs.* This fear diminishes once the person realizes that the dog is friendly. Create a useful premium to give to customers as a gift or a gesture of goodwill when cold calling. Differentiate yourself from other salespeople by establishing a friendly relationship with the client before you concentrate on the sale. Become a problem-solver for the customer.

Years ago, the president of a Swiss pharmaceutical company wistfully said, "What if our customers were dogs, would we be better off?" Months passed and he noticed that some of the orders for his antibiotics were from veterinarians. After researching the market he discovered that veterinarians had found that some antibiotics developed for humans were effective for animals, but the companies that developed these drugs refused to supply the vets. They disliked having to repackage and reformulate the drugs for animals. In addition, most thought it was a misuse of a noble medicine and were embarrassed by the thought of their drugs being used on animals.

The Swiss company approached the other manufacturers and obtained licenses for veterinary use of their drugs. Human medications have since come under price pressure and regulations, making veterinary medicine the most profitable segment of the pharmaceutical industry. The company that is harvesting the profits is the one that wondered what it would be like if its customers were dogs. Today the Swiss company is the world leader in veterinary medicine, although it never developed a single drug.

Summary

You take imaginative chances by asking imaginative questions. Spencer Silver took an imaginative chance with 3M's Post-it note pads. He discovered the sticky substance that eventually was applied to note pads, and went around 3M for five years saying, "What if we used it for this?" or "What if we used it for that?" He finally caught the attention of the right person, Arthur Fry, and Silver's glue, the glue that no one wanted, caught the attention of the world.

Percy Spencer was another person who could see "what ifs." In 1943, while prowling around Raytheon, he discovered that standing in front of a microwave guide had melted a candy bar in his pocket. Experimenting further, he found that microwaves could pop popcorn. When he was finished, he changed the eating habits of America.

Some people transform the sun into a yellow spot while others, like Silver and Spencer, can look at a mustard stain and see the sun.

COLOR BATH

"By command I mean the general's qualities
of wisdom, sincerity, humanity, courage,
and strictness."

SUN TZU

Our minds are constantly chattering away, keeping up an endless commentary about life, our problems, our feelings, our attitudes, and so on. Most of the time we aren't consciously aware of this stream of thoughts, yet it is the basis for most of our actions.

Our beliefs about what qualities we possess color our attitudes and energies. Many of these thoughts are like old tape recordings of negative thoughts we've had all our lives.

You can replace those old, negative tapes with new tapes that invoke positive qualities, and feel cheerful when overcoming difficulties, restful when working under pressure, sensitive and inspirational to your coworkers, warm toward your greatest competitor, creative when you need ideas, and strong when you need strength.

A Color Bath will activate the qualities and energies that you desire. Suppose you are feeling defeated and need strength. By bathing in the color red, you can summon feelings of strength and vitality and a strong feeling of "I can." Or perhaps you are feeling stressed and want to relax. By bathing in blue, you can bring forth restful, relaxing qualities and a strong sense of "I relax."

The seven colors of the visible spectrum are: red, orange, yellow, green, blue, indigo, and violet. The properties of these colors are:

Red excites the mind. It represents vitality, reproduction, and survival. Bathe in red when you need strength and persistence.

Orange is warm, cheerful, and emotional. Bathe in orange when you want to attract others, in your business or personal life.

Yellow is sensitive and inspirational. Bathe in yellow when you want to become more intuitive and need new ideas and concepts.

Green represents healing, harmony, and compassion. Bathe in green when you want to feel greater love and compassion for others and develop greater empathy.

Blue is restful and conservative. Bathe in blue when you are feeling stressed and need to relax.

Indigo (dark purple) represents creativity. Bathe in indigo when you want to be more creative and are looking for original concepts.

Violet brings on radical inspiration. Bathe in violet when you are looking for a radical, totally different idea, such as a revolutionary concept or invention.

BLUEPRINT

1. *Set aside about ten to twenty minutes.* Lie down on a comfortable sofa or bed and breathe deeply until you feel totally relaxed. (See "The Jell-O Syndrome" in chapter 22 for a good relaxation technique.)

2. *Select one of the basic colors and visualize the color and its qualities.* Assume that you selected the color red. When you feel relaxed, say to yourself silently, firmly, and clearly, "I now call forth the qualities of red."

3. *Imagine the color as a small ball of light above your head.* Slowly visualize that ball of red entering the crown of your head. See it filling your skull. Feel the color massaging your head and cleansing it of defeatist thoughts. Now bring red down into your throat. Allow the color to massage that area, cleaning out negative thoughts. Now move the color down through your shoulders into the chest cavity. Be aware of bathing your heart in red. Bathe your solar plexus, your abdomen, down to the root of your spine. Let your feelings of defeat emerge and let the color red wash them away. Now just let the color flow down from the top of your head through your body, down through your legs and feet. Imagine this flood of red coursing through you and eventually pouring into a drain. Check yourself. If you

feel any remaining defeatist thoughts, refocus the color and bathe that area.

4. *When you finish your color bath, affirm the desired quality.* Affirmations can be done silently, spoken aloud, or written. Take five minutes and affirm the color and its qualities. Affirmations should be short and simple words in the present tense, phrased in a positive way that feels right for you. Believe the affirmations as you do them. Suspend your doubts and put your full mental and emotional energies into them. Believe that the color bath has the power to create its quality within you.

    Be totally conscious of the affirmations as you recite or write them. Here are some sample affirmations for the color red:

    - I am red and all of its qualities of strength.
    - I feel vividly red and very strong.
    - Every day, in every way, I'm getting more and more strength.
    - I am naturally colored red.
    - I am an open red channel of persistence.
    - I exhibit the color red and its qualities every moment.
    - The more I feel like red, the stronger I feel.
    - The color red is within me and making me more vital each day.

Amazing results can be achieved when you deliberately cultivate positive qualities and energies. Consider how Jim Burke, president of Johnson & Johnson, quickly rebuilt public confidence in his company after the Tylenol cyanide poisonings shocked the world.

The color that best represents his qualities and energies is green (healing, harmony, and compassion). The quick decisions he made during the crisis were all doused in green. Among those decisions were:

- He decided that absolute candor was necessary.
- He ordered $100 billion worth of Tylenol destroyed because of his empathy with the consumer's fears.
- He told the people who threw away their tablets that the company would replace them free.

- He used real doctors to talk about the situation in television commercials.
- He constructed unique press conferences by satellite, connecting thirty cities and hundreds of reporters, so that each major city reporter had absolute open access to Johnson & Johnson. The company hid nothing from the press.

It was one of the greatest miracles in marketing history. By the time he finished, cynics had become true believers and he had won back Tylenol's market. When Burke revealed a new tamperproof package on the Phil Donahue show, people stood up and cheered. How many times have you heard anyone cheer for a consumer package?

If Burke had not exhibited the qualities of healing, harmony, compassion, and empathy, he would not have gotten the friendly media coverage he got. Because the press believed the compassion he exhibited for the consumer, they became his allies.

TALKING DOLLARS

Another way to stimulate positive qualities and energies is to feel and talk to an object. For instance, put a dollar bill in your hand. Touch it. Feel its energies and particular qualities. Smell it. Look at it. What qualities do you attribute to money? Write down what you feel. Fold it up. Unfold it. Wrinkle it and listen to it. What is it saying? What symbols come to mind when you think of money? List your feelings about money and what money can do for you. Now ask yourself: "What am I willing to do for money?" Write down your answers. Meditate on your dollar bill for a few more minutes and ask: "What am I *not* willing to do for money?" Again, write down your answers. Study all of your lists and answers. What do they tell you about the qualities of energies that you attribute to money? What do they tell you about yourself? Which of money's qualities and energies would you like to incorporate in yourself?

Suppose you identify one quality of money as "competition." People compete for money. Feel or play with a dollar bill whenever you want to be more competitive. If, on the other hand, having money makes you feel good, talk to a dollar bill when you want to feel warm and cheerful; if money reminds you of working and earning, play with money when you need to motivate yourself to work harder or longer.

As you focus on your desired quality, think about it in a positive, encouraging way. Make strong positive affirmations to yourself about the quality.

Imagine yourself filling up with the quality as you fondle your dollar bill. Continue to talk to your dollar bill until the quality or energy comes to you at will and you no longer need the dollar to summon it. Say to yourself: "I now call forth the quality of money." Feel the energy of money coming to you, or coming from someplace inside of you, filling you up, and radiating out from you. Experience the feeling and direct it toward any particular problem or situation.

You can do this with any object that you feel has strong qualities or energies, such as car keys, house keys, a military medal, your company logo, a favorite book, a poem, an inspirational quote, a photograph of someone you admire, and so on.

RING OF COLORS

While there are seven basic colors, there are estimated to be more than seven million discriminable colors, many of which we come in contact with every day. We can even create the illusion of color where none exists.

In 1838, a German psychologist by the name of G. T. Fechner twirled a ring made up of different-sized black and white spaces. He expected to see different shades of grey, and was astonished to see colors. This illusion is so mysterious that the phenomenon has been reported as a new discovery at least a dozen times since Fechner first reported it. In tribute to him, they are commonly referred to as Fechner's colors.

To see what he saw, photocopy the figure in the margin, place the straightened end of a paper clip through the center, tilt the figure slightly and spin it. You should be in moderate lighting, and you may have to experiment with several speeds before you can see the colors.

You will see light pastel colors. Some people see the colors easily, others have difficulty, but almost anyone can create this illusion.

BLUEPRINT

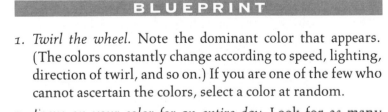

1. *Twirl the wheel.* Note the dominant color that appears. (The colors constantly change according to speed, lighting, direction of twirl, and so on.) If you are one of the few who cannot ascertain the colors, select a color at random.

2. *Focus on your color for an entire day.* Look for as many objects as possible that are or contain your color. Tune in

"blueness" (for example) and tune out the rest of the world.

3. *Look for relationships and connections between the colored objects and your challenge.* Ask questions such as:
   - What can I free-associate from the objects?
   - What are the similarities?
   - What are the contrasts?
   - What else does this make me think of?
   - What analogies can I make?
   - What connections can I force?

4. *Develop a chain of thoughts about the objects and the challenge.* Work with the chain of thoughts until you produce ideas.

Suppose my business challenge is: "In what ways might I improve the way clothes are washed?"

When I twirl the ring of colors, blue is the dominant color. I focus on it for an entire day—I see blue cars, blue shirts, a blue suit with dandruff on it, blue books, blue pens, blue eyes, blue houses, blue water, blue sky, a blue balloon, blue sweatshirts, blue clocks, a boy playing with a blue ball, and so on.

I free-associate and look for connections between the blue objects I observed and my challenge. For instance, the blue ball reminded me of an old Western I saw in which pioneer women washed clothes in a tub with water, soap, and round stones that resembled balls. When stirred, the stones created small areas of turbulence that enhanced the cleaning. This inspired an idea.

The idea: Manufacture small, reusable plastic spheres designed to create small areas of turbulence in a washing machine, to intensify the cleaning action. In addition, the balls would save on detergent and help prevent tangles. The balls could be made in fluorescent colors and sold in packs of four at supermarkets and laundromats. Add a clever name and you might have a winner.

The blue suit with dandruff reminded me of the hair and lint one has to deal with when washing clothes. I connected the blue ball with the balloon and—flash!—I had another idea.

The idea: Remove lint with an inflatable lint ball-filter. This filter would float in your washer, extracting lint and hair before it could reattach to the clothing. It would be easy to remove and clean.

When you look into a kaleidoscope, you see a pattern. If you manipulate the kaleidoscope's drum, you can see countless patterns. If you add a new piece of crystal to the kaleidoscope, you have a multitude of new patterns.

Your imagination works like a kaleidoscope. If you add a new fact, you add one new pattern. However, as soon as you manipulate, combine, and rearrange the new fact with the old, you get an even greater number of new patterns. Look what happened when an entrepreneur added "taxi" to his imagination.

An entrepreneur imported car-seat cushions made from wooden beads. These cushions had been popular in Asia for twenty years because they keep the driver cool, let air circulate beneath the driver's bottom, and give him a back and leg massage. However, Americans wouldn't buy them because they looked strange and uncomfortable. His challenge was: "In what ways might I market my seat cushion?" The entrepreneur focused on the color yellow and looked for relationships between yellow objects and his challenge. One of the yellow objects he saw was a taxi. He tugged on his imagination and saw a relationship between taxicabs and beaded seats.

The idea: He gave his seat to taxi drivers free. He met with the taxi drivers, told them the seat's history, and convinced them to try it. Taxi drivers used and liked them. Each seat has the entrepreneur's toll-free number displayed on the back where passengers can see it. Passengers inquire about the unusual seat cushion, and the cabbies would tell them about the history and virtues of the product. The taxicab became his billboard and sales skyrocketed. He now sells about 10,000 a month.

When you focus your attention, things jump out at you. For instance, when you learn a new word you tend to hear it immediately several times; if you buy a new Volvo, you suddenly see Volvos everywhere; when you are hungry you see restaurants, delis, and fast-food places everywhere; if you believe in the dignity of man, you see it everywhere; if you believe in conspiracies, you find them. Similarly, when you are looking for relationships between objects and the challenge you are working on, you will find them everywhere.

Idea

SUMMARY

When your brain is dry and ideas are scarce, irrigate it by focusing on objects of one color and searching for links between the objects and your challenge. Focusing on these relationships will stir the dull roots of your imagination, and ideas will start popping up like delicate little flowers after a spring rain.

CHAPTER TWENTY-EIGHT

DREAMSCAPE

"Supreme excellence consists in breaking the
enemy's resistance without fighting."

SUN TZU

Dreams are a rich source of ideas, as they often contain combinations and rearrangements of objects, challenges, and events that would be almost impossible to come up with while awake. Ideas twinkle in dreams like bicycle lights in a mist.

Many dreams are so bewildering, so crowded with bizarre details, that they seem to defy interpretation. Others work almost like poems, providing uncanny distillations of a situation.

On November 10, 1619, during a freezing winter in Germany, a young aristocrat dreamed throughout the night. When he awoke, he recorded his dreams in a now-famous dream diary, which detailed a new system of thought. His dreams that night changed the course of science and Western civilization. Much of the contemporary scientific method is based on the dream journals of that young aristocrat, René Descartes.

Robert Louis Stevenson dreamed his novels before he wrote them. Physicist Niels Bohr conceived of a model of the atom in a dream. James Watt revolutionized the ammunition industry with his dreams of falling lead. Dmitri Mendeleyev dreamed the solution for the arrangement of the elements. Samuel Taylor Coleridge dreamed the poem "Kubla Khan" before he wrote it.

Sleep psychologists claim that we have approximately six dreams each night, but we tend to forget most of them. You can learn to initiate a productive dream state, choose the subjects of your dreams, and remember them clearly.

1. *Formulate a question about your challenge.* Write the question several times and then, before you drift off to sleep, repeat it to yourself several more times. If necessary, do this several evenings in a row. The mind must work consciously on a challenge before the subconscious becomes employed.

2. *If you don't remember your dreams, wake up thirty minutes earlier.* This increases your chance of waking during a dreaming period rather than after one. When you awake, lie still. Prolong the quiet as long as possible as you reflect on the dream. Do not allow daytime interests to interrupt your ruminations. Dreams vanish like boats sailing into a fog bank, so record the dream after you've thought it over.

3. *Record the dream in a dream journal.* Keep the journal next to your bed, and record as many details as you remember. Sketch the vivid portions of the dream. If you can't remember a dream, record whatever is on your mind—these thoughts often come from the dream and provide a first clue to retrieving it.

4. *After the dream is recorded, ask yourself the following questions:*

   - How were the people, places, and events in the dream related to my question?
   - Who were the key players in the dream?
   - How does this relate to my question?
   - Does the dream change the nature of the question?
   - What elements in this dream can help solve my problem?
   - What associations does the dream conjure up that might help with my problem?
   - What is the answer from the dream?

5. *Take one or two dream images or ideas and free-associate from them.* Write down whatever comes to mind, and do it day after day. Soon the next dream will come along and your interpretation will go further.

6. *Keep the diary current.* Record your dreams daily. After you begin recording dreams you will remember more

dreams, in greater detail. You will begin to see patterns and themes unfolding and repeating; your dreams will become richer and richer with metaphorical meanings.

You will find that your dreams are based on a body of experiences, both past and present, that have some influence on you and your challenge. In the figure below, the black and white shapes are intermixed to form something. Can you determine what it is?

Most people cannot identify the figure without prolonged study. But once you know that it is the head of a cow, you can no longer see it as confusing. The cow's head is on the left side of the illustration; the dark area near the bottom is its mouth. If you still have trouble seeing it, try viewing the picture from a distance.

Ideas in dreams are like the cow in the picture—that elusive and that real.

The owner of a hobby store was making a reasonable profit, but wanted to do even better. His challenge was to improve his financial well-being. Trying creative dreaming, he had a recurrent dream of himself alone on a rock by a stormy sea. The wind was always blowing, and all the gold he sought was locked away below him in the rock. Then lightning would hit and split the rock, and golden disks would float out and circle in the sky. When they descended, they stacked themselves on top of the rock.

His interpretation of this dream was that he wasn't in business alone—there were other hobby and do-it-yourself stores in various locations around the city. The gold locked in the rock represented a potential profit for all of them. When the golden disks are freed by the lightning, they layer themselves on top of the rock, concentrated and available. Finally, this interpretation led to an idea.

The idea: A theme building. He bought a seven-story building and made it into a gigantic do-it-yourself, hobby, and toy center. He then convinced the other stores to lease space from him. His building is a concentration of hundreds of thousands of items that appeal to do-it-yourselfers. In addition, it offers ongoing classes in fields such as painting, bookbinding, stained-glass making, ceramics, household repairs, plumbing, and remodeling. It is *the* place to go for hobbies, toys, household repairs, or any do-it-yourself project.

Sometimes it seems like the ideas that are most deeply rooted in our minds, the most private and singular ones, came as spores on the prevailing night dreams, looking for any likely place to land, any welcome.

Frustrated by his inability to come up with a new idea for a seminar topic, a psychologist dedicated himself to creative dreaming to find one. He dreamed of a man who carried his genitals in a little box on his back and could send his penis off on adventures of its own. The man lay down to take a nap by a little stream. As soon as he fell asleep, his penis climbed out of the box, crossed the stream, and found a beautiful woman on the other side. After the penis finished its business, it returned to the box. The man woke up and continued on his way.

The psychologist pondered this dream and designed a seminar based on the question: "Is your sexuality something for which you are responsible or not?"

With creative dreaming, the "right" interpretation is the one that works for you. The unanticipated images from your dreams are starting points on which to hang your own personal meaning. Dreams weave together current experiences with ones from the past to create a unique narrative. Sometimes dreams remind you of what once was, like an Indian head nickel in a handful of new coins.

A retired dentist dreamed of a giant tooth with hair. When he awoke, he mused about the tooth walking into an old-fashioned barbershop for a haircut, and then, suddenly, he sat up straight. He had an idea for a new business venture.

The idea: Walk-in teeth cleaning services. Offer busy dental patients the same convenience they've come to expect when they want their hair trimmed. Get your teeth cleaned and polished in just thirty minutes, without an appointment, for $20. The business would be staffed by two dental hygienists working three cleaning stations. If any kind of dental problem is found, the patient would be referred back to their own dentist.

An apparently trivial dream may be very important in discovering what the dreamer's immediate difficulty actually is. Sometimes the same dream will give a clue to the solution.

Sports Illustrated reports that Nate Newton, a 320-pound Dallas Cowboy guard, has been trying to use dreams to lose weight. "Every night I tell myself, 'I'm going to dream about my girl.' But it's always ham hocks."

My nephew Karl tried creative dreaming to address the challenge of deciding on a college. He dreamed he was at the family's summer cottage. The tide was rising and gigantic, crashing waves had reached the cottage. Boats were disappearing beneath the sea. Then he saw a long object floating in the distance. A voice told him that the object was the only thing that could rescue him, that he had nothing to fear if he could reach it. He looked closely at the object and saw it was a baseball bat.

Most of the dream could be interpreted as symbolizing the feelings of any person who is about to begin some sort of independent life, but the bat was a purely personal reference. Karl associated the cottage with carefree summer life and a complete lack of responsibility, and also with financial security.

When I asked him what his association was with the bat, he said, "I have that baseball bat in my room." When I asked why, of all the objects in his room, his dream should choose this particular one, he was puzzled. Then he suddenly realized that the bat was the only thing in his life that he had bought with his own money.

The dream provided advice: "It seems I should select a college where I can try to pay at least part of my own way." He added, "It's kind of like the things you can trust most are the things that really belong to you."

SUMMARY

Dreams reveal things you did not know you knew. Elias Howe, struggling with his design for a sewing machine, reportedly dreamed he was captured by savages carrying spears with holes in their tips. Upon awakening, Howe realized he should put the hole for the thread at the end of the needle, not the top or middle. This minor modification made the sewing machine a reality.

It may be that our earliest mode of thinking was symbolic imagery—one reason, perhaps, that poetry can stir us as it does. Some dreams can haunt us with a power more pervasive even than that of poetry, shimmering in the mind like some lost city.

DA VINCI'S TECHNIQUE

"The Book of Military Administration says:
"As the voice cannot be heard in battle, drums and
bells are used. As troops cannot see each other clearly
in battle, flags and banners are used."

SUN TZU

Imagine a rectangular tray containing a rubber bag partially filled with oil. A steel marble dropped onto the bag's surface gradually sinks to the bottom, pushing the surface of the rubber bag before it. When the marble comes to rest, it is in the center of a depression. Drop a second marble and it will roll down the contour and come to rest against the first one. The second marble is *active*; it does not stay where it has been put down, but follows the slope created by the first one. All subsequent marbles will roll toward the first marble, forming a cluster.

In the same way, an active mind allows incoming information to organize itself into a new cluster, giving rise to new perspectives and new ideas.

One good way to originate new clusters of information is through pictures. In the beginning, humans communicated with pictures. The alphabet evolved from the various pictographic techniques; however, this does not mean that verbal thinking is more advanced.

Albert Einstein observed that:

The words of the language, as they are written or spoken, do not seem to play any role in my mechanism of thought. The psychical entities which seem to serve as elements in thought are certain signs and more or less clear images which can be voluntarily reproduced and combined.

Leonardo Da Vinci's technique for getting ideas was to close his eyes, relax totally, and cover a sheet of paper with random lines and scribbles. He would then open his eyes and look for images and patterns, objects, faces, or events in the scribble. Many of his inventions came forth unbeckoned from this random scribbling.

Scribbling allows you to put your abstract ideas into a tangible form. Imagine yourself flying over your challenge in an airplane to get a clear overview. While in the air, sketch what you see below you. Sketch as many alternative concepts as you think you see. You are your own audience; therefore, you can draw or sketch freely without worrying about what anyone will think. Sketching is a way of talking to yourself. Thomas Edison made hundreds of sketches and doodles before beginning to formulate an idea. GE has a collection of his doodles about the light bulb, most of which are undecipherable to anyone but Edison.

Graphic ideation (sketching, doodling, or drawing) is complementary to verbal ideation and can help you muster up new ideas.

BLUEPRINT

1. *Review a challenge you are working on.* In your mind's eye, scan its various aspects. Write the challenge on paper and reflect on it for a few minutes: What doesn't fit? What are the major obstacles? The unknown? What do I want to understand? At this point, the way I see it is . . . What's bothering me most is . . .

2. *Relax.* When relaxed, you will find your intuitive consciousness uses images and symbols more freely. (You will find a good relaxation technique in chapter 22, under "The Jell-O Syndrome.")

3. *Allow your intuition to offer images, scenes, and symbols that represent your situation.* You need not know what the drawing will look like before you draw it.

4. *Provide a format for the challenge by drawing a boundary.* This can be any size and shape you wish, and can be carefully or roughly drawn. The purpose is to separate the challenge from its surroundings and allow you to focus on it.

    A boundary also gives your drawing its own atmosphere or depth and helps establish a wholeness which in itself is meaningful and gives meaning to your drawing.

5. *Draw as your mind wants to draw.* Practice drawing without conscious direction. (Some people use their opposite hand to get less conscious control of the images.) Pretend the lines and scribbles are dictating how to draw and place them. Do not censor what you draw—the drawing is private and need not be shown to anyone. Let the drawing flow from you onto the paper.

   Chance, or randomness, gives depth to your scribbling. It points to an unknown but active principle of order and meaning that can be thought of as a secret message from your unconscious.

6. *If one drawing does not seem enough, take another piece of paper and do another one, and another—as many as you need.*

7. *Examine your drawing.* The drawing is a message from your subconscious. Look at the image as a whole and then at the separate parts. These are visual representations of your thoughts. Search the symbols and scribbles for unexpected signs and new information.

8. *Write down the first word that comes to mind for each image, symbol, scribble, line, or structure.*

9. *Combine all the words and write a paragraph.* Free-associate, writing whatever thoughts come to mind. Compare the paragraph with your drawing. If you feel the need, revise your paragraph until you are comfortable that the drawing and the words represent the same thoughts in two different languages: verbal and graphic.

10. *Consider how what you wrote relates to your challenge.* Has your viewpoint changed? Do you have new ideas? New insights? Surprises from your subconscious? What parts puzzle you? What's out of place?

    Be especially attentive to questions that pop up in your mind such as: What is that? How come? Where is that? What could that mean? If you feel it's important to find the answer to a particular question, you are on the way to a breakthrough solution.

Think of every drawing as an artichoke in which not only the heart and leaves but the spiny choke as well are edible.

One accountant drew his images on the back of scrolls of adding machine paper. He started asking himself questions about the paper he was using. He knew some of his colleagues felt so passionately about the bottom line that they rewound adding machine paper to use the other side. He designed a gadget to do the job for them: Instead of feeding onto the desk, the paper rewinds onto a roll on the back of the adding machine. It pays for itself after twenty rolls. His invention was the direct result of asking questions about *every* aspect of his drawing.

If you are unable to provoke new ideas with this technique or have failed to gain a deeper insight, keep repeating the technique each day. After you're relaxed, ask yourself, "Well now, what is the status of my challenge today?" and repeat the exercise.

University textbooks are normally sold through university bookstores. Many times, these textbooks are packaged with study guides, learning notes, course readers, and other auxiliary items. The bookstores resist stocking these extra items, pleading lack of space and low profits. Many textbook publishers had to rely on inserts and advertising to sell the auxiliary items, with minimal success. The major obstacle to overcome is reliance on the bookstore.

The challenge is: "In what ways might I create new channels of distribution for auxiliary items that accompany university textbooks?"

After contemplating this challenge for a few days, I began to draw whatever images came to mind. I drew without conscious direction and tried to draw and place the images as if they were dictating to me where to place them. I made several drawings before one galvanized my imagination. My final drawing looked like this:

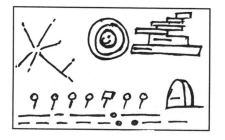

I studied the drawing, writing down the first word that came to mind for each image, combined the words, looked for and forced connections between the images and my challenge, and paid attention to every question that popped into my mind. Some of my thoughts were:

- Different channels.
- Computer programs.
- Computer floppy disk.
- Stack of coins.
- People lined up in front of a machine.
- People all converging on one spot.
- Tombstone.
- Slot for coins.
- Six round heads and one square one.

My intuitive interpretation of the images suggested an idea for a new and different channel of distribution.

The idea: Set up a system of software dispensing machines on campuses. Students can purchase a "disk" or bring one of their own, and load it, for a fee, with one of the following:

- Study guides for various textbooks.
- Lecture notes for various classes.
- Sample test questions for various classes.
- Math learning programs.
- Course readers.
- Bibliographies.
- Campus phone book.
- Games.

The software dispensing machines publish "on demand," obviating the need for the traditional marketing channel, the bookstore. The machines would be compatible with both IBM and Apple.

Once your subconscious thoughts are expressed in pictures you can hang conscious ideas, analogies, and metaphors on them. This lets you organize disparate thoughts and begin to imagine new possibilities and solutions.

Sometimes a question comes up that you can't answer but that seems very important to the solution. (For instance, "I wonder what that figure means, it seems very significant.") When this happens, your mind will not rest until an answer is found; it will search for the primal meaning slumbering beneath the world of appearances. It may take time, but eventually your mind will find the answer.

Nature's Handwriting

Leonardo da Vinci taught himself to read nature's handwriting, which can be seen everywhere: in wings, eggshells, clouds, snow, ice, crystals, and other chance conjunctions. He used these insights in his quest for new ideas and solutions to problems. Leonardo could have coaxed ideas out of a salesman's shoe. Robert McKim's *Experiences in Visual Thinking* provides this illustrative excerpt from Leonardo's notebooks:

> I cannot forbear to mention . . . a new device for study which although it may seem trivial and almost ludicrous, is nevertheless extremely useful in arousing the mind to various inventions. And that is, when you look at a wall spotted with stains . . . you may discover a resemblance to various landscapes, beautiful with mountains, rivers, rocks, trees. Or again, you may see battles and figures in action, or strange faces and costumes, and an endless variety of objects which you could reduce to complete and well-drawn forms.

Leonardo also wrote an essay agreeing with Botticelli that you can throw a paint-soaked sponge at a wall and see a host of different images in the splashes. These images are starting points for ideas; your mind superimposes the possibility of meaning onto them.

The pattern in the margin was created by splashing some ink on paper. Study the pattern. Can you free-associate from the pattern to an idea for a new product, service, or process?

A friend studied the pattern and saw:

- String.
- A spider's web.
- Coffee spill on a rug.
- McDonald's logo.

These images clustered into a new idea. He thought of fast food, liquids that spill, containers for liquids, and webbed objects. Then, bingo, he came up with an idea to replace cardboard trays at concession stands and fast-food outlets.

The idea: A cup carrier made out of plastic loops that hang from a web of strings that can tote four cups at once.

The design eliminates spilling—lids aren't even necessary. The carrier costs less and takes up less space than most paper trays.

SUMMARY

Understanding your drawings is like untying a knot. When a knot is untied, the string must be drawn back the way it traveled when the knot was tied. When you search your drawings for ideas, you are drawn back to your unconscious, which is where the drawing came from in the first place.

The ideas do not rise up from your drawing but from the deepest part of your unconscious, the secret archive stored in the soul at birth, enhanced by every waking moment of life, which has the power and the vision to let you create something never before heard or seen.

CHAPTER THIRTY

DALI'S TECHNIQUE

*"When the strike of a hawk breaks the body of
its prey, it is because of timing."*

SUN TZU

You can reach the center of a circle from any point on the compass. Similarly, you can reach into your unconscious from a variety of different starting points.

One starting point is *hypnogogic imagery.* This technique produces autonomous inner imagery that can be captured just before you fall asleep. It's a somewhat difficult technique to master, but when mastered it can provide strong images.

Can you identify the figure in the margin?

It is the letter E. It is difficult to see because it is such a strong and deep E. If you have difficulty seeing it, try looking at it from a distance. Once you understand what it is, it becomes impossible *not* to see the E. The images produced by hypnogogic imagery are like this—somehow deeper and stronger than those produced by other techniques.

This imagery can be either visual or auditory—it cannot be controlled or directed. Some people are even able to envision fantastic surreal imagery in colors that appear deeper and plusher than seemingly possible.

Salvador Dali used this technique to conjure up the extraordinary images in his paintings. He would put a tin plate on the floor and then sit by a chair beside it, holding a spoon over the plate. He would then totally relax his body; sometimes he would begin to fall asleep. The moment that he began to doze the spoon would slip from his fingers and clang on the plate, immediately waking him to capture the surreal images.

Hypnogogic images seem to appear from nowhere, but there is a logic. The unconscious is a living, moving stream of energy from which thoughts gradually rise to the conscious level and take on a definite form. Your unconscious is like a hydrant in the yard while your consciousness is like a faucet upstairs in the house. Once you know how to turn on the hydrant, a constant supply of images can flow freely from the faucet.

These forms give rise to new thoughts as you interpret the strange conjunctions and chance combinations.

BLUEPRINT

1. *Think about your challenge.* Consider your progress, your obstacles, your alternatives, and so on. Then push it away and relax.

2. *Totally relax your body.* Try to achieve the deepest muscle relaxation you can. You may wish to use the technique described in chapter 22, under "The Jell-O Syndrome."

3. *Quiet your mind.* Do not think of what went on during the day or your challenges and problems. Clear your mind of chatter.

4. *Quiet your eyes.* You cannot look for these images. Be passive. You need to achieve a total absence of any kind of voluntary attention. Become helpless and involuntary and directionless. If you fall asleep easily, hold a spoon loosely in one of your hands. You can enter the hypnogogic state this way, and, should you begin to fall asleep, you will drop the spoon and awaken in time to capture the images.

5. *Record your experiences immediately after they occur.* The images will be mixed and unexpected and will recede rapidly. They could be patterns, clouds of colors, or objects.

6. *Look for the associative link.* Write down the first things that occur to you after your experience. Look for links and connections to your challenge. Ask questions such as:
   - What puzzles me?
   - Is there any relationship to the challenge?
   - Any new insights?
   - What's out of place?
   - What disturbs me?
   - What do the images remind me of?
   - What are the similarities?

- What analogies can I make?
- What associations can I make?
- What do the images resemble?

A restaurant owner used hypnogogic imagery to inspire new promotion ideas. He kept seeing giant neon images of different foods: neon ice cream, neon pickles, neon chips, neon coffee, and so on. The associative link he saw between the various foods and his challenge was to somehow use the food itself as a promotion.

The idea: He offers various free food items according to the day of week, the time of day, and the season. For instance, he might offer free pickles on Monday, free ice cream between 2 and 4 P.M., free coffee on Wednesday nights, free sweet rolls in the spring, and so on. He advertises the free food items with neon signs, but you never know what food items are being offered free until you go there. The sheer variety of free items and the intriguing way in which they are offered has made his restaurant a popular place to eat.

Another promotion he created as a result of seeing images of different foods is a frequent-eater program. Anyone who hosts five meals in a calendar month gets $50 worth of free meals. The minimum bill is $20 but he says the average is $30 a head. These two promotions have made him a success.

The images you summon up with this technique have an individual structure that may indicate an underlying idea or theme. Your unconscious mind is trying to communicate something specific to you, though it may not be immediately comprehensible. The images can be used as armatures on which to hang new relationships and associations.

A college professor who taught a mixed-media art class was bored with the traditional first assignment of painting a self-portrait. He wanted an exercise that would explore space and perception. Using hypnogogic imagery for inspiration, he saw technicolor trees dressed up like human beings walking around and talking. He thought about this image for days, and then the idea for a new assignment struck.

The idea: He had his students personalize a two-by-four board and carry it around with them everywhere. The students shaped and designed their boards to express their experiences, personalities, and interests. The board served as a yardstick for students to relate to their environment and forced them to work with materials they wouldn't normally use.

One student made an environmental statement by painting her board blue and black, attaching tree branches and press clippings about forest fires, and scorching parts of it. Another student made his board an extension of his Mexican heritage. He decorated it like Mexican folk art, with carvings of an eagle, snake, and cactus. He depicted his family tree and attached cloth poinsettias, a rosary, and even a piñata.

SUMMARY

Treat the images as fact, but make no assumptions about them except that you experienced them, and that somehow they must make sense. One workshop contemplated ways to clean up the environment. One of the participants reported that she got the following image using this technique.

What is your interpretation? What is the associative link between the image and the challenge? Can you use the image to produce an idea to clean up the environment?

The workshop made the following associations:

- A dead bird found on a polluted beach.
- The hand that polluted the beaches killed the bird.
- The same hand tenderly holds the bird.
- The hand did not intend to kill the bird.
- The hand is a corporate hand.

These associations led to the idea of asking oil and chemical companies for a hand in cleaning up the environment. They approached Exxon Chemical and asked them to convert collected trash into plastic, barnacle-proof beach benches.

You will not always be able to convert the images into meaningful ideas. At times, the message may be too complex and difficult to link with your present situation. When that happens, certain images' meanings may remain forever out of reach like delicate balloons bouncing along the ceiling.

CHAPTER THIRTY-ONE

NOT KANSAS

"Toto, something tells me we're not
in Kansas anymore."

DOROTHY IN *THE WIZARD OF OZ*
(MGM, 1939)

It may well be that modern man's only true remaining adventure lies in the inner realm of the unconscious self. Not Kansas is a technique for using the imagination, under the guidance of the intellect and will, to take you on such an adventure. It will help you coax out messages from your unconscious.

This Thinkertoy has to be experienced before its power becomes evident. I'm always anxious when others first try it. I feel as if I am watching one of those old war movies in which a nurse is removing the last foot of white bandages from a soldier's eyes. Will he see?

BLUEPRINT

1. *Relax.* You may wish to use the technique described in chapter 22, under "The Jell-O Syndrome."

2. *Ask your unconscious for an answer to your challenge.* Write out the challenge and ask your unconscious to give you a symbol or image of how to solve your challenge.

3. *Take a guided imagery journey.* There are two model journeys described in this section: The Dakotas and Storm.

4. *Accept whatever messages emerge.* Don't censor anything. Trust your messages. The more you trust, the freer the images become, and the more truth you will find inherent in the images.

5. *Use your imagination to make the images as clear and vivid as you can.* Record or draw them immediately.

6. *If confusing images occur, conjure up others.* Become a Sam Spade of images, tracking down the ones you can use to solve your challenge.

7. *Look for qualities, patterns, relationships, and clues.* Use the messages, images, and symbols as a departure point for free-association.

After reading the following example of a guided imagery journey, The Dakotas, close your eyes and take a few minutes to visualize the scene it describes. Then, try using it to solve one of your challenges. It's a bit like sex—you can't realize what it's really like by just reading about it. You have to do it.

THE DAKOTAS

Think of a challenge you are currently working on. Write the challenge on a piece of paper as objectively as possible, as if you were a reporter writing a brief description of the challenge for the paper. Contemplate the challenge for a few minutes after you write it. Ask for an answer.

Close your eyes and relax deeply for five to ten minutes. Clear your mind. Try going to your private, inner sanctuary to breathe deeply and relax.

When you are deeply relaxed, imagine you are camping in the deep Dakotas next to a deserted mine shaft. It's late afternoon and getting cool. As the sun sets, the buttes and coulees, the cliffs and sculptured hills and ravines have lost their burned, afternoon look and are glowing with yellow and rich browns and a hundred variations of red and silver gray, all picked out by streaks of coal black. You go to a thicket of dwarfed and wind-warped cedars and junipers, and once there are stopped, surprised by the color and clarity of light.

Against the descending sun, the rocks are dark and clean-lined, while to the east, the landscape shouts with color. The night, closing around you, is lovely beyond thought, for the stars are so close that, although there is no moon, the starlight makes a silvery glow in the sky.

The air cuts your nostrils—the wind is blowing from the north and has winter in it. You collect a pile of dry, dead cedar branches and build a small fire to warm yourself, smelling the perfume of the burning wood and hearing its excited crackle. The fire makes a dome of yellow light over you, and nearby you hear an owl screech and the barking of coyotes.

Hunched over the fire, you dip a rainbow trout in cornmeal flour and fry it crisp in bacon fat. Holding the trout by its head and tail, you nibble it off its backbone, finishing with the tail, crisp as a potato chip. You finish your meal with coffee and hot homemade biscuits smothered in butter. You're warm and relaxed and feel good all over. Something rustles the thicket. As it approaches you, you realize that no danger exists for you or it. What is it? Have a dialogue with it. Ask it to speak to you; ask how it represents a solution to your challenge. Pay attention and ask for clarification where necessary. When you are satisfied, thank it for its insights, and allow it to disappear back into the thicket.

You finish your coffee and eat an apple so crisp and sweet that it seems to explode with juice when you bite into it. The campfire burns low and the thicket rustles from a strange wind that stirs mysterious feelings in you.

The night begins to turn cold. You put on your insulated underwear and the warmth gives you pure ecstatic comfort. You pick up your kerosene lamp, trim the wick, and light it to make a golden butterfly of flame. The lamp gives you warmth as well as light, and you think that no pleasanter light was ever designed. This must be like the lamps the pilgrims used.

You take your lamp to the abandoned mine, lie on the ground, and peer into the shaft to its very source. When your eyes adjust to the darkness, you see something in the depths. What is it? Study it and then let it go, but remember what you saw.

As you get up and prepare to leave the mine, you notice a weatherbeaten leather briefcase lying in the grass. You pick it up and open it. Inside you find a piece of paper folded in quarters.

As you unfold the paper, you see that on it is written a message in response to your challenge. You read the message. Contemplate the message and how it might help you solve your challenge.

When you are finished, return to your campsite. Take a deep breath and try to fix the images you received in your consciousness, then open your eyes and immediately write or draw your impressions and images.

Practice this exercise until you feel comfortable with it and images begin to appear freely and vividly. The images you invoke are clues to solutions. It may take time for the images and their import to become clear; sometimes you must wait for other images to furnish a context. Eventually, you'll find meanings for these slippery, dodging ghosts.

A community newspaper publisher wanted to make his newspaper unique and different.

He took a guided journey to The Dakotas. The images and impressions he recorded were: comfort, dogs, friendship, hunger, chickens, coldness, death, warmth, animals approaching in the dark, no danger from the animal, turning cold, dead pilgrims, and pleasant memories. The message that he found in the briefcase read: "Dead dogs are a comfort too."

He wondered, "How can dead dogs relate to my challenge?" He thought about pets, death, and grieving owners. Then the idea arrived.

The idea: An obituary column for pets. It's a journalism first and something no major publication could attempt or dare to emulate. Pet lovers liked it and, since most people have pets, circulation rose.

The obituaries are really about people's relationships with animals. The pet owners make them lively and personal by writing about what the pet did all day. For example, a typical obit reads:

Jazz, my dog, in many ways was unremarkable. Like so many of us, she liked to spend her nights on the recliner watching television. Her favorite show was "Miami Vice." Wise potato chips were her favorite snack. Her occasional outbursts of temper, often brought on when others tried to share the recliner, were just her style, and everyone understood. Jazz lived to go on vacation just once.

You certainly don't have to use The Dakotas—you may feel more comfortable writing and using scenarios that center on beaches, vacations, voyages, space trips, mysteries, or whatever. The point of any scenario is to get as many of your senses involved as possible in an imaginary setting, and guide your imagination to actively search for messages and images from your unconscious.

Remember, it doesn't matter whether the cat is black or white, so long as it catches the mouse. Nor does it matter if ideas and insights come from your conscious or unconscious psyche.

Following is another of my favorite guided journeys, titled Storm. Use the same procedures that you used in The Dakotas. Relax, write your challenge, and ask your unconscious for symbols or images to help you resolve your challenge.

STORM

You had never seen such a sunset. The sun was like a dying coal, ringed with black long before it neared the horizon. After the sun set, the rim of the earth was blood-red for a few minutes, then the red was streaked with black. When you looked at the eerie sky, it seemed as if the world had turned upside down and the road that ought to be beneath your feet was now above your head. And then the sky turned black.

You are surprised by a flicker of light to the west—so quick that you do not recognize it as lightning. But it flickers again and again and soon is almost constant. Then comes the thunder, with a sound that seems to roll over you like boulders. The lightning begins to drive into the earth, with streaks as big as poles and terrible sounds.

The rain begins, pelting down in big scattered drops that at first feel good, but the drops grow bigger and soon the rain is falling in sheets, blown this way and that by the fitful wind. In a bright flash of lightning, you see something run in front of you. What is it? Study it and then let it go, but remember what you saw.

The water beats down more heavily, pounding you and running in streams off your hat brim. The rain is now so heavy that you begin to think you might be drowned. A stream of water pours down in front of your nose while another runs down your back. You are so cold and wet that you feel you might never get warm again.

The ground is covered with water and there is nothing to do but splash along. Suddenly, you begin to slide—you have stepped into a hole and you feel water rising up to your hips. You climb out and squish along again.

Soon you get too tired to think and can only hope for morning. But the night goes on and on. Finally, the lightning dies and the hard rain slows to a drizzle. You stop to empty your shoes of water. You drop one. When you stoop down to pick it up, you notice a bottle with a slip of paper in it. You pick up the bottle and put it in your pocket.

A little while later, dawn breaks and the rain stops completely. The sky is cloudless. The first sunlight sparkles on the wet trees and bushes and on the hundreds of scattered puddles. Cold and damp, you bend over a puddle and wash the mud off your clothes. Now that the sun is beginning to warm things up, you find a grassy hill that isn't too wet and start a small fire. Starved, you fry up some eggs and thick slices of bacon. Breaking the fried eggs with your knife, you eat them with slices of bacon as you warm your body by the fire.

Remembering the bottle, you take out the note and read it slowly. What are the images? Open your eyes and write or draw your impressions and images. Write whatever comes to mind.

If the images are cloudy, repeat the exercise daily until you are comfortable with it and the images grow vivid. Begin to imagine that you are going to experience a breakthrough and the images will flow.

A lawyer who was trying to find a new business niche experienced Storm several times. He kept seeing the image of a doctor in rags running from someone in the storm. He wondered what would make this doctor so poor and scared. "Malpractice suits," he thought and decided to provide a service to protect doctors from frivolous lawsuits.

The idea: A service that helps doctors avoid malpractice claims by identifying litigious patients in advance. He discovered that 35 percent of all people who file malpractice suits have been plaintiffs in previous civil actions. His idea is to computerize all civil actions in certain target cities back to a given date. He will then sell the information to doctors for an annual fee plus a service charge for each search. The flip side is that he also plans to computerize doctors' litigation histories and provide a search service for malpractice lawyers.

Those who deny the value of asking the unconscious for ideas are those who decline to taste it. They are like people who have been eating plain boiled asparagus for so long that they begin to deny the very existence of Indian restaurants.

JUST ASK

Once you are able to summon up images from your unconscious at will, you can simply ask your unconscious for answers. The basic procedure is:

1. Formulate a challenge.
2. Address it to your unconscious.
3. Ask for the answer to emerge as a mental image.

If you are adept at imaging, the answer will emerge spontaneously and effortlessly. If a chain of images emerges, often the first one is the most significant. Spend some time studying that image for meaning.

In the figure in the margin, the lines seem irrelevant. Some appear to form right angles, but the lines do not appear to represent anything meaningful.

Now, imagine that the lines represent the shadow of the block letter H illuminated from above. Imagine that you are looking down at it. Do you see how your imagination formed the H out of a seemingly irrelevant collection of lines? You have imagined it into existence.

This is why it's important not to censor or ignore mental images that seem irrelevant. Often, after considerable attention, your imagination will coax out a message. And once you imagine the message, it exists.

Guided imagery adventures such as The Dakotas and Storm get you in touch with your unconscious, giving it an opportunity to express itself. This technique helps you overcome "conscious cramp" (the mental strain which comes from overusing your conscious mind) and allows the images and messages that are always present to come into your consciousness. Once retrieved, they may almost seem like a lonely and mysterious poetry that leads the way to ideas and insights in accordance with some secret design.

Another way to get in touch with your unconscious is The Three Doors.

THE THREE DOORS

Formulate and write a definite question about your challenge. Relax. Breathe deeply and slowly. With each breath, your lungs fill with fresh, clean air and you feel yourself becoming lighter. Keep taking deep breaths until you feel everything become effortless and easy.

Imagine you are standing before a series of doors, one behind the other. Visualize yourself opening the doors one at a time. When you've finished, write down what you saw and felt, and what you did.

Many people feel The Three Doors leads them to deeper levels of their unconscious. Each door that is opened represents going deeper and deeper into yourself. The third door seems to reveal the most significant answers.

You can search for meaning in the images generated, or free-associate from them to find ideas for solving your challenge. A city planner faced the challenge of improving city construction projects. The question he wanted resolved was: How can we avoid the chaos that city construction projects create? Tearing up pavement is unsightly, inconvenient, and causes financial harm to city merchants.

Using The Three Doors, he called up the following:

Door one: storm clouds.
Door two: long sidewalks.
Door three: long winding snakes.

The meaning he found in free-associating from these images led to a new idea for the installation of sewer pipes and cables.

The idea: Put underground cables and sewer pipes in modular concrete elements above the ground, molded as curbs (much like long concrete snakes winding through the city). These elements are easy, fast to install, repair, and will reduce the cost and inconvenience to the city and, in particular, to its merchants.

Summary

The unconscious is pure nature and, like nature, has great gifts for those who know how to find them. Songwriter and musician John Lennon taught himself to drop a hook into his unconscious and dredge up the images that he integrated into his music. He would relate the hooked images and messages to his challenge of creating original songs.

The logic of dredging for ideas is similar to the way treasure hunters search for lost booty. They suppose it's down there under the black, mysterious flowing water, and they work the grappling hooks back and forth, back and forth, back and forth, until they snag something and drag it to the surface.

You can too.

281

—

CHAPTER THIRTY-TWO

THE SHADOW

"Subtle and insubstantial, the expert leaves no trace; divinely mysterious, he is inaudible."

SUN TZU

Close your left eye and shift your gaze over the target on the left until the target on the right disappears. This means that you have found your right eye's blind spot, a small area with no light receptors. By fixating your right eye on the left target, you become blind to the target on the right. Similarly, when you fixate on your conscious mind you become blind to the value of the unconscious.

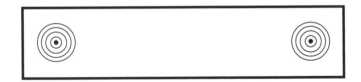

We fixate on the conscious mind because we have been taught that it is the master of the universe. If you indulge yourself with this illusion about the heroic nature of the conscious mind and disregard the unconscious as you fish for ideas, you are like a fisherman who stands on a whale while fishing for minnows.

But how do you get in touch with your unconscious? It's one thing to say, "Let ideas roll out of my unconscious mind like mighty waters," quite another to work out the irrigation system. You need a technique.

Look at the shape that appears in the margin on the facing page. Can you determine what it is?

The object is a kite, with the top of the kite at the lower right. Once you name the object, your perception changes and the figure becomes meaningful. When you name something, you create expectations and change your perceptions. Once the figure is given meaning by naming it, it is impossible to look at it and have the perception you had before.

In the same way, you can organize the irregular shapes from your unconscious into regular ones by personifying your unconscious. This technique is known as psychosynthesis, and it has incredible potential since there is no known limit to the capacities of the deep unconscious. Psychosynthesis has been used by geniuses, visionaries, artists, and inventors for centuries. Douglas MacArthur had numerous conversations with the personification of his hero-father whom he would conjure up to discuss strategy in the Pacific. Mozart was a coarse, narcissistic boor; however, when he communicated with his personified inner self, the result was some of the most complex and sensitive music the world has ever known.

Buckminster Fuller once had a conversation with his inner spiritual guide who told him: "You do not belong to you. You belong to the Universe." Fuller went on to become an architect-engineer-poet-futurist who shook the world with his technological innovations and visions of global unity. Milton referred to his inner guide as his "Celestial Patroness, who . . . unimplor'd . . . dictates to me my unpremeditated Verse."

MacArthur, Mozart, Fuller, and Milton used imagination to create a route between the conscious and unconscious and back again. By creating and interacting with their inner advisors, they learned to collect information from their unconscious and used this information to solve challenges.

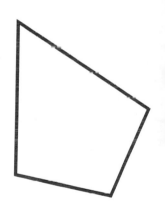

Stuart Miller, an authority on psychosynthesis, describes in *Dialogue With Higher Self* one way of initiating an interior dialogue:

Assume, with many ancient traditions, that you have within you a source of understanding and wisdom that knows who you are, what you have been, and what you can most meaningfully become in the future. This source is in tune with your unfolding purpose. It can help you direct your energies toward achieving increasing integration, toward harmonizing and unifying your life.

Having made this assumption, close your eyes, take a few deep breaths, and imagine that you are seeing the face of a wise old man or woman whose eyes express great love for you. If you have difficulty visualizing this, first imagine a candle flame, burning steadily and quietly, and then let the face appear at the center.

Engage this wise old person in dialogue, in whatever way seems best: use the presence and guidance of the sage to help you better understand whatever questions, directions or choices you are dealing with at the moment. Spend as much time as you need in this dialogue, and when you are finished, write down what happened, amplifying and evaluating further whatever insights were gained.

You can create a personal adviser to help you create associative imagery while in a relaxed awake state. Choose anyone you like, alive or dead, real or fictional: Sun Tzu, Marie Curie, Socrates, Batman, Wonder Woman, Amelia Earhart, Napoleon Bonaparte, Leonardo da Vinci, Indira Gandhi, Thomas Edison, Cornelius Vanderbilt, Buddha, Eleanor Roosevelt, Henry Ford, or an imaginary, all-knowing, mythical figure or guru to help you with your question or challenge.

With so many possible advisors available, you need to make some choices. As you move toward forming a relationship, it is important that you clearly envision the kind of adviser you want to work with. By clarifying and defining the relationship, you will know what kind of experience you hope to share and in what areas you hope to get meaningful ideas and advice.

BLUEPRINT

To invoke your personal mentor, perform the following:

Let go of your tension. Consciously take your body into a state of deep relaxation. You may wish to use the technique described under "The Jell-O Syndrome" in chapter 22.

Do not worry about achieving a deep enough level of relaxation. Just be passive and allow relaxation to occur at its own pace.

Imagine that your body is surrounded with soft, glowing white light. Let the light comfort you and bathe you in its soft radiance.

Now imagine that you are walking into a favorite place (house, boat, mountain, forest, room, whatever). Picture the details. What does it look like? Smell like? Feel like? What sounds do you hear?

Picture your spiritual mentor walking toward you. Look at his or her face. What do you see? Be aware of your emotions and reactions. Say to your mentor: "Be my guide. Introduce me to solutions and to new ideas. Lead me to the resolution of my problem." The more fully you create the pictures in your mind, the more powerful the communication with your unconscious will be.

Have your guide answer, beginning a brief dialogue. Exchange names and details of your challenges and problems. Make it as real as possible. You may get immediate answers, but if not, don't get discouraged. The answers will come to you in some form later.

There is one important rule to remember when using this technique: Give your full attention to what the mentor says or does, just as much as you would if you met your mentor in the outer world. This will keep the experience from remaining a passive fantasy.

Bring the conversation to a close. Have your guide say to you, "Listen, I'm here for you. Call me up whenever you need me. Know that I'll help you whenever you need me." Feel yourself trusting that. Open your eyes and return to the outside world.

People have different experiences in meeting their guides. Don't be surprised if your guide seems eccentric or has a sense of humor or a flair for the dramatic.

Phil Pies, who is known by his friends as the King of Batavia, related this story to me about his inner guide, whom he calls "Shadow." Phil wanted to do something to help educate the disadvantaged. But what can one person do? Phil called up Shadow, who arrived with a bulldog. He asked Shadow, "How can I generate scholarships for those students who are unable to attend college without spending a tremendous amount of money?"

"What did people use before money?" asked Shadow.

"Well, I suppose they bartered goods and services." Phil replied.

Shadow smiled and said, "Exactly."

Phil mused about this for days. How could barter be employed to help educate the disadvantaged? Then it hit him.

The idea: A not-for-profit bartering organization. The concept is simple. A business agrees to donate goods (excess equipment or inventory) to the organization, which then locates a college willing to exchange tuition credit for the donated goods. The exchange is made, and the college issues scholarship credits to the not-for-profit organization. When a disadvantaged student applies to the organization for financial aid, it pairs the student with the appropriate college and the student is issued tuition credits in the name of the business which originally donated the goods. Everybody wins, as excess shelving, computers, and so on are turned into education for the disadvantaged. The businesses can write off their tax-deductible donations.

When you first try this technique, your mentor may be hard to understand, or you may not like him or her. If your mentor is confusing, ask for another spiritual mentor who is easier for you to understand. Your mind will oblige. If you feel good with your experience, then stay with your guide. If not, change your guide. You may change guides frequently, or you may stay with the same guide for years.

This is not a mysterious technique; it is a way of personifying your conflicting ideas and emotions in the form of a specific image, of activating your unconscious through concentration. Still, some people feel awed and magical and mysterious when they become expert at this technique.

A police detective investigating a murder faced the challenge of finding the murder weapon. He consulted with his inner advisor who simply said, "Ti lo." He got the same response every time he tried. Finally, he wrote it down and free-associated from it. He reversed it to "Lo ti," which he translated to "low-tide." He directed the search to the beach at low tide and the murder weapon was found. The message was based on a body of experiences that had some significance for his challenge, but that he didn't know was influencing him.

With practice, you will find answers and associations that are extraordinarily varied and novel. You may see the associative link immediately, or the message may not be readily understandable until later.

The CEO of a major company was confronted with serious financial difficulties. Since he viewed the company as the source of his happiness, he ignored the problems and refused to discuss them with other officers of the company. He began to project the problems on the other people involved. Finally, he tried to repress these projections as being disloyal to his friends.

Up against the wall, he created a personal spiritual advisor he called "Companion." Companion told him: "You drowned the employees of the company whom you feared. But now you are attacked by a greater enemy. If you had not drowned the employees, you might have received help from them, where without them you have little chance."

He chewed on this like a rubber meatball. After several days, he interpreted it to mean that he had covered up an increasingly bad situation for fear that the situation would not be solvable and would lead to the dissolution of the source of his happiness—the company. The greater enemy was the unconscious guilt, resentment, and anger that were overwhelming him and making it impossible for him to work. In the end, he revealed all the disturbing and negative aspects of the financial situation and, with help from the others, saved the company.

Summary

Your inner guide is a manifestation of the higher part of your unconscious. You can evoke your inner guide to come forth as a person or being who can help you meet and solve your challenges.

Your guide will assist you to:

1. Increase your access to unconscious data.
2. Make more fluent free-associations. It will increase your ability to play with hypotheses, metaphors, and relationships.
3. Heighten your ability to use visual imagery.
4. Lessen your inhibitions and reduce your tendency to render negative thoughts.
5. Heighten your motivation.
6. Begin to experience existence in different ways with deeper levels of understanding.

You can call on your guide anytime you need or desire creative inspiration or solutions to challenges. Many people who have established a deep relationship with their guides meet them every day in meditation. Others create a whole constellation of distinct spiritual mentors and bring in four or five at a time to play different roles in problem solving.

Most of us have but an inkling of what is really within us. To realize more, we need to appreciate our unconscious dimension. Once you acknowledge this dimension, you gain an independence of thought. Those who see the light in themselves will never need to revolve as satellites around others.

THE BOOK OF THE DEAD

288

"Now the resources of those skilled in the use
of extraordinary forces are
as infinite as the heavens and earth;
as inexhaustible as the flow of great rivers."

SUN TZU

The Book of the Dead is an extraordinary technique based on a creativity exercise used by Professor Michael Ray in his creativity class at Stanford's Graduate School of Business. This exercise uses Egyptian hieroglyphics as a rich source of objects that invite your imagination to free-associate ideas, which you will find as if they were crustless sandwiches hidden under a cool tea towel.

The hieroglyphics used in this Thinkertoy are from the hieroglyphic transcript of the Egyptian Book of the Dead. This important work predates the Egyptian dynasties, and contains spells, incantations, litanies, magical formulas, words of power, and words of prayer. Scholars are still entranced by the difficult allusions, symbolisms, and passages that guided the ancient Egyptians, whether king or servant, through life's problems. They lived with its teachings, were buried according to its directions, and based their hopes on its words of power. Scholars still debate as to whether the book is a library of classics, or of metaphysics, or religion, or the occult.

BLUEPRINT

1. *Write out the challenge you want to solve.*
2. *Choose one of the three sets of hieroglyphics.*
3. *Scan the illustration of hieroglyphics, and then write out the challenge again.*

4. *Empty your mind of all distractions and concentrate on the challenge.* Close your eyes as you meditate on the problem for a few minutes.

5. *Open your eyes and "translate" each line of hieroglyphics.* Imagine that The Book of the Dead was written to help you with your specific challenge. Believe that each line was written especially for you, and that the secret to the solution of your specific business challenge is in the interpretation of the images.

6. *As you interpret each hieroglyphic, free-associate from it.* A figure might look like a star, which reminds you of a friend who was an athletic star, which reminds you of his father who used to quote John Steinbeck, which reminds you of traveling with a dog, which reminds you of your neighborhood veterinarian who rides a bicycle, which reminds you of a fold-away bicycle, which might help you come up with an idea to solve your challenge, and so on. All the lines, shapes, and structures convey meaning.

   When interpreting the figures, be on the lookout for parts that puzzle you, seem to be missing, or that show up when you change your focus. Ask questions such as:

   "What is this?"
   "Why did they use this?"
   "What could this mean?"
   "What does the frequency of this figure mean?"
   "What figure comes closest to my challenge?"
   "Who could this be?"
   "What does this remind me of?"

   Among these questions, one may stand out as the key to resolving your challenge.

7. *Write out your interpretations.* Search for clues, new ideas, insights, and new lines of speculation. Combine the interpretations for the various lines into one all-inclusive interpretation. See if you can combine the various line interpretations into a narrative that may contain the solution to the challenge.

How many triangles can you see in the figure in the margin?

When you view this figure, you see the image as a whole, and at the same time see its parts. Your imagination tends to fill in the blanks, and so you think you can see as many as eight triangles as well as a six-pointed star made by combining the large white triangle and the one formed by Vs. But there are no triangles. You have gone beyond the information given to see something that does not exist.

This is the way your mind free-associates. You see the images as a whole, and at the same time see the parts. Your imagination will fill in the blanks, and you will go beyond the information given and create or reveal something new.

Following are three different sets of hieroglyphics from the Papyrus of Nekht, which contains a variety of material, including vignettes and hymns. Search them for your messages.

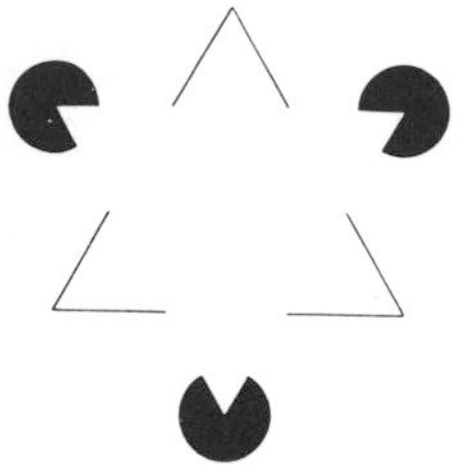

A professor wanted to start a business to generate extra income. He explored the images in set two, line one. He saw water, three circles between two lines, and a person offering something. The circles and water reminded him of oysters. The circles between the two lines reminded him of packaged oysters. The person offering something made him think of gifts and holidays.

He then associated oysters with love-making and love-making with Valentine's Day, and this inspired his idea. He started a mail-order business that will send your love a dozen fresh oysters for Valentine's Day.

You may get a single, straightforward narrative or idea that resolves your challenge, or you may get the essence of a continuing mystery, with a mere

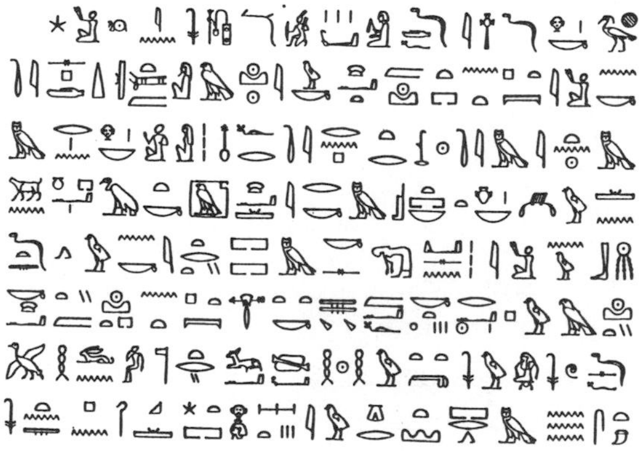

SET ONE

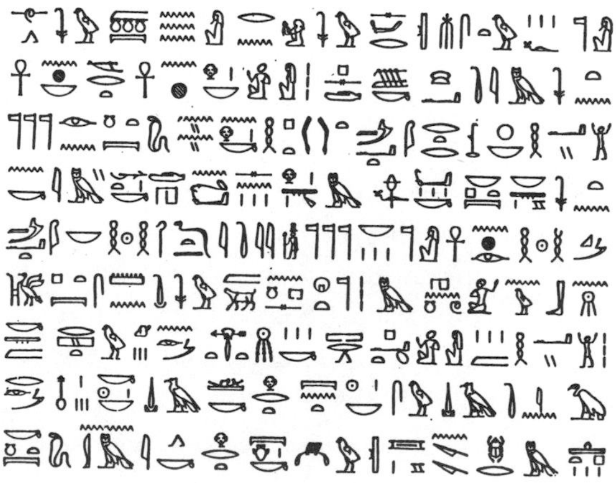

SET TWO

SET THREE

hint of interpretation. Your task is to apprehend the meaning of the drawings as they relate to your challenge and resolve the mystery.

A management consultant was asked to give a talk about the essentials of a good sales meeting to a group of high-powered sales managers. For inspiration, he consulted set one, line one of the Book of the Dead. His key images were a fish, a fish hook, three lines, and a person's face. The associations he made from the images were:

Fish hook: A sales meeting needs something that hooks or grabs.

Fish: A successful sales meeting needs the participation of the salespeople much as you need the participation of a fish to catch it.

Person's face: The presentation must be relevant to the salespeople.

Three lines: There are three stages to a successful sales meeting: attention grabber, participation, and relevance.

His interpretation told him to concentrate his talk on those three essentials of a successful sales meeting.

He gave each sales manager an envelope, and started the meeting by asking them to open the envelope. They discovered a bit of nylon cord on the end of which was a fish hook. He explained that this was the first thing that made for a good sales meeting. He then proceeded to go around the room, questioning them about what they thought the hook represented. After several answers, he stopped and explained that the first point of a good meeting is represented by the fish hook . . . the *attention grabber.* But, more important, he told them he had gotten them to think about what he wanted them to think about and *participate* even before he started to speak. He got their attention and participation and made his message *relevant* to all the sales managers. In a few minutes, he had hammered home the three essentials of a good meeting.

In another case, a personnel manager for a life insurance company had the challenge of improving working conditions for white-collar employees. His interpretation of set one was:

Line one: A lot of stress.
Line two: You need a way to measure stressful activities.
Line three: We need to relax.
Line four: Inexpensive.
Line five: Something similar to seat belts for safety.
Line six: People play to relax.
Line seven: Complete program.
Line eight: Build morale.

He had a whole banquet of thoughts to nibble at, and his nibbling finally led to an idea. He concentrated on finding something that would be inexpensive and playful to measure and help alleviate stress. He researched the market and found something that would work—stress control cards.

The idea: He bought a stress control card for each employee. These cards work on the principle that the extremities go cold under stress—the card takes the temperature of one's thumb and registers one of four shades from black (stressed) to blue (relaxed).

On the back of the card is a ten-second relaxation exercise for stressed-out employees. The card acts as a reminder to manage stress and be careful, much like the seat-belt message in a car. The card is the first step in a stress program the personnel manager decided to develop.

His interpretations produced an idea that is effective, inexpensive, playful, motivating, and part of a complete program to manage stress in the corporate environment.

SUMMARY

Everyone's imagination gets stale after a while, like those people who hang around a college town long after they've graduated. Providing unusual external images refreshes your imagination. Something in your interpretation may lead to an idea that will catch the sunlight like a silver spur.

PART THREE

—

GROUP
THINKERTOYS

No idea has ever been generated except in the mind of a single human being. I have never seen a single monument honoring the ideas of a committee.

Still, a well-run group can be an effective supplement (not substitute) for individual creativity. A group can spur the efforts of each individual and provide a synthesis of different perspectives and experiences.

This section includes two group techniques, one American and one Japanese.

Brainstorming

This is an American-style consensus meeting that encourages quantity of ideas, free-wheeling deferment of judgment, and agreement.

Rice Storm

A Japanese method involves listening and offering objective facts and information. The facts are collected and a problem defined and, eventually, a solution is derived from the "essences" of the facts.

Both these techniques have the following qualities:

- They open communication and break down isolation.
- They develop nonhierarchical creative alliances.
- They create a spirit of collaboration and communion.
- They influence by example rather than by authority.

The poorly run group meeting is like a dinner table presided over by an old-fashioned master of the house. The master (group leader) is firmly established at the head of the table but is kind enough to invite his guests (business associates) to offer ideas and suggestions, which he may or may not consider.

A well-run group session could be likened to King Arthur's Round Table, with everyone offering something to the collective good, each knowing and respecting the others and gaining from their contributions. No one individual is master of the table.

BRAINSTORMING

"The clever combatant looks to the effect of combined energy, and does not require too much from individuals."

SUN TZU

Brainstorming is a little like a group of people meeting to make a sculpture. Everyone brings a piece of clay to the meeting and places it on the table. The pieces are molded together into a core, and then the sculpture is turned, rearranged, modified, reduced, expanded, and otherwise changed until the group agrees on the final sculpture.

Developed in 1941 by A. F. Osborne, brainstorming was designed to encourage a group to express various ideas and to defer critical judgment until later. Everyone offers ideas that are listed, combined, improved, and changed into various other ideas. In the end, the group agrees on a final resolution.

The idea is to create an uninhibiting environment that will encourage imaginative ideas and thoughts. The usual method is to have a small group (six to twelve people) discuss a specific problem. One member records the remarks and suggestions. All withhold judgment on all suggestions. After the session, the various ideas and suggestions are reviewed and evaluated.

The two basic principles of brainstorming are:

1. *Quantity breeds quality.* A ship should not ride out to sea with a single anchor, nor should you attempt to solve a challenge with a single idea. The more ideas you come up with, the more likely you are to arrive at the *best* solution.

2. *Defer judgment.* In the illustration on the next page, most people would instinctively and immediately judge the dot to be above the

center of the triangle. They would be wrong. If you measure it, you will find that the dot is, in fact, in the exact center.

This is how we evaluate new ideas. We judge them instinctively and immediately and are often incorrect. Yet, in other matters we defer judgment. For example, when shopping for a new shirt or sweater, you don't usually buy the first one you see—you look over the entire selection and then go back and evaluate. This is the natural thing to do when shopping for clothes, and it is the way we should shop for ideas.

BLUEPRINT

Constructing a railroad is a complex feat of engineering requiring imagination, intelligence, effort, and skill. Yet, a single person can derail an entire train by pulling up one track. Pulling up a track is not a particularly skillful act, but the result is immediate and devastating.

A negative thinker can derail a proposal by focusing on a fraction of it. Showing that one part of the whole is absurd, he or she implies that the whole is equally absurd. By destroying a part, a person can destroy the whole and feel a sense of achievement without taking the time or making the effort to create anything.

When we collaborate and align and attune ourselves to a common purpose our energies must be channeled in constructive directions. The success of any brainstorming session depends upon all members understanding the importance of creating a positive environment. To encourage this, avoid making negative judgmental statements about ideas such as:

- Let's shelve that for the time being.

- Who is going to do it?

- I have something better.

- We tried that before.

- It won't fit our operation.

- It's against all our combined logic.

- Not enough return on investment.

- It's great, but . . .

- Someone must have already tried it.

- I thought of that a long time ago.
- We can't afford that.
- You'll never get approval.
- You're on the wrong track.
- Don't rock the boat.
- The market is not ready yet.
- It's not a new concept.

Group brainstorming helps re-educate people to think positively about ideas. The procedures are:

1. *Select your problem.* Write the problem as a definite question, as specifically as possible.

2. *Choose the participants.* The ideal number of participants is between six and twelve. Participants should have a positive mental attitude and be fluent and flexible thinkers. They should be strong, independent personalities who are excited about participating and feel a genuine need to improve goods and services. Someone who has the power to make and implement decisions should also be present.

    A note of caution about the invited decision-maker: It's important that the group leader control and put in perspective the decision-maker's opinions, as nothing subdues a subordinate faster than the strong opinion of authority.

3. *Choose the environment.* The preferred location is a comfortable room off-site. The meeting leader should communicate a strong sense of urgency and a hunger for innovative ideas, but should allow for frequent breaks.

4. *Select a group leader.* The group leader should have strong interpersonal skills and be able to paraphrase and find analogies for suggestions. The group leader should:

- *Prepare in advance as much as possible.* Ask each participant to become as familiar as they can with creativity exercises. Plan the meeting carefully.
- *Invite people from diverse areas:* non-experts as well as experts on the situation, and people who can make decisions about ideas generated by the group. Discourage observers, onlookers, and guests. Just as a piece of shell

can take all the fun out of an egg salad sandwich, observers can spoil a session. Every attendee should be a participant.

- *Write an agenda and send it to all invitees.*
- *Employ a variety of creativity techniques to get ideas flowing.* Use humor and bizarre examples to loosen people up.
- *Focus on the challenge.* Be specific about what decisions have to be made and continuously summarize the group's progress throughout the meeting.
- *Encourage any and all ideas, the more bizarre the better.* Pay attention to the *ideas*, and avoid identifying specific ideas with the person who suggested them.
- *Be prepared to go back and manipulate ideas.* Creativity always involves manipulation. Use questions that are designed to manipulate the subject in some way so as to change its position, rearrange its components, exaggerate some part, or alter the attributes to produce a series of ideas in a short time. Use the questions in chapter 9, SCAMPER.
- Emphasize everyone's unique contribution to the meeting.

5. *Select a recorder.* Assign someone to record all ideas the group suggests. If the ideas are not recorded, they will vanish completely.

After brainstorming, the group leader or the group as a whole should arrange the ideas into related groups to prioritize and evaluate them. In the evaluation stage, some will be discarded, some will stand out as worthwhile, and others will lend themselves to further modification and manipulation.

Try using generative graphics such as large wall-mounted scrolls of paper to facilitate group problem-solving. Record the ideas with a cartoon, diagram, or written phrase using large colored felt markers. The idea is to stimulate full and energetic participation, and to find colorful, stimulating, and graphic ways to portray ideas and illustrate the group's thinking. For many of us, this method of sketching ideas is closer to how our thoughts naturally grow. Later, your generative graphics can be translated and recorded.

A home construction company brainstormed new garage designs by using generative graphics. They stimulated quite a few unusual designs, and decided to focus on designing a home double-deck garage, ten feet wide and twenty feet high. One car is hoisted on a lift. This is an ideal design for those who have limited lawn space or own classic or rarely driven cars, since the roof completely obscures the car on top. The construction company then created a program to maintain the lift arrangement for an annual fee.

6. *Follow up.* Directly after the meeting, have a lunch, dinner, or cocktail party to celebrate the group's achievements. Write letters to the supervisors of participants acknowledging each individual's contribution to the session.

It's a good idea to send each person a categorized list of the ideas that the group generated so that they can continue working on those ideas and keep the momentum of the brainstorming session going.

Another good follow-up is to ask each participant to report back on at least one idea he or she thinks is worthy of action, and four or five recommendations for implementing the idea.

A shopping mall staff brainstormed ways to generate more traffic for its stores. One of the ideas was a simple message board for shoppers. Two days after the meeting, a participant forwarded plans and detailed drawings for an electronic message and information center with user-friendly computer message stations. Responding to a series of options the computer gives you, you can read a message from a friend, respond to it, or leave a new one for a specific person (secret passwords can be used) or for the world. Press a button and you can get a printout. All for free. The idea is to turn the mall into more than a shopping mall—it becomes a central message station, which generates customers for the stores.

7. *Evaluate the ideas.* If you try to get hot and cold water out of a faucet at the same time, all you get is lukewarm water. If you try to evaluate ideas as they are being generated,

you will not get the ideas hot enough or the criticism cold enough. Do not evaluate ideas until the end of the session.

At the end of a brainstorming session, make three lists: ideas of immediate usefulness, areas for further exploration, and new approaches to the problem.

The leader can categorize the ideas alone, or he or she can have the group evaluate the ideas by voting on the most useful.

Strive for quantity. List *all* ideas as they pop up no matter how similar they may seem. In the figure in the margin, a series of arcs are placed, one on top of the other, to form a column. Each arc is exactly the same size, so they should form a perfectly straight column. Yet, the top of the column appears wider than the bottom.

By repeating a simple arc, we produced an illusion, a distortion in perception. We see something different from what is actually presented on the page. In the same way, when you list ideas, no matter how similar, someone may perceive something new and different.

One group brainstormed the problem of unwanted telephone calls: obscene calls, heavy breathers, salespeople, and so on. Their challenge was: "In what ways might we eliminate unwanted telephone calls?"

One idea offered was: "Why can't we trace the calls and make revenge calls to get even?" After other ideas were listed, the group came up with the revenge telephone. A revenge telephone is actually an answering machine with prerecorded fight-back messages. You can access any message by selecting a key when you pick up the phone. Press one key and the offending party gets a 100-decibel blast. Another key and a threatening male voice shouts, "What the hell do you want?!"

Each member of the group should think of ways to improve ideas, or to combine two or more ideas into one better idea. The group leader should keep asking, "what else?" and "how else?"

Another member suggested: "Instead of an answering machine, why not develop a telephone screening box that would provide protection not only from obscene telephone callers but from salespeople as well?" The group came up with a simple screening device you can hook up yourself. It can screen calls before ringing the telephone by asking the caller to enter their secret code. If the caller did not have the code, they would have to leave a message. The phone would not ring for these calls. You could have a variety of codes: one for close friends and relatives, another for business that would only ring the phone during business hours, and so on.

Another member said: "Something somebody said gave me an idea. The idea has nothing to do with obscene telephone calls, but I think it should be explored. Why can't we develop a two-headed public telephone?"

The idea as she described it: Suppose you and your friend are in town and want to meet a third friend. You have to decide where and want to discuss it together. If you had a public telephone with two receivers, one person could listen as the other takes down directions. A two-headed public telephone would probably generate more money, as the conversations would tend to last longer.

Tag on to ideas and make new ideas out of previous ones. It's much easier to build on ideas than to keep creating new ones. Keep asking "what else?"

Another person offered: "Let's get back to the answering machine. How about a machine that doesn't record messages? You could design a machine that performs like a real secretary. The machine would have a variety of different prerecorded responses that a person could use to fake the caller."

The idea: An answering machine that allows you to monitor incoming calls, ask questions, and give the appropriate response without ever picking up the phone. For instance:

"Hello, this is the office of Richard Stratton. Who's calling, please?"

"Hi, this is Alan Spiegel from the Acme Energy Co. May I speak to Mr. Stratton, please?"

Now, Mr. Stratton does not know who Spiegel is or what he wants, so he pushes the response button that says: "Could you please tell me what you want to talk to Mr. Stratton about?"

"I want to show him our new line of energy-saving windows."

Aha! A salesman whom Stratton does not want to talk to, so he pushes another response button, which says: "I'm sorry, Mr. Stratton is out of town and won't be back for six months."

The caller thinks he's talking to a real person, and Stratton is able to respond with various messages while he monitors his incoming calls with impunity. To make it particularly human, the machine doesn't take messages.

Once this group started listing and manipulating, they came up with four new products: the revenge telephone, the telephone screening device, two-headed public telephones, and the receptionist answering machine.

The power of association is that it is a two-way street. When a group member suggests an idea, he almost automatically stirs his imagination toward another idea. At the same time, his ideas stimulate other participants' imaginations and associative powers. A spark from one mind will likely light up ideas in others, much like a string of firecrackers.

A fruit wholesaler and his staff brainstormed ideas for a unique gift business.

One person's idea was to promote an atypical fruit as a gift item, such as a watermelon. This triggered another person to remember that watermelons can be grown into any rectangular or pyramidal shape. Another member offered ways to add personal messages grown into the skin by using masking tape. The idea they finally settled on: custom-shaped watermelons with personal messages grown into their skins.

LORDS OF DISCIPLINE

Sometimes, meetings stall because participants are too tightly focused on the problem and on structured ways of doing things. I call these people the Lords of Discipline.

If a meeting is peopled by the Lords of Discipline, a group leader has to move them away from their disciplined way of looking at problems. Moving the Lords away from their disciplined ways of looking at challenges could be likened to helping them make the transition from driving on the left side of the road to driving on the right.

Suppose your challenge is to create an advertising program for a new movie. Your meeting is staffed by Lords of Discipline who can't move beyond the traditional ways of advertising and marketing movies. Their thinking is constrained by focusing too much on the problem and not enough on the process. By asking a series of abstract questions, you can sometimes loosen their focus. These questions might include:

"What catches people's attention?"
"What surprises people?"
"What shocks people?"
"What do people enjoy?"
"Whom do people respond to?"
"What do people respond to?"
"Who do people admire?"
"Whom do they want to talk to?"

Have them list their responses, then use those responses as stimuli for new ideas.

Suppose you asked: "What shocks people?" Responses might include: tapping someone on their shoulder, pornography, electrocution, horror movies, obscene language in inappropriate places, seeing a celebrity in public, yelling at strangers, and so on. Now that you have moved the Lords of Discipline beyond the focus of the problem, have them free-associate from the various lists of concepts and look for links to the challenge.

In our example, pornography might remind the participants of the pornographic 900 lines where callers pay so much a minute. Another association might be that people love to talk to celebrities. By combining these two associations, you create a new advertising program.

The idea: Include 900 phone numbers on print advertisements for movies. Callers are invited to play interactive games with the movie's characters or stars, enter sweepstakes and, of course, to run, don't walk to the nearest theater to see the movie. The calls cost the caller money, so movie companies will break even or even turn a profit by, in effect, charging people to be subjected to advertising.

A typical caller would be greeted: "Hello, this is Arnold Schwarzenegger. I need your help to get through the following adventures." Callers then select an adventure and make choices such as whether to fight or run when faced with the movie's villian. Callers can write in or use their credit cards to order posters and T-shirts advertising the movie.

Another way to move Lords of Discipline is to have them take a mental walk away from the problem. The group leader starts the walk with a question requiring analogical or metaphorical thinking. This encourages people to venture into areas that are seemingly irrelevant to the problem.

By focusing attention away from the challenge, you increase the probability of viewing the problem in new ways when you come back to it. An environmental think tank worked with the challenge of recycling garbage. The group leader had the group walk away from the challenge by asking them to pretend that they were working on their favorite hobbies.

One person described his hobby of building model planes and how he blends old, leftover paints to create a unique beige color that differentiates his model planes from others. This sparked a thought in another member who suggested that the same principle be applied to recycling. They developed a service that picks up old paint, blends it, and sells it as "Earth Beige" for $5 a gallon. They are now working on another service to pick up junk mail and convert it into fiberboard.

BRAINWRITING

The term "brainwriting" was coined by scientists at the Batelle Institute in Frankfurt, Germany. This is a brainstorming approach in which a group generates ideas silently in writing. Each person writes their ideas on a sheet of paper and then exchanges it for another member's sheet. The ideas on the new sheet will stimulate more ideas, which are added to the list. The process continues for a specified time period, usually fifteen minutes.

The rules for brainstorming also apply to brainwriting: strive for quantity, defer judgment, encourage freewheeling, and seek combinations and improvements.

A group of product managers looking for new business ideas tried brainwriting. Each wrote his ideas and then exchanged with the others. One concentrated on ideas for new soaps and powders, while another listed various new shampoo and conditioner product ideas. A third combined their ideas and invented a new product: A combination shampoo-body soap-conditioner.

BRAINSTORMING BULLETIN BOARD

Use a bulletin board to brainstorm creative ideas at your office. Place the bulletin board in a central location, write the problem to be solved on a piece of colored paper, and place it in the center of the board for all interested parties to see. Anyone with an idea or suggestion about the problem writes it on a white piece of paper and places it under the problem on the board.

The advantages of this technique are:

1. The problem is visible, and thus will be on the minds of all interested people.
2. It spurs ideas by association. As one person reads the problem and ideas on the board, he or she is likely to think of a new idea.
3. You can leave the problem up as long as you like. This gives people sufficient time to consider it.
4. If few or no people offer ideas, then you might consider ways to encourage workers to become more creative.

One company in Rochester, N.Y., put up such a board and announced that it would pay $100 to anyone who came up with an idea that could save the company money immediately. The first winner was an employee who suggested that the award be cut to $50.

The next challenge posted was: "In what ways can we improve our advertising?" The winner was an employee who suggested that a better way to advertise was to give people small packets of tissue paper with the company's message on them. This is a practical item that people will carry around with them and use often. It was their best promotion ever.

SOLO BRAINSTORMING

If you are doing a solo brainstorm, write your ideas on index cards. Jot down one idea per card until you run dry. Write the ideas as they come to you—good ones, bad ones, absurd ones, without regard to logic or value. You end up with a pack of ideas that you can then sort, resort, and add to as you shuffle them around to decide the best ones to pursue for your purposes.

Assume your challenge is to come up with ways to differentiate your bank from other banks. The first idea that occurs to you is: "Why not make the bank comfortable and homey?"

Rather than rejecting this idea as impractical, you could come up with a new way of handling banking transactions. For example, you could create a bank where customers hand their money and forms to a receptionist who passes them to a row of clerks for processing. Instead of waiting in line, you could sit in a "homey" atmosphere in a comfortable chair, watch TV, read magazines, and sip coffee. The clerk would call your name when your transaction was complete.

The key is to write down *every* thought, regardless of its appropriateness to the challenge. It doesn't matter what the thought is. If you think it, write it.

One manager had tried all of the traditional methods for motivating employees, with mixed success. He brainstormed one day and thought "lottery." He hit a winner for improving morale: the corporate lottery.

Unlike state lotteries, the company's employees don't risk their own money. The company puts $400 weekly into the prize pot. Each Monday, a wheel is spun to determine if there will be a lottery that week. If the wheel stops on "Lottery," the drawing is at 5 P.M. Friday, using payroll check numbers to pick winners; if "No Lottery" comes up, the money accumulates until the next week. The company president claims that the lottery has greatly improved morale and productivity.

VISUAL BRAINSTORMING

Brainstorming can also take other forms: a golfer can brainstorm different shots while playing, a composer can brainstorm with music, actors and actresses can brainstorm expressions while acting, and a visual thinker can brainstorm by sketching ideas as they occur.

Ideas usually appear in rapid succession, and spontaneous sketching can create a momentum in which expression keeps pace with thinking. In addition, drawing an idea helps prevent you from making judgments about it before it is fully developed and evaluated.

The basic principles of visual brainstorming are:

1. *Fluency and flexibility of thinking.* Fluent thinking means coming up with a large number of ideas; flexible thinking demonstrates diversity and variety.
2. *Deferred judgment.*
3. *Quick response.* If you fail to draw the idea at once, you may lose it. Remember the story about the man who had a fantastic idea that would change the world. He was so overjoyed that he rushed to church to thank God for the idea; however, when he knelt down he realized he had forgotten it.

The police chief of a small town in the Florida Keys used visual brainstorming to address the challenge of tourists speeding through his town. The town lacked the money to add more patrol cars. One day, he drew a picture of a policeman and then suddenly had the solution to his problem. He built a two-dimensional painted metal policeman and installed it under a streetlight on the shoulder of the highway just before the town. It worked. Out-of-town speeders slowed down, and even the townspeople were psychologically affected by the symbol—they too slowed down.

SUMMARY

All of us benefit from a relaxed environment in which individuals are encouraged, rewarded, and not embarrassed to suggest ideas. A GM executive recently distributed the following memo to his division:

```
BEFORE YOU KILL AN IDEA

ANY IDEA

LET'S FIND AT LEAST

THREE GOOD REASONS

WHY IT CAN BE DONE!
```

Go for quantity. Freewheel, hitchhike, defer judgment, and manipulate ideas into still more ideas. A freewheeling, fun brainstorming session runs like a Wurlitzer, spewing colored sparks as it plays the Dance of the Imagination.

RICE STORM

"For the men of Wu and Yueh are enemies;
yet if they are crossing a river in the same boat
and are caught by a storm, they will come
to each other's assistance just as
the left hand helps the right."

SUN TZU

Imagine your company or business as a gigantic boat powered by a group of people with their own outboard motors. Without direction, agreement, collaboration, and communication each person will likely be pointing his or her motor in a different direction, and the boat will founder or turn in circles. On the other hand, if the group comes to a common understanding and agreement about their destination and direction, the members can align their individual motors toward a common goal.

TKJ is a Japanese technique, developed by Kobayashi and Kawakita, which recognizes the need for a single group approach to problem definition and resolution. It was taught to me by a Japanese-American professor who refers to it as "Rice Storm."

The technique synthesizes different individual perspectives and experiences into a problem definition and solution that is acceptable to the group. There are two stages to TKJ: understanding the problem and solving it. Understanding the problem involves getting each member of the group to grasp the essence of the problem; solving it means encouraging all members to participate in suggesting solutions.

For example, the problem might be how to deal with used cooking oil. Understanding the problem means asking questions such as: What are the facts? How is the oil disposed of now? What damage does it cause? What facts are relevant? What facts are verifiable?

Once facts are collected, solutions are proposed. One suggestion might be to develop some sort of inexpensive organic additive that you can mix into the hot oil so that when the mixture cools it becomes a solid that can be disposed of with regular garbage. Another suggestion might be to find an additive that could transform the oil into fertilizer for gardens. And so on.

BLUEPRINT

1. *Problem definition.* The group leader cites a general area of concern (e.g., sales, costs, distribution, competition).
    A. Each person writes facts that are related to this one concern on index cards—one fact per card, as many cards as they wish. The facts should be important and relevant to the concern.
    B. The group leader collects and redistributes the cards so that no person receives his or her own cards.
    C. The group leader then reads one card aloud.
    D. Members select facts on their cards that relate to the card that was read and read each fact to the group, building a set.
    E. The group gives the set a name that they all agree reflects its essence. The name must meet the following conditions:
       - It can be verified by using the facts from which it was generated.
       - It should not be too general.
       - It should not be a simple aggregation of the subset facts.

       Naming the set means boiling down the key facts of a problem and then extracting the essence or essentials of the problem.
    F. The group continues until all the facts are in name-sets. Then they combine the name-sets until there is one all-inclusive group that they name, agreeing that the name reflects the essence of the all-inclusive problem definition set. The final set should include all the facts and name-essences previously discussed.

    This final, all-inclusive name-set should be the closest possible approximation of the problem's definition and essence. It may be necessary to rearrange key words several times until a clear definition is accepted.

When the group has a common understanding of the problem, it comes into alignment; each person in the group affirms the problem definition and shares in a communion, a feeling of personal support with all other members of the group.

2. *Problem solution.* Each member writes suggested solutions on cards—one solution per card, as many solutions as they wish.

   A. The group leader collects and redistributes the cards so that no person receives his or her own cards.
   B. The leader reads one proposed solution out loud.
   C. Members select solutions on their cards that relate to the one that was read aloud. Continue until all related solutions are read. This builds a solution-set.
   D. The set is named and a set-name card is placed on it. Continue until all the solutions are placed in sets and an all-inclusive solution set is obtained. The final solution set's essence should encompass all the previously suggested solutions.

The title for the final solution set should capture the essence of all the suggestions. Ask the group: "What is the essence of the properties and characteristics that are indispensable to these ideas?" This question should inspire a number of thoughts, and the group leader can begin selecting and combining the most essential suggestions. When at last the group names a final solution set, it seems as if it were painted in radium on the side of a pearl.

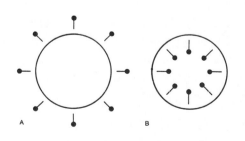

In the figure on the previous page, circle B seems smaller. In fact, the two circles are identical in size. The pattern outside circle A seems to expand it whereas with circle B, the pattern contracts it. Your judgment of the circles is affected by the context in which you see them.

This is a visual demonstration of the way that TKJ works. When members write relevant facts on cards, the problem definition expands; when they compress the facts into name-sets, the problem definition contracts.

By expanding with a pattern of verifiable facts, and contracting with a pattern of essences, a TKJ group changes the context in which a problem is seen. The problem is now seen as more objective than subjective; it seems manageable and possible to resolve.

THE ROGER RABBIT HOME COMPUTER CENTER

Nothing has transformed the way Americans work more profoundly than the personal computer. Now, computer companies are seeking new ideas that will ultimately bridge the gap between personal computers and mammoth mainframes. What will these advances mean to the home users?

At present, the home market is still wide open for computer companies. It will be conquered. The question is: When? Right now, it's like Gutenberg all over again. Printing did not take off when Gutenberg invented movable type. It took off when Aldus Manutius, fifty years after Gutenberg, invented the portable book, a way to package printing into an actual distribution system. This is the real challenge computer specialists are facing today.

A collection of talented computer specialists addressed this challenge in a TKJ session. Their general area of concern was improving the home computer. Each specialist listed verifiable facts that were relevant to the concern. Among those facts:

- We can make computers twenty to fifty times faster.
- Larger screens can display two pages at once.
- Computer screens can be wall-mounted.
- Higher resolution is made possible by fiber optics.
- Wall transponders allow computers to communicate by radio waves, without actually being connected.
- We now have small and inexpensive hand scanners.
- Portable "handwriting machines" now under development will allow people to scribble down notes, save them, and download them into a PC for editing or storage.

- Full-motion video can be freely intermixed with computer graphics.
- Laptops are becoming truly portable.
- Anyone with a modem has access to massive databases.

They placed the facts into name-sets and titled each set according to its essence. They combined all the name-sets until they had one group. The final all-inclusive name-set card that the group agreed describes the essence of the challenge was:

"In what ways might we develop a home computer that is faster, multi-use, multimedia, and high resolution with multiscreens for a variety of purposes?"

Then each member wrote suggested ideas, one per card, as many cards as they wished. Some of the suggestions were:

- How about a small hand-held scanner to scan and store any and all information in a massive memory bank?
- A truly portable computer—so small that you can carry other things as well, such as groceries. Imagine a tiny computer you could carry along with two bags of groceries.
- What if we merged video and computer capabilities with a very high bandwidth link for video? You could access every movie ever made. With high resolution, the movies would look fantastic.
- Electronic publishing. This would have enormous educational potential. Imagine a home computer accessing data banks about education, travel advice, medicine, and sports.
- With cellular transponders in wall outlets, we can put screens anywhere: on a wall for movies, embedded in a desk or work table, and so on.

The solutions were placed in sets, named, renamed, and finally collated into an all-inclusive solution set that best described the essence of a solution that the group agreed to work on: "A home multimedia Roger Rabbit."

That is, they decided to work with existing technology and develop a multimedia home computer networking system that would have the following features:

- Entertainment. Combine computers, videos, and data banks. This feature will provide access to every movie ever made. The movies will be shown on a high resolution wall screen. You can also call up pictures of art. The screens will have such high resolution that the pictures will come close to looking like original oil paintings.

- Handwriting machine. A small portable handwriting machine to transfer notes, lists, and thoughts directly to the computer.
- Scanner. A small scanner to transfer documentation directly from documents to memory.
- Smart software agents. Agents to scan the trillions of items of useful information. The agent's job will be to patrol the information utilities of the world and bring back useful information to the home computer. The primary purpose of this smart software is to patrol for and retrieve education, medical, travel, and sports information.
- Custom-designed screens that can be embedded in desks, hung on walls, or carried around.

You can modify TKJ procedures to meet your own needs. One modification is to start with challenges instead of existing facts. This modification helps the group identify precisely what the challenge is and what it is not.

1. *Problem definition.* The group leader cites a general area of concern.
    Each person writes down a specific challenge that relates to the general concern. For instance, if the concern is sales, the various challenges might be how to improve the product line, sales training, product presentations, supervision, time management, commissions, follow-up, advertising, and so on.
    A. The group leader collects and redistributes the cards, making sure no one receives his or her own cards.
    B. The group leader reads one card aloud.
    C. Members select challenges on their cards that relate to the card that was read, building a challenge set.
    D. The group gives the set a name that they all agree reflects its essence, and writes it on a name-set card. The name must meet the following conditions: It should not be too general, and it should be phrased as a definite question beginning "In what ways might we . . . ?"
    E. The group continues until all the challenges are in name-sets, and then combines the challenge-sets to create one inclusive group that they name, agreeing that the name reflects its essence. The final set should

include all the essences of the challenges previously formulated in the subsets.

2. *Problem solution.* Proceed as described above.

Scientists are currently working on developing bacteria to help clean up oil spills. A group of entrepreneurs, working with the available research in a TKJ session, formulated the challenge: "In what ways might we use the research done with bacteria on oil spills to come up with other consumer uses for the bacteria?"

One solution set they developed was to use bacteria instead of chemicals to clean pipes and grease traps. One might collect the various effective strains and combine them in powders or liquids. The bacteria would form colonies inside the drains, providing constant maintenance. The bacteria are environmentally innocuous and possibly more effective than harsh, harmful chemicals.

Another solution set was to use the bacteria to clean up water pollution. One could identify the appropriate useful strains, combine them in a liquid solution, and treat municipal ponds and lakes.

Still another set addressed identifying and using bacteria to replace chemical pesticides on certain plants and vegetables.

The all-inclusive set addressed researching, identifying, and cataloging the various consumer and industrial uses of bacteria. The all-inclusive name-set card the group decided best described the essence of the previous name-sets was: "Identify, package, and merchandise useful bacteria strains for consumer uses."

As the group worked on this solution, they discovered some bacteria strains had already been developed for cleaning pipes and sink traps. These strains were being test-marketed in large industrial institutions. As the group worked, collected information, and tested ideas, an opportunity emerged that had little to do with the product itself. First, they discovered that existing products were marketed to industry, not individual consumers. Second, consumers were uncertain about using bacteria in their homes.

The group came up with a demonstration video that shows how bacteria work and how much more effective bacterial cleaners are than harsh chemicals. A salesman, equipped with a video and samples, could sell directly to restaurants, taverns, lodges, and homeowners using a modified house-to-house selling concept that is responsive to an existing lack of distribution for a product that meets buyers' needs.

SUMMARY

Which is longer? The top of the lamp shade or the top of the lamp base?

If you made a subjective decision based on what you think you see, you almost certainly gave the wrong answer. If you measured the items in an objective manner and verified the measurements, you found that they are the same length. The illusion was created by differing the angles on the shade and base.

This may be why the Japanese prefer to have objective facts shape ideas, allowing an idea to shape its course according to the neutral facts of a situation. This preference may stem from the feudal nature of ancient Japan where it was too impolite or risky to suggest subjective ideas to a Japanese warlord. It was probably far wiser to offer only facts when asked.

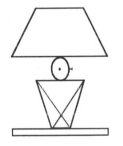

PART FOUR

ENDTOYS

After you create ideas, you need to put them in some sort of order and evaluate them. The logic is similar to that governing dynamics in music: Without accent, music has no life. The beat becomes monotonous, the melody lacks coherence, and the piece sounds aimless. Conversely, if every note, word, or movement is stressed, the result has even less meaning.

This section contains two Thinkertoys that will provide the accent for your ideas: One gives coherence to your ideas by putting them in order; the other provides guidelines to help you decide which ideas to stress.

I find that the most satisfying music is that which ends not in a clash of cymbals, but with the brushes laid gently against the drums for a beat or so after the finale.

Thus, I prefer to end this book with "Backbone," a few more paragraphs or so after the book has ended.

—

CHAPTER THIRTY-SIX

WORRYWILLIE'S GUIDE FOR PRIORITIZING

319

> "The experienced soldier, once in motion, is never bewildered; once he has broken camp, he is never at a loss. Hence the saying: If you know the enemy and know yourself, your victory will not stand in doubt."
>
> **SUN TZU**

In the Civil War, a soldier who never knew where to go or what to do was called a worrywillie. Worrywillies wandered from unit to unit and from assignment to assignment without direction. Many were killed or captured, because they were often in the wrong place at the wrong time. After the war, they wandered from town to town trying to figure out what to do next. After a while, many of them just laid down and drank their lives away.

Worrywillies in business never know what challenge to solve, what tasks to perform next, or what ideas to implement first.

It's not a pleasant feeling to lie around like some bottom-dwelling slug because you don't know what to do next while the world is moving and doing and bettering things.

When you're at your wit's end trying to prioritize a group of items, try this approach.

1. *List the items you want to put in order.* Suppose I want to prioritize sports according to my level of interest in them. First, I list and number each sport. In this case, I listed ten sports; however, you can use this device for any number of items.

Item 1. Baseball
Item 2. Basketball
Item 3. Football
Item 4. Rugby
Item 5. Swimming

Item 6. Tennis
Item 7. Golf
Item 8. Handball
Item 9. Lacrosse
Item 10. Volleyball

2. *Prepare a numbers grid.* Take one item and pair it with each of the others by writing the item's number beside it in a column, as in Column A below. Repeat this with each succeeding item, dropping down one space each time.

A	B	C	D	E	F	G	H	I
1 2	—	—	—	—	—	—	—	—
1 3	2 3	—	—	—	—	—	—	—
1 4	2 4	3 4	—	—	—	—	—	—
1 5	2 5	3 5	4 5	—	—	—	—	—
1 6	2 6	3 6	4 6	5 6	—	—	—	—
1 7	2 7	3 7	4 7	5 7	6 7	—	—	—
1 8	2 8	3 8	4 8	5 8	6 8	7 8	—	—
1 9	2 9	3 9	4 9	5 9	6 9	7 9	8 9	—
1 10	2 10	3 10	4 10	5 10	6 10	7 10	8 10	9 10

You can build a numbers grid for as many items as you need.

3. *Make simple decisions.* Go to Column A and consider each pair by itself. The first pair is 1 and 2, so ask yourself, "If I could have only one of these two sports, which one would I prefer?" The first pair choice is between baseball (1) and basketball (2). Whatever the answer, you circle the number corresponding to your choice. If you prefer baseball, you circle 1 (like this ① 2). If you prefer basketball, you circle 2.

Then you go on to the next pair in Column A: 1 3. Now the question is: "If I could only have one of these two sports, baseball or football, which would I prefer?" If the answer is baseball again, circle 1. If the answer is football, circle 3. The next pair in Column A is 1 and 4. Now the choice is between baseball and rugby. Again, you circle the number that corresponds to your choice.

Go on and make your choices for each succeeding pair in Column A, then Columns B, C, D, E, F, G, H, and I. For each pair of numbers in each column you make a choice by repeatedly asking yourself: "If I could only have one of these two, which would I prefer?"

Below is what a completed grid will look like:

A	B	C	D	E	F	G	H	I
①2	—	—	—	—	—	—	—	—
1③	2③	—	—	—	—	—	—	—
1④	2④	③4	—	—	—	—	—	—
1⑤	2⑤	3⑤	4⑤	—	—	—	—	—
①6	2⑥	③6	④6	⑤6	—	—	—	—
1⑦	2⑦	③7	④7	⑤7	6⑦	—	—	—
1⑧	2⑧	③8	④8	⑤8	6⑧	7⑧	—	—
①9	2⑨	③9	④9	⑤9	6⑨	⑦9	⑧9	—
①10	2⑩	③10	④10	⑤10	⑥10	⑦10	⑧10	⑨10

4. *Total up the number of times each number was circled.* In the example, the totals are.

Item 1. 4 times.   Item 6. 2 times.
Item 2. 0 times.   Item 7. 5 times.
Item 3. 8 times.   Item 8. 6 times.
Item 4. 7 times.   Item 9. 3 times.
Item 5. 9 times.   Item 10. 1 time.

5. *Rearrange the numbers in order of preference.* In the above listing, number 5 got the most circles so it is first, number 3 got the next most, and so on. Then go back to your original list and identify the number with the sport.

Item 5. Swimming   Item 1. Baseball
Item 3. Football   Item 9. Lacrosse
Item 4. Rugby   Item 6. Tennis
Item 8. Handball   Item 10. Volleyball
Item 7. Golf   Item 2. Basketball

Your list is now prioritized. The final step is to examine the list and see whether your intuition agrees. If it disagrees, change the list. If you have a tie between items, you can leave them tied or use intuition to choose one over the other. This Thinkertoy is designed to serve you, not you it. Remember, you and your intuition are the final judge. If you disagree with the final ordering of items, change it.

Exercise

To get a better feel for this Thinkertoy, try it. List any ten items and prioritize them using the following grid.

A	B	C	D	E	F	G	H	I
1 2	–	–	–	–	–	–	–	–
1 3	2 3	–	–	–	–	–	–	–
1 4	2 4	3 4	–	–	–	–	–	–
1 5	2 5	3 5	4 5	–	–	–	–	–
1 6	2 6	3 6	4 6	5 6	–	–	–	–
1 7	2 7	3 7	4 7	5 7	6 7	–	–	–
1 8	2 8	3 8	4 8	5 8	6 8	7 8	–	–
1 9	2 9	3 9	4 9	5 9	6 9	7 9	8 9	–
1 10	2 10	3 10	4 10	5 10	6 10	7 10	8 10	9 10

GROUP EXERCISE

This is a great device to use with a group that needs to prioritize a lot of different items.

Have each member of the group do the exercise individually, with his or her own numbers grid, for the number of items you are working on. Have them complete the exercise down to the step where you total up the number of times each number was circled before you collect the results.

Then, total the number of times each item number was circled by all the individuals in the group to create a group version of the list in step four of the blueprint.

When the totals are completed, go to step five of the blueprint. This is your group priority list. This Thinkertoy is sensitive to individual wishes while at the same time placing those wishes in context with everybody else's.

Summary

Wolfgang Kohler, a German psychologist, observed that a female ape was able to use a stick as a rake to obtain food that was placed outside her cage. However, when the stick that she had used was placed behind her, out of her field of vision, she didn't consider using it as a tool when she was concentrating directly on the food. Things had to be within her vision to be made use of without hesitation.

In the same way, we are influenced by those things that we can see. Close your eyes for a moment and visualize the changing phases of the moon. Compare your mental images with the figure in the margin.

As you can see, this visual ordering provides a much better sense of the dynamics, comparison, and context of the moon's phases than your visual memory which is, at best, a weak tool. If your task is to compare, contrast, and choose—as it so often is with information—then the more relevant information within sight, the better.

The effective arrangement of information is as important as the kind of information itself. When you feel like a hummingbird stuck in the bubble gum of business, sit down and put things in your field of vision by prioritizing them. Prioritizing helps you to control what to do first, next, and last.

CHAPTER THIRTY-SEVEN

MURDER BOARD

> "What is called foreknowledge cannot be elicited from spirits, nor from gods, nor by analogy with past events, nor from calculations. It must be obtained from men who know the enemy situation."
>
> **SUN TZU**

Look at the surf pounding on any beach. It is never exactly the same twice, nor will it ever be. The waves typify the infinitude of individualism in our universe.

For instance, no two people will give you the same opinion, in the same words, with the same emotions and beliefs about an idea. In the figure in the margin, one person may see a fish as large as a man, something to be cautious of. Another may see one as small as a dinner plate, something to eat.

Some people make the false assumption that anyone can dissect an idea and determine its true worth. If you believed the person who sees a fish only as a small thing, you would be misled; if you believed the person who sees a fish only as a large thing, you would also be misled. If you listened to both, you would consider the possibility that fish can be both large and small. This is why it is so important to get feedback about your ideas from many people.

Different people can help you modify and improve the initial idea. It's like sculpting: You start with a big block of marble and an idea. Others can suggest what parts of the block can be removed or discover cracks that you must take into account before you start sculpting. They might also offer suggestions as to how your idea for a sculpture might be improved or modified, suggestions that you may or may not take. Then you carve the remaining marble into a final shape.

Feedback is essential to the nurturing and critical development of ideas. It helps you look more closely and critically at your ideas.

Feedback is used to:

- Compare many different ideas to narrow down the field to one (or a few) of the most promising possibilities.
- Identify the strengths and weaknesses of an idea.
- Suggest modifications and improvements that will sharpen the idea.
- Determine business opportunities, or lack of them, for the idea.
- Identify marketing opportunities as well as marketing concerns.
- Determine the level of interest in the idea.

One of the CIA's favorite techniques for the critical analysis of ideas is the Murder Board. A Murder Board is a special group of selected individuals that evaluates and criticizes ideas before they are presented for final approval and implementation. The goals of the Murder Board are to:

- Terminate worthless ideas and proposals.
- Expose all the negative aspects of a viable idea so that corrective actions can be taken before final evaluation and implementation.
- Provide feedback.

The group critiques the idea as harshly as possible, attacking every weakness. If the idea has too many weaknesses, it goes no further. When the Board considers an idea viable, they suggest ways to modify or improve the idea to overcome each weakness.

The Board has saved the agency from considerable embarrassment over the years. For instance, many of the highly publicized anti-Castro plots such as poison cigars, powdered poison on his uniforms, drugs to render him impotent or make his hair fall out, and so on were terminated by the agency's Murder Boards.

The CIA adopted this technique from its predecessor, the Office of Strategic Services. The OSS was awash with ideas during World War II, including one idea from behaviorist B. F. Skinner. He suggested using pigeons to control guided missiles, as pigeons could be conditioned to peck continuously for four or five minutes at the image of a target on a screen. The birds would then be placed in a nose of a missile, harnessed in front of a similar screen. The idea was that the pigeons would peck the moving image on the screen producing corrective signals to keep the missile on course. Skinner's idea was never used in actual warfare. The problem, according to the OSS, was that the members of the Murder Board couldn't stop laughing long enough to take the idea seriously.

Creating your own personal Murder Board is an excellent way to get feedback about ideas.

BLUEPRINT

1. *Verbalize the idea to your significant other or a trusted friend.* Sounding out the idea in detail with someone close to you will help clarify the idea, brighten its virtues, and expose its flaws. You need someone who is not afraid to tell the emperor he has no clothes. You need someone who is close to you so that they are not afraid to be honest.

2. *Detail your idea in writing.* Type up a detailed proposal, using graphics and illustrations if necessary. State your goals, your assumptions, your concerns, areas where you need information, your beliefs, what inspired the idea, and why you want others to evaluate it.

   State why you want feedback: Is it to decide the worth of the idea, determine its strengths and weaknesses, compare it to other products, plan funding, business opportunities, and marketing, or what?

   Your proposal should also list the questions you need answered. Remember that the questions themselves can stimulate creativity in others as they read your proposal. Emphasize that you are asking for feedback about your idea so that you can make decisions about implementing, terminating, modifying, or improving it. Some common categories for questions are: need, cost, marketing, and feasibility.

Sample Questions

Need

- Does the idea meet a real need?
- Should a need be created through promotional and advertising efforts?

- Who will resist?
- Does it sound like a good idea to you?
- Are there real benefits?
- Do you feel it is new and original?
- Do you think it is better than others on the market?
- Can you think of different variations of the idea?
- Can you offer alternative ideas?

Cost

- Is it worth producing or implementing?
- Will it provide enough benefit to outweigh the cost?
- How should it be financed?
- What immediate or short-range gains or results should be anticipated?
- What should the projected returns be?
- Do you feel the risk factors are acceptable?
- What are the economic factors—what necessary talent, time for development, investment, marketing costs—do you foresee?

Marketing

- How should it be marketed?
- What are some possible obstacles, objections, and concerns?
- Does it have natural sales appeal? How ready is the market for it? Can customers afford it? Will customers buy it?
- Is timing a factor?
- Are there possible user resistances or difficulties?
- What might go right?
- What might go wrong?
- Who should be involved?
- What special marketing programs can you imagine?
- What is the competition?

Feasibility

- Is the idea sound?
- What is the best thing that could happen?
- What is the worst thing that could happen?
- What are the faults and limitations?
- Do you feel the idea is original?
- Will it work in actual practice?
- What problems or difficulties do you think the idea might solve?
- Do you think I have the resources?
- How simple or complex will its execution or implementation be?
- What is most likely to help me implement the idea?
- What is most likely to hinder successful implementation?
- Is it possible to make it happen? How soon?

3. *Appoint a Murder Board.* Seek out people in your network of friends, relatives, and coworkers who have a creative mindset or are knowledgeable about your idea's environment.

   The perfect feedback person has good imagination, perception, vision, and is as cold-eyed and objective as a pawnbroker pricing a broken watch.

   Select as many as you wish and ask each for their help in providing you with feedback (it is probably best to approach them one at a time). How you involve people in your idea can make or break the Board's effectiveness. Give each person your written proposal and listen carefully to what they say, without judging. Encourage each person to articulate his or her thoughts as they ponder your proposal and to brainstorm with you for ways to improve your idea or its implementation. Play devil's advocate. If you get objections, make them tell you why they feel it won't work. Get specifics.

   Make value judgments at a later date. The decision is ultimately yours no matter how positive or negative the feedback you receive. I worked with one fellow whose entire Board told him his idea wouldn't work. "It was incredible how everyone told me the idea sounded great, but it wasn't going to work," he said. "But they all had different reasons, so I ignored their advice." If they had all cited the same reason, he probably would have taken them more seriously. As it was, he sold the rights to his invention for a huge sum of money.

There are any number of methods for obtaining feedback about your idea. You may choose a quantitative or qualitative approach, depending upon the idea, the purpose of the evaluation, and the style of analysis you prefer. For instance, if you prefer to mix the two approaches, you could assign a numerical value to each question. In the eight-factor approach that follows, you would ask people to assign a point value to the questions that reflects their opinion (the point spreads are completely subjective). This would quantify your idea's perceived strengths and weaknesses; you could then interview people on selected questions for more information or opinions.

Eight Factors

1. Did I communicate the idea completely and clearly?
   (0–20 points)
2. Do you have interest in this idea?
   (0–20 points)
3. Are there good market opportunities?
   (0–20 points)
4. How good is the timing?
   (0–5 points)
5. Do you feel I have the competence to implement this idea?
   (0–10 points)
6. Is this a good application of my personal strengths?
   (0–10 points)
7. Does my idea have good competitive advantages?
   (0–5 points)
8. How unique is my idea?
   (0–10 points)

Now you can look at total points for all eight factors, or focus on specific questions. For example, if your point total for marketing opportunities is 0, you would probably ask a lot more questions about the market or marketing opportunities.

One inventor developed a commercial hair dryer that could dry hair in five minutes. He used the eight-factor method and got a 0 for marketing opportunities from hairdressers. The reason there was no market, he found out, was that stylists wanted slower dryers to keep patrons occupied for thirty minutes or so while they worked on other customers.

PMI

Edward de Bono, international authority on thinking, recommends using "PMI" to get people away from simply reacting to ideas and situations.

Subjects are asked to observe and list the pluses, minuses, and most interesting aspects of an idea or situation. The "most interesting" category is for all those things that are worth noting but do not fit under either "plus" or "minus."

PMI forces people into action, thinking and focusing their attention in a specific direction rather than just reacting to an idea or situation.

A PMI list can help you:

- *Compare many different ideas and narrow them down to one or a few.* I know a sales manager who sends his staff several different sales strategies and asks them to do a PMI on each before he decides on a final strategy.
- *Focus objectively on the pluses and minuses of a proposition.* An inventor proposed a new hinged bottle top to make drug bottles "elder accessible." His friends did PMIs on this idea, and their feedback led him to a better idea. He decided to create a cap that works like a combination lock: turn right, turn left, lift off.
- *Make a decision about the worth of an idea.* An executive who had been arguing for weeks with his management team about an idea finally gathered everyone involved and asked them all to do a PMI. Once the problem had been laid out, a route could be chosen, and the matter was resolved in minutes.

OPUS

Opus is modeled after the market research technique used by TerraFirma AB, a Swedish research company that gets an amazing 92 percent response to its surveys.

Although you can certainly improvise, Opus seems to work best when you use a sleek, elegant-looking box, about 16 inches by 4 inches by 1 inch.

The interior of the box should be divided into four compartments, and contain a description of your idea, instructions for performing Opus, and about 100 cards. On each card, type a statement of concern (not a question) about your idea. Examples:

I believe my product is superior to Brand X because . . .
The major benefit is . . .
I can produce this for a cost of . . .
People will buy it because . . .
The best way to market it is . . .
I plan to finance it by . . .
The problems it will solve are . . .
I expect the following results . . .

You ask the respondent to put each card into one of the four compartments, labeled agree, partly agree, disagree, or no opinion. The cumulative results will give you a feel for how your idea will be received. You can reuse the box with several different people. It works because it's fast and easy to do, and most people enjoy doing this kind of physical survey.

An obscure artist had the idea to sell advertising space on his canvases. He had absolutely no idea whether or not this could work, so he used an Opus box to survey nightclubs, clothing boutiques, hair salons, art galleries, and trendy restaurants. He found that advertisers seemed happy to pay up to $1000 for space on a painting.

He has been successful in selling these paintings, which are heavy on stylized images of celebrity idols, with as many as a dozen ads, presented in foot-square boxes, adorning both sides and the bottom of each canvas. One art collector calls them "the cutting edge." The demand for his work became so heavy that he hired a full-time salesperson to sell advertising space and is planning a solo exhibition.

DEVIL'S FOOD

Most people love to help others with their business ventures or challenges, and their cooperation and compassion can be invaluable to you in your quest for feedback. An ancient story illustrates the radical difference cooperation and compassion can make. A man who led a basically good life died, and was assigned to Hell for a short time. He discovered that the main torture in Hell was that everyone was forced to eat with spoons that were longer than their arms. The condemned spent eternity in the midst of excellent food they couldn't eat. When he was finally transferred up to Heaven, he found that the blessed were given the same spoons. In Heaven, however, no one went hungry because they fed each other.

An effective feedback system is one that works for you. A Murder Board is one way to get honest information and create an ongoing creative climate for modifying and improving ideas. Of course, advice and feedback mean nothing unless you listen to and evaluate them properly.

SUMMARY

When your idea feels final, implement it. Do not spend days, weeks, or months refining it. If you delay, you may find yourself in a situation like that of the Victorian portrait painter who chose not to seek immediate benefits from his talents. Instead, he spent years refining his craft and art until he finally reached a pitch of dazzling brilliance—just in time to be rendered obsolete by photography.

CHAPTER THIRTY-EIGHT

BACKBONE

"All we need do is to throw something odd
and unaccountable in his way."

SUN TZU

Associating seemingly disparate elements in new ways by finding a novel connection between them is the backbone of creativity. It is also the backbone of this book.

To associate elements in new ways, you must think flexibly. Flexibility of thought is the ability to produce a large number of original ideas.

For a quick test of your mental flexibility, try the Remote Associates Test (Mednick 1962). For each set of three words, the goal is to find an associated word that all three have in common. For example, the words "wheel," "electric," and "high" can all be paired with "chair."

1.	piggy	green	lash	_____
2.	surprise	line	birthday	_____
3.	mark	shelf	telephone	_____
4.	stick	maker	tennis	_____
5.	blue	cottage	cloth	_____
6.	motion	poke	down	_____
7.	gem	wall	stepping	_____
8.	chorus	bee	side	_____
9.	lunch	car	gift	_____
10.	foul	ground	pen	_____

If you are like most people, you probably did not make all the associations. To learn how to think more flexibly, you need guidelines. This book is packed with techniques, exercises, and eye-opening illustrations in the shape of

Thinkertoys that effectively document how to think more flexibly. (The answers are: back, party, book, match, cheese, slow, stone, line, box, and play.)

To go a step further you have to truly *understand* the techniques. An artist, seeing a man run the 100-yard dash, should be able to complete a drawing of him by the time he crosses the finish line. Such a drawing could not be made by careful analysis, accurate measurements, application of the laws of physics, a study of perception, or any other such deliberation. The artist gains understanding *while* drawing the lines, not before or after.

In much the same way, your understanding of the techniques can only unfold when you use them. You have to draw the lines, so to speak, to understand them. When you use Thinkertoys, your spark of creativity, however dim it may have become, will be rekindled to the brightest flame possible.

To keep your creative fire, you need variety. Variety is the essence of all sensation; our senses are designed to respond to change and contrast. When a stimulus is unchanging or repetitious, sensation disappears.

Hold your hand over one eye and stare at the dot in the middle of the circle. After a few moments, the circle will fade and disappear. It will only reappear if you blink or shift your gaze to the X.

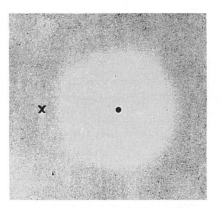

What happens is that the receptors in your eye get "tired" and stop responding, and nerve cells higher up in your sensory system switch off. This process is called *sensory adaptation*. You become blind to what is right before your eyes. The same phenomenon explains what is going on when you can no longer smell a gas leak that you noticed when you first entered the kitchen.

When your method for getting ideas is routine and unchanging, your imagination gets bored and switches off. One might term it "imagination adaptation." You become blind to the opportunities right before your eyes, but do not realize it until someone else points out your blindness. Then, and only then, can you see what you had been looking at all along. If you can no longer recall your last original idea, you are suffering from this condition.

The final message of the book is this: To realize life's possibilities, think flexibly and use a variety of techniques to keep your imagination fresh. The joy of creating original ideas is right here within your grasp, if you accept it.

More for the creative business person

THINKPAK
by Michael Michalko

From the author of *Thinkertoys*, nationally renowned creativity expert and consultant Michael Michalko brings you this handy pack of brainstorming cards. Designed to stimulate creative, innovative ideas, and help you solve tough problems.

LEADING CHANGE, OVERCOMING CHAOS
by Michael L. Heifetz

"This volume will function as a Virgil through the Inferno of corporate change."
—Michael Cohen, KRC Research & Consulting

A seven stage process for making change succeed in your organization. Contains proven tools and insights to help you manage transition in any field and use it to your advantage.

THAT'S A GREAT IDEA!
by Tony Husch
and Linda Foust

How to get, evaluate, protect, develop, and sell new product ideas—anything from a silly game to a plan for real estate development. A wealth of possibilities for entrepreneurs, inventors, tinkerers—and anyone who's ever had a great idea.

THINKING WITH A PENCIL
by Henning Nelms

". . . an inviting pragmatic introduction to the full range of image representation. Nelms makes it look easy and fun."—*The Next Whole Earth Catalog*

Covers sketches, diagrams, tables, architectural renderings, graphs, and figure drawing.

RUNNING A ONE-PERSON BUSINESS (Revised)
by Claude Whitmeyer
and Salli Rasberry

Advice for one-person businesses—which can range from realtors to caterers to accountants to florists to plumbers. Based on the authors' varied experiences, and interviews with successful businesspeople, this book simplifies setting up shop, bookkeeping, marketing, legal matters, and more.

TEN SPEED PRESS
P. O. Box 7123
Berkeley, California 94707

Available from your local bookstore, or call 1-800-841-BOOK for information on how to order direct from the publisher. Write for our free catalog of over 500 books, tapes, and posters.